Human M

Scт
CPT OK
9/19

Human Morality and Sociality

Evolutionary and Comparative Perspectives

Edited by

HENRIK HØGH-OLESEN

First published 2010 by
PALGRAVE MACMILLAN

Palgrave Macmillan in the UK is an imprint of Macmillan Publishers Limited,
registered in England, company number 785998, of Houndmills, Basingstoke,
Hampshire RG21 6XS.

Palgrave Macmillan in the US is a division of St Martin's Press LLC,
175 Fifth Avenue, New York, NY 10010.

Palgrave Macmillan is the global academic imprint of the above companies
and has companies and representatives throughout the world.

Palgrave® and Macmillan® are registered trademarks in the United States,
the United Kingdom, Europe and other countries

ISBN: 978-0-230-23799-5 hardback
ISBN: 978-0-230-23800-8 paperback

This book is printed on paper suitable for recycling and made from fully
managed and sustained forest sources. Logging, pulping and manufacturing
processes are expected to conform to the environmental regulations of the
country of origin.

A catalogue record for this book is available from the British Library.

A catalog record for this book is available from the Library of Congress.

10 9 8 7 6 5 4 3 2 1
19 18 17 16 15 14 13 12 11 10

Printed in China

Contents

Contributors

Christophe Boesch
Department of Primatology,
Max Planck Institute for Evolutionary Anthropology,
Leipzig, Germany

Leda Cosmides
Center for Evolutionary Psychology,
University of California, Santa Barbara, USA

Azar Gat
Department of Political Sciences,
Tel Aviv University, Israel

Henrik Høgh-Olesen
Department of Psychology,
Aarhus University, Denmark

Dennis Krebs
Department of Psychology,
Simon Fraser University, Canada

Ara Norenzayan
Department of Psychology,
University of British Columbia, Canada

Michael Bang Petersen
Department of Political Science,
Aarhus University, Denmark

Aaron Sell
Center for Evolutionary Psychology,
University of California, Santa Barbara, USA

John Tooby
Center for Evolutionary Psychology,
University of California, Santa Barbara, USA

Frans B. M. de Waal
Living Links, Yerkes National Primate Research Center &
Department of Psychology,
Emory University, Atlanta, USA

1

Human Mind – Human Kind:
An Introduction

Henrik Høgh-Olesen

In the hands of philosophers, human nature has proven to be a slippery thing. Are we cruel, selfish creatures or good, merciful Samaritans? And what is the natural condition of humanity? Is humanity the primeval state of *"warre of every man against every man,"* that Thomas Hobbes (1588–1679) pictured in his great work Leviathan (1651), deeming us to *"solitary, poor, nasty and short"* lives, or is it closer to the blissful pastoral envisioned by Jean-Jacques Rousseau (1712–1778) in his Discurse sur L´ineqalite (1755) roughly a hundred years later, in which man, the noble savage, governed by innate compassion, lives peacefully among his fellow kinsmen? Are we wolves – *Homo homini lupus* – bloody on tooth and claw as the rest of nature, or lambs peacefully grazing the pastures together?

Perhaps it is time to raise our mutual tolerance of ambiguity and accept that the answer may be slightly more complex than the above stereotypes suggest. Asking if humans are good or bad, selfish or caring, peaceful or hostile equates to asking if light is particles or waves. The answer is, "Yes." Physical entities can have contradictory properties, but some of these contradictions are complementary, as modern physics has shown (Bohr 1999), and both characteristics coexist simultaneously, even if we can only perceive and measure one at a time.

Another thing to remember is that nature is all about functionality and adaptive fitness, and as such beyond good and bad, or any

1

other socially constructed duality for that matter. Additionally, many aspects of human sociality and morality have to be captured and understood in this complex, functional and complementary way in order to make sense. Humans are neither egoists nor altruists in the absolute. Instead we are exactly as selfish and self-sacrificing as it has evolutionarily paid off for us to be!

The essays collected in this volume share this understanding, just as they share an evolutionary and comparative approach to the study of human mind and kind. To understand how a capacity as morality evolved – i.e., to understand what it was for, and how it was helpful in optimizing the organisms' survival and general fitness – helps us to understand what morality is. And if we wish to understand what is uniquely human, why not take a closer look at the other creatures around us, both inside and outside the primate line, and compare similarities and differences?

The ambition has not been to create an "all inclusive" volume like a textbook in the traditional sense in which no study is left untouched. Instead the idea was to compile a stimulating and hopefully thought-provoking reader that brings students and scholars face-to-face with some of the main protagonists of the field by offering their outlooks and perspectives on human morality and sociality.

Psychology has never been a unified science, collected under one paradigmatic hat, as for example physics, and different paradigms – covering the whole range from realist to social constructionist perspectives – coexist, even often in the same department.

During some periods, major movements have dictated the agenda and led the masses, and in the history of psychology we usually refer to the major paradigmatic "forces" that have dominated the field.

Behaviorism, psychoanalysis and humanistic psychology constituted the first three forces. Now, after some 30 years interregnum, a fourth unifying force, which integrates an evolutionary and cognitive angle to the study of man, has emerged strong and vital, generating hypotheses, boosting research and inspiring interdisciplinary collaborations on a scale not seen before.

Some may look at this force as a delta of minor streams spreading from the spring of Darwinian thinking, and there are differences between "socio-biology," "human behavioral ecology," "gene-culture coevolution," "memetics," "evolutionary psychology broad and narrow," etc., as there were between "Watsonian," "Pavlovian" and "Skinnerian" behaviorism and between "humanistic" and "existential" psychology.

However, let us not indulge in "the narcissism of the little difference," as Freud put it. It is not the aim of this book to stress the variations of the basic theme. The different "regiments" in this force may wave different colors (and it is mutually stimulating that they do), but it is still the same force united in a common evolutionary understanding.

Scope and Outline

A solitary organism has no need for moral rules, nor does a creature living among others without mutual dependency. Humans, however, have evolved from a long lineage of social-hierarchical and interdependent animals, for which life in groups are not an option but a survival strategy. We simply are each other's means to the common goals, and as such are a species whose sociality and morality are communicating vessels. It is meaningless to treat one without the other.

We are also animals with large brains. Hominine brain size has increased more than 250 percent in less than 3 million years, and much of this increase has occurred within the past 500,000 years (Flinn, Geary, and Ward 2005). A multitude of selective forces (ecology, climate, foraging, tool use, predators, etc.) may have influenced this increase, and among these, perhaps first and foremost the force of our own social relations: The necessity of dealing continually with conspecifics in social circumstances that became ever more complex as the human line evolved. Nothing would select more potently for increased encephalization and social cognition than such an intraspecific, coevolutionary arms race in which success was dependent on skills in social competition (Alexander 1987; Dunbar 1998).

Furthermore, human nature is complex and the idea is not just to understand and comparatively analyze our altruistic and pro-social inclinations, from in-group helping, caring and sharing, to solidarity and large-scale collaboration with unrelated strangers, but also to examine the complementary, "darker" sides of our sociality, such as free-riding, cheating, cheater-detection and punishment, distrust and stranger hostility, and last but not least, inter-group conflicts and warfare.

In Chapter 2 Dennis Krebs opens the discussions by challenging the logic behind traditional biological theory: Does it necessarily follow that anything that has evolved by natural selection should be selfish, as biologists from Huxley (1893) to Williams (1989) and Dawkins (1989) hold, and does a disposition really have to be "unselfish" in order to qualify as moral?

What if both premises are wrong, and what does it actually mean when something is "selfish"? This mischievous concept is used by biologists, psychologists, theologians, and ordinary people alike, but unfortunately, not in the same way.

In a careful analysis, Krebs clarifies this conceptual mess and shows us (1) that moral inclinations can be naturally selected; (2) that psychologically unselfish dispositions can be genetically self-ish and enhance the fitness of those who emit them; and (3) that even in many cases, where "good manners" are taught and culturally tutored, social learning and cultural indoctrination are often medi-ated by evolved mechanisms, rendering people more susceptible to some forms rather than others.

These views are further consolidated in Chapter 3 as Frans de Waal presents evidence of the continuity between humans and other primates and shows how some of the building blocks of mor-ality – such as reconciliation, empathy, reciprocity and a sense of fairness – are older than our species and a natural outgrowth of the social instincts that we share with other group-living animals.

Later on, these comparisons are used by de Waal to make the important distinction between morality proper and social conven-tions. To an obligatory gregarious species as ours, morality is a group-oriented phenomenon primarily related to Helping or (not) Hurting others. Anything unrelated to the two H´s (such as bare breasts in prime time TV, or headscarves to cover women's hair) falls outside of morality and into the domain of social conventions couched in moral language.

Religion tops the list of species-specific human universals, and to many people religion is seen, as the God-given, or socially constructed, antidote to our alleged venomous nature. The contributions in this book take another stand, allowing moral building blocks and pro-social inclinations to be part of our natural endowment. But, of course, reli-gion has a part to play in the staging of human morality and sociality, not least by way of its ability to facilitate social cohesion and large-scale, high-risk cooperation among unrelated strangers, as we shall see.

In Chapter 4 Ara Norenzayan guides us into this strange suite of propensities called religion, and shows us some of their adaptive characteristics.

On the one hand, social organisms are motivated to engage in fitness-maximizing behaviors that are often detrimental to other conspecifics and, on the other hand, group-living collapses if too many reap the benefits of it without contributing to the group. So whom do we trust, and how do we spot a fair collaborator?

Genuine religious sentiments, emotions, and participation in time-consuming religious rituals may serve as "costly signals" – which may show that a person has stamina, perseverance, and is conscious and concerned about rules –, which may curb the free-rider problem inherent in collaboration among strangers. And just as two eyespots installed over the moneybox will enhance the payments in a self-administered beer sale, the installation of a morally concerned and omni-present supernatural agent, in the mindset of a group of humans, will help the members of this group to pay their social dues, as Norenzayan's fascinating studies show. Experimentally induced religious thoughts reduce rates of cheating and increase altruistic behavior among anonymous strangers. And cross-cultural evidence suggests an association between the presence of morally concerned deities and large group size in humans, so religion may serve as a cohesive force in our in-group relations (Norenzayan here; Norenzayan and Shariff 2008).

But we have other devices to help us with the recurrent problems of cheating and exploitation.

In Chapter 5 Michael B. Petersen, Aaron Sell, John Tooby and Leda Cosmides show us that humans have evolved psychological adaptations that allow us (1) to detect and respond to cheating conspecifics; (2) to evaluate the prospective return of continued association with the perpetrator; and (3) to react with punitive and/or conciliatory strategies, calibrated according to the anticipated future net value of our association with the exploiter.

Humans are score-keepers, and our interactions are regulated by "welfare trade-off ratios," which are internal regulatory variables that set the threshold for acceptable cost-benefit transactions between us and others, and which index the degree to which we are willing to trade-off our own welfare against others when we take action.

We also have to take into account that in the small groups in which our ancestors evolved, some perpetrators were more valuable to our mutual survival than others, and this programmed calculus apparently still plays a part in modern humans' spontaneous moral intuitions and political attitudes toward punishment and criminal justice. Making us more disposed to forgive and apply reparative strategies, when the transgressor is perceived as valuable. Moreover, what goes for in-group members certainly does not apply to outsiders.

Not even religious pro-sociality is extended indiscriminately. The drawback of intra-group collaboration is inter-group competition and conflict, and very often the same mechanisms involved in intra-group altruism may also facilitate inter-group antagonism and war between groups.

Anthropologist have long thought that war was uniquely human, and more or less absent until we became sedentary, territorial agriculturalists that accumulated resources and developed high population densities (Keeley 1997; Kelly 2007), but primatologists have shown that we do not have to settle down, grow vegetables, and be possessive in order to fight wars. Of the more than 10 million animal species that exist, one other species, besides our own, has been documented to show male-initiated coalitions that raid neighboring territories and carry through lethal attacks on out-group members of their own kind, and this other species is our closest relatives: the chimpanzees (*Pan troglodytes*).

Jane Goodall (1979) was the first to describe the dramatic war-like fights that occurred between chimpanzee communities in her study site, the Gombe National Park in Tanzania. Over a period of 4 years she watched a group split into two fractions after which one fraction systematically killed all the males and some of the females in the other fraction.

In Chapter 6 Christophe Boesch presents us with a fresh field study of inter-group fights and violence of four neighboring chimpanzee communities in the Tai National Park, Côte d'Ivoire.

Direct aggression between groups has been observed in species such as lions, African wild dogs, wolves, and a range of monkeys; these physical confrontations, however, do not appear to be premeditated, coalitional, or collaborative.

War is distinguished from ordinary conflicts and physical brawls, carried out in the heat of the moment, by exactly these insignias. War is planned, organized, and coordinated. It entails a division of labor that goes beyond one based on age and gender alone, and implies the envisioned harm on others, and the purposeful act of taking up means in order to accomplish this goal (Kelly 2007).

War's most elementary form is the raid, in which a small group enters enemy territory undetected in order to ambush, kill, or harm unsuspecting, isolated individuals, and then withdraws to their own ground after their mission has been accomplished. So far, this distinct coalitional behavioral pattern has only been observed in humans and chimpanzees.

Boesch's observations document these fascinating inter-specific similarities and indicate that there may be differences in inter-group violence between chimpanzee populations. Attacks with lethal consequences may be fewer, female participation higher, and the level of violence directed at stranger infants may be reduced among the Tai chimpanzees compared to other flocks.

Others, like Wrangham, Wilson and Muller (2006), have compared death rates from conflicts between groups of chimpanzees in five long-term study sites, with data for inter-group conflicts in several hunter-gatherer and subsistence-farmer societies, and found comparable levels of violent death between species. All in all, the similarities are obvious, but so are the differences, as we shall later see.

Already in The Descent of Man, Darwin recognized, that war, inter-group conflict, and competition over resources were powerful evolutionary forces that could foster intra-group solidarity and altruism. Conflict being the midwife of altruism, so to speak. Guiding behaviors according to a rationale running something like: "stick together, help each other, and endure personal sacrifices for the common good of the tribe in order not to be overrun by those over there." And recent anthropological evidence (Keeley 1997; Kelly 2007), indicating that inter-group violence killed a considerable proportion of our ancestors, has renewed the interest in war as a force for robust group- and multi-level selection.

Along the same lines, Choi and Bowles´(2007) computer simulations have shown that war drives the joint evolution of altruism and inter-group hostility, and that altruism and intra-group solidarity flourish only in the company of competitive, aggressive outgroup forces, leaving us once again with the profound irony that one of our noblest achievements – morality – has evolutionary ties to one of our bloodiest and most brutal behaviors – warfare (Alexander 1987; de Waal 2006; Bowles 2008)!

In Chapter 7, one of the leading authorities on human warfare, Azar Gat, addresses the causes of fighting and shows that societies throughout history have manifested a remarkably similar set of reasons for fighting, reflecting "the human motivational complex."

War is a continuation of human aims, and the behavior designed to achieve them, by violent means, the thesis goes. Universally the primary cause of conflict and fight is the competition over (a) subsistence resources (hunting territories, water, shelter, raw materials) and (b) reproduction, followed by the subordinate and derivative causes of (c) dominance (rank, power, status, prestige) and (d) revenge and retaliation. Gat shows how these motives, rather than being separate, come together in an integrated motivational complex, shaped by the logic of evolution and natural selection.

We call exploitations perpetrated by in-group members "crimes," while the same or similar acts by sets of outgroup members will often be categorized as "attacks," which activate a different set of evolved defenses related to our coalitional psychology. The finer nature of these evolved mechanisms are outlined by John Tooby and Leda Cosmides in Chapter 8.

The human mind is equipped with a rich multicomponent coalitional psychology in the form of species-specific programs, designed by natural selection to regulate intra-coalition cooperation and inter-coalition conflict.

A fight is an aggressive conflict between two individuals involving no cooperation. A war, in turn, is an aggressive conflict between two coalitions of individuals, involving cohesion and complex cooperation, which may explain, (1) why it is so rare among animal species, and (2) why human males find it so psychologically appealing!

Cooperation depends on the ability to detect and exclude cheaters – on the ability to track the performance of multiple individuals over time and through ambiguous situations, while at the same time orchestrating one's behavior so that it mixes simultaneously with that of the others. Such operations require sophisticated cognitive programs – for example, the above-mentioned "welfare trade-off ratios"; "formidability indexes," designed to track the ability of self and others to inflict costs; and "conferral indexes," designed to track the ability of self and others to confer benefits – which most other species may not possess.

Finally, the connections between war and morality are treated. Our norms and values are seen as anchored in our adaptations for evaluating situations that allow us to choose and plan more fitness-enhancing actions over lesser ones. Add to this our natural propensities to unite in groups and to influence (persuade as well as force) others to act in conformity with our evaluations, and the fine line between intra-group solidarity and outer-group hostility – in the form of tugs of war between neighboring groups with colliding interests – is suspended.

So, contrary to common belief, warfare is not a denial of our capacity for social cooperation – it is just the most destructive expression of it. Neither is it a denial of human morality, but one of its basest foundations!

But let us return to the inter-specific comparisons to put this in perspective.

It may not appear so, but comparatively speaking, humans are a much more peaceful species than our chimpanzee relatives. Humans may be on guard when confronted with strangers of their own kind, but chimpanzees are nothing less than xenophobic. They simply lack any friendly ties between groups, and know only varying degrees of hostility (de Waal 2005), whereas human groups mingle and trade all the time, share habitats and resources, practice inter-marriage, go on holidays to or settle down permanently in foreign territories, etc. In contrast, in intra-group conflicts and killings, chimpanzees turn on their own up to 200 times more frequently than humans in small-scale societies (Wrangham et al. 2006).

These and other findings suggest that the human brain is not just an enlarged chimpanzee brain, and that evolution seems to have favored an altogether more collaborative kind of sociality in our species. These and other comparisons on what makes us humans are the objects of discussion by this author in Chapter 9.

Humans have one thing in common with ants, bees, and naked mole rats: we are "ultra-social" creatures (Campbell 1983) who live in highly cooperative groups of hundreds or thousands of individuals with a refined division of labor. The insects and the mole rats accomplish this magnificent interdependence by a trick of genes. They are all siblings, and from a genetic standpoint helping a sibling is almost like helping oneself, whereas humans have other ways, as we shall see.

Humans are mind readers by nature, and will automatically infer social intentions in objects, animals, or other human beings on the basis of minimal cues, as Heider and Simmel (1944) demonstrated in their classic experiment involving "chasing" triangles and "evading" circles (see also Barrett et al. 2005 for more recent cross-cultural confirmations). We also have a deeply felt need for social inclusion. Participants left out of a face-to-face ball toss react with depressed mood and lowered self-esteem (Williams and Sommer 1997); deprivation of social contact produces anxiety and depression (Baumeister and Leary 1995); and brain studies suggest that being ostracized activates the same brain regions involved in the sensation of physical pain (Eisenberg, Lieberman, and Williams 2003). Furthermore, this acute social sensitivity makes sense in an organism built to survive in collaboration with others, and who depends on a close knit support system for its survival.

Four central fields of activity related to (1) complex symbolic capacities, (2) tool making and tool use, (3) culture and social transmission, and (4) sociality and morality, are surveyed and comparatively analyzed for similarities and differences.

The main focus is on our social and moral capacities; but since these characteristics are situated in – and part and parcel of – a unique language–using, tool-producing, and culture-accumulating organism, these features will also be reviewed and compared. Data from a broad range of sciences, from archaeology to economics and neuroscience, is brought together to introduce light and shade into the picture.

On paper this may look like plain sailing, but history shows that identifying what is uniquely human is a hazardous endeavor. As late as 1962, one of the leading "New synthesis" biologists, T. Dobzhansky, laid down as a fact that: *"Homo sapiens is not only the sole tool-making animal and the sole political animal, he is also the sole ethical animal"* (1962, p. 339), just to find himself corrected in everyone of these areas a few years later by primatologists such as Goodall (1969, 1986) and de Waal (1982, 1996). A similar fate most likely awaits some of the claims presented in this book. Nevertheless, these demarcations simply have to be drawn once and again. They focus our attention, make us wonder, and direct and stimulate research because they provoke and challenge other researchers to take up the glove and prove us wrong.

So here we go again.

References

Alexander, R. D. (1987). *The biology of moral systems*. New York: Aldine de Gruyter.

Barrett, H. C., P. M. Todd, G. F. Miller, and P. Blythe. 2005. Accurate judgements of intention from motion alone: A cross-cultural study. *Evolution and Human Behavior* 26:313–31.

Baumeister, R. F., and M. R. Leary. 1995. The need to belong: Desire for interpersonal attachments as a fundamental human motivation. *Psychological Bulletin* 117(3):497–529.

Bohr, N. 1999. *Causality and complementarity: Epistemological lessons of studies in atomic physics*. UK: Oxbow Press.

Bowles, S. 2008. Conflict: Altruism's midwife. *Nature*, V 456:326–7.

Campbell, D. T. 1983. The two distinct routes beyond kin selection to ultrasociality. In *The nature of prosocial development: Theories and strategies*, edited by D. Bridgeman, 11–39. New York: Academic Press.

Choi, J. K., and S. Bowles. 2007. The coevolution of parochial altruism and war. *Science* 318:636–40.

Darwin, C. 1998 [1874]. *The descent of man*, 2nd ed. New York: Prometheus Books.

Dawkins, R. 1989. *The selfish gene*. Oxford: Oxford University Press.

De Waal, F. B. M. 1982. *Chimpanzee politics* London: Jonathan Cape.

De Waal, F. B. M. 1996. *Good natured. The origins of right and wrong in humans and other animals*. Cambridge, MA: Harvard University Press.

De Waal, F. B. M. 2005. *Our inner ape*. London: Grania Books.

De Waal, F. B. M. 2006. *Primates and philosophers*. Princeton: Princeton University Press.

Dobzhansky, T. 1962. *Mankind evolving: The evolution of the human species*. New Haven: Yale University Press.

Dunbar, R. I. M. 1998. The social brain hypothesis. *Evolutionary Anthropology* 6(5):178–90.

Eisenberger, N. I., M. D. Lieberman, and K. D. Williams. 2003. Does rejection hurt? An fMRI study of social exclusion. *Science* 302:290–2.

Flinn, M. V., D. C. Geary, and C. V. Ward. 2005. Ecological dominance, social competition, and coalitionary arms races: Why humans evolved extraordinary intelligence. *Evolution and Human Behavior* 26:10–46.

Goodall, J. 1969. *My friends the wild chimpanzees*. Washington DC: National Geographic Society.

Goodall, J. 1979. Life and Death at Gombe. *National Geographic*, May, 592–621.

Goodall, J. 1986. *The chimpanzees of Gombe*. Boston: Bellknap Press.

Heider, F., and M. Simmel. 1944. An experimental study of apparent behavior. *American Journal of Psychology* 57:243–59.

Hobbes. T. 1985 [1651]. *Leviathan*. Harmondsworth: Penguin Books.

Huxley, T. 1893. *Evolution and ethics*. London: Macmillan.

Keeley, L. H. 1997. *War Before civilization*. Oxford: Oxford University Press.

Kelly, R. C. 2007. *Origin of war*. Michigan: University of Michigan Press.

Norenzayan, A., and A. F. Shariff. 2008. The origin and evolution of religious prosociality. *Science* 322:58–62.

Rousseau, J. J. 1997 [1755]. *Discurse sur L'ineqalite*. Translated and edited by Victor Gourevitch as *The discourses and other early political writings*. Cambridge: Cambridge University Press.

Tooby, J., and L. Cosmides. 1988. The evolution of war and its cognitive foundations. Institute for Evolutionary Studies, Technical Report 88–1.

Williams, G. C. (1989). A sociobiological expansion of evolution and ethics. In *evolution and ethics: T. H. Huxley's evolution and ethics with new essays on its Victorian and sociobiological context*, edited by Paradis, J. and G. C. Williams, 179–214. Princeton: Princeton University Press.

Williams, K. D and K. L. Sommer. 1997. Social ostracism by one´s coworkers. *Personality and Social Psychology Bulletin*, 23:693–706.

Wrangham, R. W., M. L. Wilson, and M. N. Muller. 2006. Comparative rates of violence in chimpanzees and humans. *Primates* 47:14–26.

2

Born Bad? Evaluating the Case against the Evolution of Morality

Dennis Krebs

A great many people, laypeople and scholars alike, believe that humans are born fundamentally bad, or immoral, in "Original Sin." Consider some prominent examples. Calvin preached that, following Adam and Eve's fall from grace, humans were cursed with: "a hereditary corruption and depravity of our nature, extending to all parts of the soul" (I: 217).[1] The colonial preacher Jonathan Edwards asserted that children are born as "young vipers and infinitely more hateful than vipers" (p. 12).[2] And Anna Freud wrote that "we know that the child acts throughout the period of development [from birth to age five] as if there was nothing more important than the gratifying of his own pleasures and fulfilling of his powerful instincts, whereas education proceeds as if the prevention of these objects was its most important task" (p. 101).[3]

Although evolutionary biologists do not have much in common with religious scholars and psychoanalysts, some very prominent evolutionary theorists appear to agree with them about the fundamental selfishness of human nature. Darwin considered the implications of his theory of evolution for the selection of moral dispositions and asserted that "it is extremely doubtful whether the offspring of the most sympathetic and benevolent parents, or of those which were the most faithful to their comrades, would be reared in greater numbers than the children of selfish and treacherous parents of the same tribe.

He who was ready to sacrifice his life, as many a savage has been, rather than betray his comrades, would often leave no offspring to inherit his noble nature (p. 127).'[4] A couple of decades after the publication of *Descent of Man*, Darwin's cousin, Thomas Huxley, gave a series of lectures on the relation between evolution and ethics, and concluded that "the practice of that which is ethically best – what we call goodness or virtue –involves a course of conduct which, in all respects, is opposed to that which leads to success in the cosmic struggle for existence. Ethical nature may count upon having to reckon with a tenacious and powerful enemy as long as the world lasts" (p. 83).[5]

Almost a century later, the eminent evolutionary biologist, George Williams, reexamined Huxley's position in light of refinements in Darwin's theory of evolution and reached an even bleaker conclusion: "There is no encouragement for any belief that an organism can be designed for any purpose other than the most effective pursuit of... self-interest.... Nothing resembling the Golden Rule or other widely preached ethical principles seems to be operating in living nature. It could scarcely be otherwise, when evolution is guided by a force that maximizes genetic selfishness" (pp. 195–7).[6]

Richard Dawkins, the author of one of the most influential books of our times, *The Selfish Gene*, appears to agree. He wrote: "I think 'nature red in tooth and claw' sums up our modern understanding of natural selection admirably... If you look at the way natural selection works, it seems to follow that anything that has evolved by natural selection should be selfish.... Much as we might wish to believe otherwise, universal love and welfare of the species as a whole are concepts that simply do not make evolutionary sense.... Be warned that if you wish, as I do, to build a society in which individuals cooperate generously and unselfishly toward a common good, you can expect little help from biological nature" (pp. 2–4).[7]

There are no scholars whom I admire more than Charles Darwin, George Williams, and Richard Dawkins; however, I am quite sure that the pessimistic conclusions about human nature implied in the passages I have extracted from their writings are wrong, or at least misleading. Let us examine carefully the basis for these conclusions.

The Case against the Evolution of Morality

Reduced to its essence, the inference that moral dispositions cannot evolve is the product of two premises: (a) all evolved dispositions are selfish and (b) to qualify as moral, a disposition must be unselfish. Evolutionary theorists hold that all evolved dispositions are selfish because they define selfishness in terms of behaviors that enhance the fitness of actors at the expense of the fitness of recipients. As explained by Kurland and Gaulin, selfish behaviors "confer a fitness benefit on the actor, while placing a fitness cost on the recipient" and "altruism refers to interactions where the actor incurs a fitness cost while benefiting the recipient" (p. 448).[8] By fitness, modern evolutionary theorists mean the number of genes that individuals contribute to the next generation, usually by way of the number of surviving offspring they produce, which defines their "reproductive success." "By definition altruists have lower fitness than the selfish individuals with whom they interact. It therefore seems inevitable that natural selection should eliminate altruistic behaviour, just as it eliminates other traits that diminish an individual's fitness" (p. 189).[9]

With respect to the second premise, evolutionary theorists assume – usually implicitly – that selfishness violates the criteria for morality. The kinds of behaviors that people consider immoral seem selfish, and the kinds of behaviors that people consider moral seem unselfish.

Beastly Behaviors

To support his contention that evolved dispositions are selfish, George Williams offered "obvious examples of the pursuit of self-interest as practiced in the biological cosmos," noting that, "I will need no theoretical subtleties to show their gross selfishness and moral unacceptability" (p. 197). With respect to relations between parents and offspring, Williams alluded to evidence amassed by Robert Trivers[10] demonstrating that "evolution favors offspring that try to get more than their fair share of resources from parents," but that parents "try for maximal reproductive success per unit of expenditure" (p. 197). With respect to relations between mates, Williams argued that "recent accounts of reproductive behavior in wild animals are tales of sexual intrigue full of deception, desertion, double-dealing, and sometimes lethal violence" (p. 198). Males attempt to mate with as many females as possible, and may force sex on unreceptive females. For example, "Cheng, Burns, and McKinney (1982)[11] have shown that rape is a normal part of mallard reproductive behavior.... An unguarded female mallard may be raped so persistently by gangs of males that she drowns (Barash 1977)" (p. 200).[12] In turn, females cuckold males. "Besides adultery and rape, just about every other kind of sexual behavior that has been regarded as sinful or unethical can be found abundantly in nature" (pp. 201–2).

Williams goes on to review evidence that, "the killing of other members of the same species is a frequent phenomenon in a wide variety of forms and contexts. Simple cannibalism is the commonest form of killing, ... [which] can be expected in all animals except strict vegetarians" (p. 202). Several researchers have "documented the previously unappreciated frequency of various forms of infanticide among mammals, including many primates. Among rodents and carnivores the killer often eats the victim" (p. 203). "Many conspecific killings result from violent contests over resources .... Death from strife among neighbors tends to be recorded for any wild animal population carefully observed for a thousand hours or more" (p. 204). Although males of "most vertebrate species are more likely than females to kill or injure others of their own kind ... competitions among females may not be so much of lesser intensity as of greater subtlety. Females commonly deprive each other of resources in various ways, aggressively interfere with one another's reproduction, attack one another's young, and actively aggravate male competition when it serves their interests" (p. 205).

Williams closes his case supporting the "triumph of selfishness" by noting that "none of the [examples of immorality] are really needed for the argument being advanced; the inescapable arithmetic of predation and parasitism should be enough to show that nature is morally unacceptable ... The survival of one organism is possible only at great cost to others. The moral message in this obvious fact has been recognized by many philosophers and humanists, despite the general prevalence of romanticism" (p. 229).

Although humans are different from other animals in many ways, humans also engage in beastly behaviors. Members of families compete for resources, sometimes to the point of killing one another. As documented by Daly and Wilson,[13] stepchildren are especially susceptible to abuse. Mates commit adultery and rape women. Women cuckold men. Jails are bursting with people who assault others, steal their possessions, and cheat them out of their money. Infanticide is common in some cultures. Although cannibalism is rare in the human species, people kill one another at a relatively high rate, especially during wars and bouts of "ethnic cleansing."

You might argue that only a small portion of the population – the bad guys – behave badly, and that most people are nice most of the time. It is tempting to divide the world into "us" good guys and "them" bad guys, but a great deal of evidence suggests that this dichotomy is misguided. Social psychologists have demonstrated that it is quite easy to induce ordinary people to commit dishonest, hurtful, unfair, and irresponsible acts. Milgram's study on obedience[14] and Zimbardo's prison study[15] are probably the best known examples. On a larger scale, a large number of ordinary German people participated in the suppression and extermination of Jews, and previously-friendly neighbors commonly turn on one another during ethnic conflicts such as those that occurred in Rwanda and Bosnia. When nations are freed from external control, people often roam the streets, looting, burning buildings, and killing one another. To some, this reveals the emergence of a previously suppressed, inherently evil human nature.

Apparently Altruistic Behaviors

Let us accept the conclusion that humans and other animals sometimes – perhaps even often – behave badly. Really, it can't be denied. This granted, evidence of badness is only part of the story. Members of all social species also may treat one another quite kindly. Parents make sacrifices for their offspring, friends support one another, and individuals help members of their groups. Social insects probably display the most dramatic of all caring behaviors, willingly sacrificing their lives to protect their groups.

Psychologists have documented countless examples of apparently altruistic and cooperative behaviors in human beings,[16] but we don't need this evidence to establish that people frequently behave in pro-social ways. We need only look around us. People customarily help their friends and relatives, cooperate with members of their groups, sacrifice their interests for the sake of others, and behave fairly. Indeed, many people help perfect strangers. They donate blood, contribute to charities, and help starving people from other countries.

The Challenge of Altruism to the Theory of Evolution

Evidence that animals behave in selfish ways seems consistent with the basic tenets of the theory of evolution, but evidence that animals behave in altruistic ways seems to challenge these tenets. Indeed, Darwin wrote that the altruistic self-sacrifice of social insects presented "one special difficulty, which at first seemed insuperable, and actually fatal to my whole theory [of evolution]."[17] Huxley considered it paradoxical that "ethical nature, while born of cosmic nature, is necessarily at enmity with its parent" (pp. 94, 9: viii),[18] and Williams asked, "How could maximizing selfishness produce an organism capable of often advocating, and occasionally practicing, charity toward strangers and even towards animals?" (p. 208).[19] The answer, according to Williams, is that "altruistic behavior is limited to special situations in which it can be explained by ... factors [that are not] of any use as a romantic's 'exemplar for human conduct'" (pp. 190–1).

Explaining Altruism Away

Skeptical evolutionary theorists have accounted for the seemingly altruistic behaviors of animals in four main ways. First, they have questioned whether such behaviors are really altruistic. Theorists such as Ghiselin have suggested that, if probed deeply enough, seemingly altruistic behaviors will be exposed as disguised forms of selfishness: "Scratch an altruist and see a hypocrite bleed" (p. 247).[20] You see one animal helping another animal survive or reproduce. When viewed out of context, the helping behavior seems biologically altruistic. However, it could be a tactic aimed at fostering the fitness of the helper – a means to a selfish end. Animals could help other animals instrumentally in order to foster their own survival and reproductive success, either directly or indirectly. For example, they could help other animals in order to curry favor, to cultivate an ally, or to obtain a mate.

When examined from a biological perspective, the thing we want to know about apparently altruistic acts is whether they are really costly, or whether they actually produce ultimate payoffs to the animals that emit them relative to the payoffs of behavioral alternatives and to the benefits to recipients. In evolution, payoffs are reckoned in terms of fitness, or the propagation of genes. (As I will explain, when examined from a psychological perspective, we want to know whether the behavior is aimed at helping the other as an end in itself, or whether it is a means of maximizing the helper's personal benefits.) No one questions that animals behave in ways that have the immediate effect of helping others; however, Ghiselen, Williams, and other evolutionary theorists believe that most of these behaviors stem from behavioral strategies that evolved because they increased the probability that those who possessed them would survive and reproduce.

The second way in which evolutionary theorists have accounted for altruism is as a product of manipulation: As expressed by George Williams, "As a general rule, a modern biologist seeing one animal doing something to benefit another assumes either that it is manipulated by the other individual or that it is being subtly selfish" (p. 195)[21]. Manipulation probably played an important role in the evolution of morality. When animals succeed in manipulating others into behaving in ways that enhance the recipients' fitness at an expense to the fitness of the manipulated animals, they induce the manipulated animals to behave in biologically altruistic ways. Although evolutionary theorists such as Williams acknowledge that such behaviors are biologically altruistic, they do not consider them moral, or at least up to the standards of "a romantic's exemplar for human conduct" (pp. 190–1), presumably because the animals that emit them do not intend to sacrifice their interests for the sake of the recipient. The animals are tricked into behaving altruistically.

The third explanation for apparent acts of altruism advanced by skeptical evolutionary theorists is similar to the second in a certain respect, but different in another. Evolutionary theorists have suggested that altruistic and moral behaviors may be incidental byproducts of mechanisms that evolved for other purposes. Mechanisms that induce animals to adopt *strategies* that pay off in the end may induce them to emit altruistic *behaviors* in some contexts. The short-term costs of the altruistic "mistakes" may be outweighed by the long-term benefits of the strategy. Although natural selection tends to hone the design of evolved mechanisms in increasingly fitness-enhancing ways, the mechanisms that end up being selected are often far from perfect. Mechanisms that produce the greatest ultimate net gains in fitness relative to other mechanisms in the population may induce those who inherit them to emit biologically costly behaviors in some contexts. For example, alluding to mental mechanisms that endow humans with the capacity to reason, Williams asserted that "reasoned analysis prompted by suspicion ... undoubtedly aided the receivers of messages in deciding (1) whether they gain or lose by complying, and (2) if they are likely to lose, whether defiance will bring a retaliation worse than the loss .... The ability to deal with such questions was designed by natural selection to spread selfish genes [but] in its boundless stupidity, this evolutionary process incidentally designed machinery capable of answering other sorts of questions, such as, Is the message one of help or harm for what I really want for the world?" (p. 212).[22]

Finally, related to all three arguments discussed above, skeptical evolutionary theorists have joined many lay people and social scientists in attributing altruistic behaviors to social learning and cultural indoctrination. For example, Dawkins wrote, "Let us try to *teach* generosity and altruism, because we are born selfish.... Our genes may instruct us to be selfish, but we are not necessarily compelled to obey them all our lives" (p. 3)[23]. In a similar vein, Donald Campbell suggested that, "in man, genetic competition precludes the evolution of... genetic altruism. The behavioral dispositions that produce... self-sacrificial altruism must instead be products of culturally evolved indoctrination that has had to counter self-serving genetic tendencies. Thus, ... man is profoundly ambivalent in his social role – as Freud noted. ... The commandments, the proverbs, the religious 'law' represent social evolutionary products directed at inculcating tendencies that are in direct opposition to the 'temptations' representing, for the most part, the dispositional tendencies produced by biological evolution" (pp. 52–3).[24]

It is important to remember that social learning and cultural indoctrination are mediated by evolved mechanisms. The questions that need to be answered about these mechanisms pertain to their design and decision-making rules. Social learning and cultural internalization mechanisms that rendered people indiscriminately susceptible to fitness-reducing forms of social influence and manipulation would not have evolved. To be selected, the genes that guide the development of these mechanisms must have enhanced the fitness of those who inherited them relative to alleles that designed alternative mechanisms.

An Evaluation of the Case against the Evolution of Morality

To evaluate the case against the evolution of morality, we need to determine whether the premises on which the conclusions are based are valid. Let us first examine the premise that all evolved dispositions are selfish, then turn to the premise that to qualify as moral, a behavior must be unselfish.

Must All Evolved Dispositions Be Selfish?

If you carefully compare the excerpts from the writings of Darwin at the beginning of this chapter with the excerpts from the writings of contemporary evolutionary biologists, it should become apparent that although modern biologists seem to be saying the same thing as Darwin was, their arguments differ in several significant ways. First, Darwin viewed evolution in terms of the survival of the fittest individuals and the reproduction of offspring. (Darwin also believed that traits could evolve through group selection.) Modern theorists view evolution in terms of the propagation of genes. Second, when Darwin alluded to "selfish and treacherous" parents, he was referring to parents who behaved in *personally* selfish ways. Modern theorists focus on *genetically* selfish behaviors. Finally, although Darwin felt that it was "*extremely doubtful*" that "the most sympathetic and benevolent parents" would produce more offspring than those who inherited more "selfish and treacherous" traits, he did not, like contemporary theorists, conclude that they *could not* produce more offspring.

In contemporary evolutionary biology, the ultimate criterion of fitness is the number of genes an individual contributes to the next generation, relative to the number of alleles contributed by others. When selfishness and altruism are defined in terms of genetic fitness, the assertion that all evolved dispositions are selfish, or more exactly, *were* selfish *when they were selected*, is true by definition. To characterize a disposition as evolved is to assert that it enhanced the fitness of the individuals who possessed it at the expense of the fitness of individuals who did not possess it, which is what evolutionary theorists mean by "selfish." As expressed by Randolph Nesse, "It is correct beyond question that genes shape brains that induce individuals to do whatever best gets copies of those genes into future generations. This principle follows from the logic of how natural selection works, and is not an empirical issue. When this is combined with our intuitive notion that altruism consists of costly acts that benefit others, and genes are seen as the ultimate currency, then altruism is impossible" (p. 228).[25]

It would have been more exact for Nesse to have said "*got* copies of those genes into future generations." The conclusion that all evolved traits are genetically selfish pertains only to the generation in which they were selected, because changes in physical, social and cultural environments may render previously adaptive (genetically selfish) strategies maladaptive (genetically unselfish). In a book called *Mean genes*, Burnham and Phelan[26] describe the maladaptive effects in the modern world of previously adaptive mechanisms governing hunger, thrill-seeking, greed, and sexual relations. The adaptiveness of social strategies also may depend on their frequency in the population. Maladaptive traits can evolve in several ways.

Genetic selfishness vs. individual selfishness

Animals can propagate their genes in two ways. They can propagate them directly, by fostering their own survival and reproductive success at the expense of the survival and reproductive success of others; and they can propagate them indirectly, by fostering the survival and reproductive success of individuals who possess replicas of their genes. As Richard Dawkins has acknowledged, although the indirect way of enhancing one's fitness is selfish at a genetic level, it can be altruistic at an individual level: "there are special circumstances in which a gene can achieve its own selfish goals by fostering a limited form of altruism at the level of individual animals" (p. 6).[27] It follows that even if all evolved strategies were genetically selfish, they would not necessarily be individually (or biologically) selfish.

Psychological selfishness vs. genetic selfishness

To complicate matters further, evolutionary definitions of selfishness do not correspond to the ways in which people define selfishness in their everyday lives. If you look up the word selfish in a dictionary, you will find such definitions as: "caring chiefly for oneself or one's own interests or comfort, esp. to the point of disregarding the welfare or wishes of others" (Funk and Wagnalls), "concerned excessively or exclusively with oneself: seeking or concentrating on one's own advantage, pleasure, or well-being without regard for others" (Merriam-Webster), and "deficient in consideration for others [and] concerned chiefly with one's own profit or pleasure" (Oxford Dictionary). I will label the type of selfishness described by these definitions *psychological selfishness*.

Psychological selfishness differs from genetic selfishness in three significant ways. First, whereas genetic selfishness is defined in terms of the consequences of behaviors (the frequency of genes in a population, which is related to the effects of a behavior on survival and reproductive success), psychological selfishness is defined in terms of a motivational state of "concern," "caring," or "consideration" for oneself and a deficiency in concern for others. Second, when individuals behave in psychologically selfish ways, they seek to obtain things they want for themselves, such as "pleasure," "well-being," "comfort," "advantage," and "profit. " When individuals behave in genetically selfish ways, they succeed in propagating their genes. Whether the pursuit of profit and pleasure helps individuals propagate their genes is an open question. Finally, whereas the standard for genetic selfishness is the number of genes that one contributes to future generations relative to, or at the expense of, the genes' alleles, the standard for psychological selfishness is "excessive" or "exclusive" concern for one's own needs, desires, interests, and welfare, and disregard for the welfare of others. It is not necessarily psychologically selfish to be concerned about, or to care for, oneself, to satisfy one's own needs, to foster one's own welfare, or to seek one's own advantage, as long as one does not pursue these self-interested goals excessively without due regard for the welfare, comfort, and wishes of others.

As explained by such theorists as Daniel Batson,[28] Randolph Nesse,[29] Elliot Sober and David Sloan Wilson,[30] there is no necessary connection between genetic and psychological forms of selfishness and altruism. To quote Sober and Wilson, "The automatic assumption that individualism in evolutionary biology and egoism in the social sciences must reinforce each other is as common as it is mistaken. More care is needed to connect the behaviors that evolved ... with the psychological mechanisms that evolved to motivate those behaviors" (p. 205). And to quote Batson, "as I once heard Richard Dawkins provocatively but accurately point out, an allele that produces bad teeth in horses (and leads to less effective grazing and more grass for others) is an example of evolutionary altruism. Similarly, an allele that leads one to smoke cigarettes, which may cause impotence, birth defects, and early death, is also an example of evolutionary altruism; it reduces one's procreative potential, thereby providing relative reproductive benefits to others. Most people interested in the existence of altruism are not thinking about bad teeth in horses or smoking cigarettes; they are thinking about psychological altruism" (p. 208).

Whether individuals who seek to obtain benefits for themselves without regard for others fare better biologically and contribute more copies of their genes to future generations than those who behave in less psychologically selfish ways is an open question. They might, or they might not. Certainly, there is nothing in the process of natural selection that dictates that individuals who are motivated to behave in psychologically selfish ways will prevail in the struggle for existence and reproduction. On the other side of the coin, there is no logical inconsistency in the assertion that behaving in psychologically unselfish ways may pay off biologically and genetically in the end. Cooperative individuals motivated to benefit both themselves and others, and altruistic individuals motivated to help others as an end in itself, could end up being more likely to survive, to produce offspring, and to propagate their genes than individuals who were motivated to help themselves at the expense of others.

Clearly, the first premise in the case against the evolution of morality – that all evolved dispositions are selfish – is valid only with respect to genetic forms of selfishness in the environments in which they were selected. The process of evolution leaves the door open for the evolution of the kinds of dispositions and behaviors that people commonly characterize as unselfish, as Darwin implicitly realized. Inasmuch as psychologically unselfish dispositions can be genetically selfish (i.e., can enhance the fitness of those who emit them), they can evolve.

Is Unselfishness Necessary for Morality?

I believe that the essence of morality lies in behaving in socially responsible, caring, cooperative, and fair ways. Character traits that dispose people to care for others, respect others' rights, and do their share are considered virtuous. Character traits that dispose individuals to behave in unfair and unkind ways are considered vices. On this definition of morality, the second premise in the case against the evolution of morality (that to qualify as moral, a disposition must be unselfish) is valid only with respect to psychological forms of unself-ishness. Trying to take more than one's share and give less – devoting one's efforts excessively to meeting one's own needs and advancing one's own interests without due regard for the needs and interests of others – is both selfish and immoral.

Defined in this way, all forms of conduct and character traits that people consider moral should be psychologically unselfish. I'm not positive that this is the case, but I believe it is safe to say that people consider most of the behaviors they classify as immoral psychologic-ally selfish. In contrast, people do not necessarily consider biologic-ally and genetically selfish behaviors immoral. Indeed, many believe that people have a moral duty to preserve their lives and to foster the welfare of their offspring. In itself, it is not immoral to foster your genetic interests by helping your kin (though it may be if it is done in nepotistic ways).

The genetic consequences of behaviors are irrelevant to most people's attributions of morality. Most people do not consider psy-chologically selfish behaviors aimed at maximizing people's profit and pleasure excessively at the expense of others moral even if these behaviors end up elevating others' fitness at actors' expense – for example, by ruining their health or turning others against them. Most people do not consider self-indulgent dispositions that induce individuals to eat or drink themselves to death or to kill their off-spring in fits of rage moral, even though such dispositions lower the fitness of the individuals who possess them. In contrast, most people consider individuals who are genuinely motivated to sacrifice their profit and pleasure for the sake of others moral, even if such sacri-fices ended up incidentally elevating their fitness (and therefore are genetically selfish). Morality does not pertain to individuals' success in surviving, reproducing, and propagating their genes; it per-tains to how individuals go about achieving these goals – whether through behaviors that are aimed at maximizing their own profit and pleasure at others' expense, or through more psychologically unselfish means.

It is important to note that concluding that psychological unselfishness is necessary for morality does not imply that psychological *altruism* is necessary for morality or that psychological unselfishness is *sufficient*. On the definition of morality advanced here, people can behave morally without behaving altruistically by, for example, tak-ing their fair share or advancing their interests in cooperative ways. People also can behave altruistically without behaving morally by, for example, helping someone cheat or saving the life of one friend at the expense of the lives of many strangers. To qualify as moral, a behavior must not only be unselfish, it also must be fair. It is relatively easy to meet the first criterion – unselfishness –, because it involves extending one's helping behaviors to individuals other than oneself. Meeting the second criterion – fairness – is much more challenging, because it requires individuals not only to help others, but also to distribute their helping in fair and equitable ways. As explained by philosophers of ethics such as Peter Singer,[31] the broader the range of others encompassed by a moral decision-rule (i.e., the more univer-sal the application), the more moral the behaviors it produces, when evaluated on objective criteria.

To summarize, the case against the evolution of morality seems to be strong because the two premises on which it is based seem to be valid. It is reasonable to assume that all evolved dispositions are self-ish and that selfish dispositions cannot be moral. However, neither premise is valid with respect to the form of selfishness assumed in the other premise. There is nothing in the process of natural selec-tion that prevents the evolution of psychologically unselfish coopera-tive and altruistic dispositions, and there is nothing about genetically selfish dispositions that prevents them from qualifying as moral. When one asks whether moral dispositions can evolve, it is not helpful to set genetic unselfishness as a necessary condition and then reach a negative conclusion, because all evolved dispositions are genetically selfish when they are selected. When selfishness is defined in this way, there is no question to ask, because the answer is contained in the definitions of the constructs.

Establishing that psychologically unselfish cooperative and altruistic dispositions *can* evolve opens the door for the evolution of moral dispositions, but it does not get us through. All kinds of dispositions could evolve, but they have not. The question we must answer is: What kinds of mental mechanisms enabled the ancestors of humans and members of other social species to solve the adaptive problems they encountered and to propagate their genes most effectively in the social and physical environments in which the mechanisms evolved – mechanisms that enabled or motivated them to benefit themselves at the expense of others; mechanisms that enabled or motivated them to benefit both themselves and others; or mechanisms that enabled or motivated them to benefit others at their own expense? I think that the correct answer to this question is, "all of the above."

The Adaptive Strengths and Limitations of Selfishness

As recognized by Darwin and many other evolutionary theorists, there is good reason to expect early humans who were psychologically disposed to enhance their own welfare at the expense of others to have fared better biologically and genetically than early humans who were motivated to sacrifice their welfare for the sake of others. Early humans who made selfish choices could have fared better than those who made cooperative choices, because they could have reaped the benefits of being treated cooperatively without suffering the costs of reciprocating. However, unconditionally selfish strategies suffer from several adaptive limitations.

For openers, the unmitigated pursuit of pleasure may be dangerous to one's heath. For example, as documented by Burnham and Phelan,[32] gluttony and the unconstrained consumption of alcohol and drugs may jeopardize people's survival and reproductive success. As explained by Gangstad[33] and Lack,[34] unrestrained promiscuity may jeopardize animals' reproductive success. Perhaps the most significant limitation of unconditionally selfish behaviors – especially those that people consider morally repugnant – is that they tend to evoke costly reactions from others. Animals bent on maximizing their profit by taking more than their share of resources or by exploiting one another could end up in a conflict that diminished their survival and reproductive success. In addition, animals that try to maximize their benefits at the expense of others may provoke their intended victims and other members of their groups to punish them – by refusing to help them when they are in need, by inflicting physical and material sanctions on them, by turning others against them, and by ostracizing them from their group.

More indirectly, selfish motives to maximize one's gains without regard for others may destroy beneficial relationships, undermine coalitions, and diminish the welfare of one's group as a whole, thereby jeopardizing the social environment that one needs to survive and to reproduce. In contrast, less selfish motives to help one's friends and other members of one's group may help preserve valuable resources, and therefore pay off physically, materially, biologically, and genetically in the end.

It is important to remember that the evolutionary consequences of motivational states, decision-making strategies, and forms of conduct are a function of the net genetic costs and benefits to the actor and to everyone else affected by the actor's behavior, including those with the same genes. Although we would expect psychologically selfish motives to be selected when they induced individuals to behave in ways that helped them propagate their genes at the expense of those who possessed alleles of their genes, we would not necessarily expect them to be selected when they induced individuals to behave in ways that jeopardized the genetic success of those who possessed copies of their genes.

The adaptive limitations of psychologically selfish forms of conduct open the door for the selection of dispositions to behave in psychologically unselfish ways. Although the benefits that animals behaving in cooperative and altruistic ways bestow on others could be byproducts of their desire to benefit themselves, this is neither the only, nor the most plausible, possibility. If we assume that animals that benefit themselves are motivated to benefit themselves, why not assume that animals that benefit others are motivated to achieve this goal?

Given the limitations of unconditionally selfish strategies, what kind of adaptive strategies would we expect to evolve? Not unconditionally cooperative or altruistic strategies, because they are susceptible to exploitation by selfish strategies. Indeed, we would not expect any kind of unconditional strategy to evolve, at least not in unpredictable environments. We would expect evolved social strategies to be designed in terms of implicit "if-then" types of decision rules of the form, "if the (internal or external) conditions are similar to those in which selfish behaviors paid off genetically in ancestral environments, then behave selfishly; if the conditions are similar to those in which unselfish behaviors paid off genetically in ancestral environments, then behave unselfishly." Different "if" conditions may activate different neurological, hormonal, emotional and motivational systems. It is inappropriate to characterize conditional strategies as either selfish or unselfish, because they give rise to both types of behavior, depending on the conditions. It follows that it is inappropriate to characterize species in which such conditional strategies have evolved as either selfish or unselfish; they are more appropriately characterized as both.

Summary

Evolutionary theorists have argued that all species are selfish by nature, but the type of selfishness meant by these theorists is quite different from the type of selfishness that is relevant to attributions of morality. When selfish dispositions are defined in a way that corresponds to the meaning that most people assign to the concept, such dispositions may or may not prevail in the process of natural selection. The evidence suggests that although psychologically selfish forms of conduct are adaptive in some conditions, they are limited in other conditions. The mechanisms regulating selfish (and unselfish) forms of conduct are designed in terms of conditional decision rules. The key to understanding human nature and the nature of other animals lies in deciphering these decision rules, mapping the ways in which the mechanisms that produce them are shaped during development, and identifying the internal and external stimuli that activate them in everyday life.

Notes

1. Calvin, J. (1559/1995). *Creation of sacred*. Cambridge, MA: Harvard University Press.
2. Elkind, D., and Weiner, I. B. (1978). *Development of the child*. New York: Wiley.
3. Freud, A. (1963). The infantile instinct life. In H. Herma and G. M. Karth (Eds.), *A handbook of psychoanalysis*. New York: World Publishing Company.
4. Darwin, C. (1874). *The descent of man and selection in relation to sex*. New York: Rand, McNally & Company.
5. Huxley, T. (1893). *Evolution and ethics. The second Romanes Lecture*. London: Macmillan.
6. Williams, G. C. (1989). A sociobiological expansion of "Evolution and Ethics," *Evolution and Ethics* (pp. 179–214). Princeton: Princeton University Press.
7. Dawkins, R. (1989). *The selfish gene*. Oxford: Oxford University Press.
8. Kurland, J. A., and Gaulin, S. J. C. (2005). Cooperation and conflict among kin. In D. Buss (Ed.) *The handbook of evolutionary psychology*, pp. 447–482. New York: John Wiley & Sons.
9. Sober, E., and Wilson, D. S. (1998). *Unto others: The evolution and psychology of unselfish behavior*. Cambridge MA: Harvard University Press.
10. Trivers, R. (1974). Parent-offspring conflict. *American Zoologist, 14*, 249–264.
11. Cheng, K. M., Burns, J. Tl, and McKinney, F. (1982). Forced copulation in captive mallards (*amas platyrhynchos*). *Animal Behavior, 30*, 695–699.
12. Barash, D.(1976). The male response to apparent female adultery in the mountain bluebird Sialia currucoides: An evolutionary interpretation. *American Naturalist, 110*, 1097–1101.
13. Daly, M., and Wilson, M. (1983). *Sex, evolution, and behavior*. Boston: Willard Grant Press.
14. Milgram, S. (1974). *Obedience to authority*. New York: Harper.
15. Zimbardo, P. Gl, Hane, C., Ganks, W. C., and Jaffe, D. A. (1973). Pirandellian prison: The mind is a formidable jailer. *New York Times Magazine*, pp. 38–60.
16. For example, see Staub, E. (1978). *Positive social behavior and morality*. New York: Academic Press; Oliner, P. M., Oliner, S. P., Baron, L., Krebs, D. L., and Smolenska, M. Z. (Eds.). (1992). *Embracing the other: Philosophical, psychological, and historical perspectives on altruism*. New York: New York University Press; and review chapters in the handbooks of social and developmental psychology.
17. Darwin, C. (1874). The descent of man and selection in relation to sex. New York: Rand, McNally & Company.

18. Huxley, T. (1893). *Evolution and ethics. The second Romanes Lecture.* London: Macmillan.
19. Williams, G. C. (1989). A sociobiological expansion of "Evolution and Ethics," *Evolution and Ethics* (pp. 179–214). Princeton: Princeton University Press.
20. Ghiselin, M. T. (1974). *The economy of nature and the evolution of sex.* Berkeley, CA: University of California Press.
21. Williams, G. C. (1989). A sociobiological expansion of "Evolution and Ethics," *Evolution and Ethics* (pp. 179–214). Princeton: Princeton University Press.
22. Williams, G. C. (1989). A sociobiological expansion of "Evolution and Ethics," *Evolution and Ethics* (pp. 179–214). Princeton: Princeton University Press.
23. Dawkins, R. (1989). *The selfish gene.* Oxford: Oxford University Press.
24. Campbell, D. (1978). On the genetics of altruism and the counterhedonic components of human nature. In L. Wispe (Ed.). *Altruism, sympathy, and helping,* pp. 39–58. New York: Academic Press.
25. Nesse, R. M. (2000). How selfish genes shape moral passions. L. D. Katz (Ed.). *Evolutionary origins of morality: Cross-disciplinary perspectives.* (pp. 227–231). Thorverton, UK: Imprint Academic.
26. Burnham, T. and Phelan, J. (2000). *Mean genes.* New York: Perseus Publishing.
27. Dawkins, R. (1989). *The selfish gene. (2nd ed.)* Oxford: Oxford University Press.
28. Batson, C. D. (2000). Unto others: A service ... and a disservice. *Journal of Consciousness Studies,* 7, 207–210.
29. Nesse, R. M. (2000). How selfish genes shape moral passions. L. D. Katz (Ed.). *Evolutionary Origins of Morality: Cross-disciplinary perspectives.* (pp. 227–231). Thorverton, UK: Imprint Academic.
30. Sober, E. and Wilson, D. S. (2000). Summary of "Unto others: The evolution and psychology of unselfish behavior." *Journal of Consciousness Studies,* 7, 185–206.
31. Singer, P. (1981). *The expanding circle: Ethics and sociobiology.* New York: Farrar Straus Giroux.
32. Burnham, T. and Phelan, J. (2000). *Mean genes.* New York: Perseus Publishing.
33. Gangestad, S. W. (2007). Biological adaptations and human behavior. In C. Crawford and D. L. Krebs (Eds.) *Foundations of evolutionary psychology.* London: Taylor & Francis.
34. Lack, D. (1954). *The natural regulation of animal numbers.* Oxford: Oxford University Press.

3

Morality and Its Relation to Primate Social Instincts

Frans B. M. de Waal

The question whether we are naturally good or bad is a perennial one. The past quarter of a century has seen biologists weigh in with a thoroughly pessimistic view according to which we are not naturally moral. This is a curious position, because it presents us as going against our own nature when striving for a moral life. Accordingly, we are moral only thanks to culture and religion. I will call this view "Veneer Theory," as it postulates morality as a thin layer disguising the less noble tendencies seen as the true core of human nature (de Waal 2006). Veneer Theory radically breaks with Charles Darwin's position that morality is an outgrowth of the social instincts, hence is continuous with the sociality of other animals (Darwin 1871).

Veneer Theory suffers from several unanswered questions. First, why would humans, and humans alone, have broken with their own biology? Second, how is such a feat even possible? And third, where is the empirical data? The theory predicts that morality resides in recently evolved parts of our enlarged brain and leads to behavior substantially at odds with that of animals. Both are verifiably wrong. For the latest human evidence, I refer to Haidt (2001) and Greene and Haidt (2002). This chapter discusses the animal evidence. Animals may not be moral beings, but they do show signs of empathy, reciprocity, and a sense of fairness. I will review evidence for the continuity between humans and other primates expected by Darwin, and suggest that the building blocks of morality are older than our species.

31

Veneer Theory

In 1893, Thomas Henry Huxley publicly tried to reconcile his dim view of a nasty natural world with the kindness occasionally encountered in human society. Huxley realized that the laws of the physical world are unalterable. He felt, however, that their impact on human existence could be softened and modified provided people kept nature under control. He compared us with a gardener who has a hard time keeping weeds out of his garden. Thus, he proposed ethics as a human cultural victory over the evolutionary process in the same way as the gardener conquers the weeds in his garden (Huxley 1894).

This position deliberately curbed the explanatory power of evolution. Since many consider morality the essence of our species, Huxley was in effect saying that what makes us human could not be handled within an evolutionary framework. It was an inexplicable retreat by someone who had gained a reputation as "Darwin's Bulldog" owing to his fierce advocacy of evolutionary theory. His solution was quintessentially Hobbesian in that it stated that people are fit for society only through education, not by their nature (Hobbes 1651).

If we are indeed Hobbesian competitors who don't care one bit about the feelings of others (*Homo homini lupus,* or Man is wolf to man), how did we decide to transform ourselves into model citizens? Can people for generations maintain behavior that is out of character, like a school of piranhas which decide to become vegetarians? How deep does such a change go?

Darwin saw morality in a totally different light. As Huxley's biographer, Desmond (1994, 599), put it: "Huxley was forcing his ethical Ark against the Darwinian current which had brought him so far." Two decades earlier, in *The Descent of Man,* Darwin (1871) had unequivocally stressed continuity between human nature and morality. The reason for Huxley's departure has been sought in his suffering on the cruel hand of nature, which had taken the life of his daughter, as well as his need to make the ruthlessness of the Darwinian cosmos palatable to the general public. He could do so only, he felt, by dislodging human ethics, declaring it a cultural innovation (Desmond 1994).

Huxley's dualism was to get a respectability boost from Sigmund Freud's writings, which throve on contrasts between the conscious and subconscious, the ego and super-ego, Love and Death, and so on. As with Huxley's gardener and garden, Freud was not just dividing the world in symmetrical halves: he saw struggle everywhere. He let civilization arise out of a renunciation of instinct, the gaining of control over the forces of nature, and the building of a cultural super-ego (Freud 1930).

That this remains a theme today is obvious from the statements by outspoken Huxleyans, which are still found among biologists. Declaring ethics a radical break with biology, George Williams has written extensively about the wretchedness of nature culminating in his claim that human morality is an inexplicable accident of the evolutionary process: "I account for morality as an accidental capability produced, in its boundless stupidity, by a biological process that is normally opposed to the expression of such a capability" (Williams 1988, 438).

Richard Dawkins (1996) suspects that we are nicer than is good for our "selfish genes," and has explicitly endorsed Huxley: "What I am saying, along with many other people, among them T. H. Huxley, is that in our political and social life we are entitled to throw out Darwinism, to say we don't want to live in a Darwinian world" (Roes 1997, 3).

Like Huxley, these authors generally believe that human behavior is an evolutionary product, except when it is unselfish. And like Freud, they propose dichotomies: we are part nature, part culture, rather than a well-integrated whole. The same position has been echoed by popularizers, such as Robert Wright (1994), who in *The Moral Animal* went so far as to claim that virtue is absent from people's hearts and souls. He bluntly stated that our species is potentially but not naturally moral. But what if people occasionally experience in themselves and others a degree of sympathy, goodness, and generosity? Wright's answer is that the "moral animal" is a fake:

> ...the pretense of selflessness is about as much part of human nature as is its frequent absence. We dress ourselves up in tony moral language, denying base motives and stressing our at least minimal consideration for the greater good; and we fiercely and self-righteously decry selfishness in others. (Wright 1994, 344)

This recalls the famous synopsis of Veneer Theory by Ghiselin (1974, 247): "Scratch an 'altruist,' and watch a 'hypocrite' bleed." To explain how we manage to live with ourselves despite this travesty, theorists have called upon self-deception (e.g., Badcock 1986). The problem is, of course, that self-deception is a

cognitively demanding process compared with the sentiments proposed by Hume (1739), Darwin (1871), Westermarck (1906; 1908),
and myself (de Waal 1996a; Flack and de Waal 2000). In the latter view, morality flows naturally from inborn social tendencies.
To illustrate these tendencies, I will review evidence for conflict
resolution, empathy, reciprocity, and an aversion to unfairness in
nonhuman primates.

Conflict Resolution

Reconciliation

In the summer of 2002 various national European behavioral biology
and ethology societies came together for a conference on animal conflict resolution. Research in this field started out with simple descriptive work, but is now rapidly moving toward a theoretical framework
supported by observational as well as experimental data (reviewed by
de Waal 2000; Aureli and de Waal 2000; Aureli et al. 2002).

Reconciliation was first reported by de Waal and van Roosmalen
(1979). A typical example concerns two male chimpanzees who
have been chasing each other, barking and screaming, and afterwards rest in a tree (Figure 3.1). Ten minutes later, one male holds
out his hand, begging the other for an embrace. Seconds later, they
hug and kiss, and climb down to the ground together to groom each
other. Termed a *reconciliation*, this process is defined as a friendly
contact not long after a conflict between two parties. A kiss is the
most typical way for chimpanzees to reconcile. Other primates have
different styles. Bonobos do it with sex, and stumptail macaques
wait until the subordinate presents, then hold its hips in a so-called
hold-bottom ritual. Each species has its own way, yet the basic principle remains the same, which is that former opponents reunite following a fight.

Primatology has always shown interest in social relationships, so
the idea of relationship repair, implied by the reconciliation label,
was quickly taken seriously. We now know that about 30 different
primate species reconcile after fights, and recent studies show that
reconciliation is not at all limited to the primates. There is evidence
for this mechanism in hyenas, dolphins, and domestic goats (Schino
2000). Reconciliation seems a basic process found, or to be found, in
a host of social species. The reason for it being so widespread is that
it restores relationships that have been disturbed by aggression but

Figure 3.1 Reconciliation ten minutes after a protracted, noisy conflict between two adult males at the Arnhem Zoo. The challenged male (left) had fled into the tree, but ten minutes later his opponent stretched out a hand. Within seconds, the two males had a physical reunion. (Photograph by the author.)

are nonetheless essential for survival. Since many animals establish cooperative relationships within which conflict occasionally arises, many need mechanisms of repair.

A standard research method is the PC/MC method (de Waal and Yoshihara 1983). Observations start with a spontaneous aggressive encounter after which the combatants are followed for a fixed period of time, say 10 minutes, to see what subsequently happens between them. This is the PC or post-conflict observation. Figure 3.2, which concerns stumptail macaques, shows that approximately 60 percent of the pairs of opponents come together after a fight. This is compared with control observations that tell us how these monkeys normally act without a preceding fight. Since control observations are done on a different observation day but matched to the PC observation for the time of the day and the individuals involved, they are called MC's, or matched controls.

Notice that there is far more contact after fights than in the control observations, which is exactly the opposite picture from that

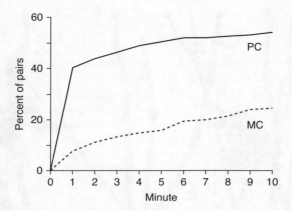

Figure 3.2   Primates show a dramatic increase in body contact between former
opponents during Post-Conflict (PC) as compared to Matched-Control
(MC) observations. The graph provides the cumulative percentage of
opponent-pairs establishing friendly contact during a ten-minute time
window following 670 spontaneous aggressive incidents in a zoo group
of stumptail macaques. (Based on de Waal & Ren (1988))

presented by the textbooks I read as a graduate student. In those days,
Lorenz's (1963) *On Aggression* was influential. The popular idea was
that aggression is a dispersive behavior, which serves to space out
individuals. This idea was developed on territorial species, which
were the first studied. With social animals, however, things are quite
different. In primates, we actually see the opposite: aggression literally brings individuals together.

If the same observations and analyses are conducted on human
children, as a co-worker and I did at a preschool near our university,
one finds the familiar PC/MC pattern (Verbeek and de Waal 2001).
An extensive review of recent child studies by Verbeek et al. (2000)
confirms that the data looks essentially the same for children, chimpanzees, monkeys, and goats. After fights, individuals come together
more than normally, often with intense contact patterns, doing so
especially with partners whom they need for one reason or another.
This behavior is explained by the Valuable Relationship Hypothesis,
according to which reconciliation will occur especially between individuals who stand much to lose if their relationship deteriorates. This
hypothesis has been well-supported by observational studies as well as
by an elegant experiment on monkeys, which manipulated relationship value by promoting cooperation (Cords and Thurnheer 1993).

Empathy

Emotional Linkage in Animals

When Zahn-Waxler visited homes to find out how children respond to family-members instructed to feign sadness (sobbing), pain (crying), or distress (choking), she discovered that children a little over one year of age already comfort others. This is a milestone in their development: an aversive experience in another person draws out a concerned response. An unexpected finding from this classical study, however, was that some household pets appeared as worried as the children by the "distress" of a family-member. They hovered over them or put their heads in their laps (Zahn-Waxler et al. 1984).

Intersubjectvtity has many aspects apart from emotional linkage, such as an appraisal of the other's situation, experience-based predictions about the other's behavior, extraction of information from the other that is valuable to the self, and an understanding of the other's knowledge and intentions. When the emotional state of one individual induces a matching or related state in another, we speak of *emotional contagion* (Hatfield et al. 1993). With increasing differentiation between self and other, and an increasing appreciation of the precise circumstances underlying the emotional states of others, emotional contagion develops into empathy. Empathy encompasses – and could not possibly exist without – emotional contagion, yet goes beyond it in that it places filters between the other's state and the own, and adds a cognitive layer. In empathy, the subject *does not* confuse its own internal state with the other's. These various levels of empathy, including personal distress and sympathetic concern, are defined and discussed in detail by Eisenberg (2000).

Empathy is a social phenomenon with great adaptive significance for animals in groups. That most modern textbooks on animal cognition do not index empathy or sympathy does not mean that these capacities are not essential; it only means that they have been overlooked by a science traditionally focused on individual rather than inter-individual capacities. Inasmuch as the survival of many animals depends on concerted action, mutual aid, and information transfer, selection must have favored proximate mechanisms to evaluate the emotional states of others and quickly respond to them in adaptive ways. Even though the human empathy literature often emphasizes the cognitive side of this ability, Hoffman (1981, 79) rightly noted early on that "humans must be equipped biologically to function effectively in many social situations without undue reliance on cognitive processes."

Empathy allows us to relate to the emotional states of others. This is critical for the regulation of social interactions, such as coordinated activity, cooperation toward a common goal, social bonding, and care of others. It would be strange indeed if a survival mechanism that arises so early in life in all members of our species would be without animal parallels.

Early Experiments

An interesting older literature by experimental psychologists addresses empathy (reviewed by Preston and de Waal 2002 a, b). In a paper provocatively entitled "Emotional reactions of rats to the pain of others," Church (1959) established that rats that had learned to press a lever to obtain food would stop doing so if their response was paired with the delivery of an electric shock to a neighboring rat. Even though this inhibition habituated rapidly, it suggested something aversive about the pain reactions of others. Perhaps such reactions arouse negative emotions in those who see and hear them.

In the same year as Church's rat study, Miller et al. (1959) published the first of a series of pioneering papers on the transmission of affect in rhesus macaques. They found that monkeys react with avoidance to pictures of conspecifics in a fearful pose, and that this reaction is stronger than that toward a negatively conditioned stimulus. This was an astonishing discovery, suggesting that to see the fear of a two-dimensional, soundless image of another monkey is more disturbing than the anticipation of an actual electric shock.

Perhaps the most compelling evidence for the strength of the empathic reaction in monkeys came from Wetchkin et al. (1964) and Masserman et al. (1964). They found that rhesus monkeys refuse to pull a chain that delivers food to themselves if doing so shocks a companion. One monkey stopped pulling for five days, and another one for twelve days after witnessing shock-delivery to a companion. These monkeys were literally starving themselves to avoid inflicting pain upon another, and maintained this response to a far greater degree than reported for rats.

Evidence of Primate Empathy

Qualitative accounts of great apes support the view that these animals show strong emotional reactions to others in pain or need. Yerkes (1925, 246) reported how his bonobo, Prince Chim, was so extraordinarily concerned and protective toward his sickly chimpanzee companion, Panzee, that the scientific establishment might not accept his claims: "If I were to tell of his altruistic and obviously sympathetic behavior toward Panzee I should be suspected of idealizing an ape" (Figure 3.3). Ladygina–Kohts (1935, 121) noticed similar empathic tendencies in her young chimpanzee, Joni, whom she raised at the beginning of the previous century, in Moscow. Kohts, who analyzed Joni's behavior in the minutest detail, discovered that the only way to get him off the roof of her house after an escape (much better than any reward or threat of punishment) was by appealing to his sympathy:

> If I pretend to be crying, close my eyes and weep, Joni immediately stops his plays or any other activities, quickly runs over to me, all excited and shagged, from the most remote places in the house, such as the roof or the ceiling of his cage, from where I could not drive him down despite my persistent calls and entreaties. He hastily runs around me, as if looking for the offender; looking at my face, he tenderly takes my chin in his palm, lightly touches my face with his finger, as though trying to understand what is happening, and turns around, clenching his toes into firm fists.

Similar reports are discussed by de Waal (1996a; 1997a), who suggests that, apart from emotional connectedness, apes have an appreciation of the other's situation and a degree of perspective-taking. Apes show the same empathic capacity that was so enduringly described by Smith (1759, 10) as "changing places in fancy with the sufferer."

O'Connell (1995) conducted a content analysis of thousands of qualitative reports, counting the frequency of three types of empathy, from emotional contagion to more cognitive forms, including an appreciation of the other's situation. Understanding the emotional state of another was particularly common in the chimpanzee, with most outcomes resulting in the subject comforting the object of distress. Monkey displays of empathy were far more restricted, but did include the adoption of orphans and reactions to illness, handicaps, and wounding.

This difference between monkey and ape empathy is also evident from systematic studies of a behavior known as "consolation," first documented by de Waal and van Roosmalen (1979). Consolation is defined as friendly, reassuring contact directed by an uninvolved bystander at one of the combatants in a previous aggressive incident. For example, a third–party goes over to the loser of a fight and

Figure 3.3   Robert Yerkes with two apes in his lap. This photo was taken in 1923, before the discovery of the bonobo as a distinct species. We know now that the ape on the right, named Prince Chim, was a bonobo. Prince Chim was described by Yerkes as gentler and more empathic than any other ape he knew. In debates about human evolution, the bonobo is largely ignored. (Photograph by Lee Russell, courtesy of the Yerkes National Primate Research Center)

Figure 3.4   Consolation among chimpanzees: a juvenile puts an arm around a
screaming adult male who has just been defeated in a fight with a rival.
(Photograph by the author)

gently puts an arm around his shoulders (Figure 3.4). Consolation is
not to be confused with reconciliation, which seems selfishly motivated (see above). The advantages of consolation for the actor remain
unclear. The actor could probably walk away from the scene without
negative consequences.

Chimpanzee consolation is well-quantified. De Waal and van
Roosmalen (1979) based their conclusions on an analysis of hundreds
of post-conflict observations, and a replication by de Waal and Aureli
(1996) included an even larger sample in which the authors sought to
test two relatively simple predictions: If third-party contacts indeed
serve to alleviate the distress of conflict participants, these contacts
should be directed more at recipients of aggression than at aggressors,
and more at recipients of intense than of mild aggression. Comparing
third-party contact rates with baseline levels, we found support for
both predictions.

Consolation has thus far been demonstrated in great apes only. When de Waal and Aureli (1996) set out to apply exactly the same observation protocols as used on chimpanzees to detect consolation in macaques, they failed to find any (see also Watts et al. 2000). This came as a surprise, because reconciliation studies, which employ essentially the same design, have shown reconciliation in species after species. Why, then, would consolation be restricted to apes?

Targeted helping in response to specific, sometimes novel situations, may require a distinction between self and other that allows the other's situation to be divorced from one's own while maintaining the emotional link that motivates behavior. Possibly, one cannot achieve cognitive empathy without a high degree of self-awareness. In other words, in order to understand that the source of a vicarious affective state is not oneself but the other and to understand why the other's state arose (e.g., the specific cause of the other's distress), one needs a distinction between self and other. Based on these assumptions, Gallup (1982) was the first to speculate about a possible connection between cognitive empathy and mirror self-recognition (MSR). This view is supported both developmentally, by a correlation between the emergence of MSR in children and their helping tendencies (Bischof-Köhler 1988; Zahn-Waxler et al. 1992), and phylogenetically, by the presence of complex helping and consolation in hominoids (i.e., humans and apes) but not monkeys. Hominoids are also the only primates with MSR.

I have argued before that, apart from consolation behavior, targeted helping reflects cognitive empathy. Targeted helping is defined as altruistic behavior tailored to the specific needs of the other even in novel situations, such as the highly publicized case of Binti-Jua, a gorilla female who rescued a human boy at the Brookfield Zoo, in Chicago (de Waal 1996a; 1999). Targeted helping is common in the great apes, but also striking in dolphins (Caldwell and Caldwell 1966) and elephants (Poole 1996; Douglas-Hamilton et al. 2006). The recent discovery of MSR in dolphins (Reiss and Marino 2001) and elephants (Plotnik et al. 2006) thus fits the proposed connection between increased self-awareness, on the one hand, and cognitive empathy, on the other.

Russian Doll Model

The literature includes many accounts of empathy as a cognitive affair, even to the point that apes, let alone other animals, probably lack it (Povinelli 1998; Hauser 2000). This "top–down" view equates empathy with mental state attribution and theory of mind (ToM). The opposite position has recently been defended, however, in relation to autistic children. Contra earlier assumptions that autism reflects a deficit in ToM (Baron–Cohen 2000), autism is noticeable well before the age of 4 years at which ToM typically emerges. Williams et al. (2001) argue that the main deficit of autism concerns the socio–affective level, which then negatively impacts more sophisticated down–stream forms of inter–personal perception, such as ToM (see also Baron–Cohen 2004).

Preston and de Waal (2002a) propose that at the core of the empathic capacity is a relatively simple mechanism that provides an observer (the "subject") with access to the subjective state of another (the "object") through the subject's own neural and bodily representations. When the subject attends to the object's state, the subject's neural representations of similar states are *automatically* activated. The more similar the subject and object, the more the object will activate matching peripheral motor and autonomic responses in the subject (e.g., changes in heart rate, skin conductance, facial expression, body posture). This activation allows the subject to understand that the object also has an extended consciousness including thoughts, feelings, and needs, which in turn fosters sympathy, compassion, and helping. Preston and de Waal (2002b) and de Waal (2003) propose evolutionary continuity in this regard between humans and other mammals. Their Perception–Action Model (PAM) fits Damasio's (1994) somatic marker hypothesis of emotions as well as recent evidence for a link at the cellular level between perception and action (e.g., "mirror neurons," di Pelligrino et al. 1992).

The idea that perception and action share common representations is anything but new: it goes as far back as the first treatise on *Einfühlung*, the German concept later translated into English as "empathy" (Wispé 1991). When Lipps (1903) introduced *Einfühlung*, which literally means "feeling into," he speculated about *innere Nachahmung* (inner mimicry) of another's feelings along the same lines as proposed by the PAM. Accordingly, empathy is often an automatic, insuppressible process, as demonstrated by electromyographic studies of invisible muscle contractions in people's faces in response to pictures of human facial expressions (Dimberg et al. 2000). Accounts of empathy as a higher cognitive process neglect these "gut level" reactions, which are far too rapid to be under voluntary control.

Perception–action mechanisms are well-known for motor perception (Prinz and Hommel 2002), causing researchers to assume similar processes to underlie emotion perception (Gallese 2001; Wolpert et al. 2001). Data suggests that observing and experiencing an emotion involve similar physiological substrates (Adolphs et al. 1997; 2000), and that affect communication creates similar physiological activity in subject and object (Dimberg 1982; 1990; Levenson and Reuf 1992). Recent investigations of neural mechanisms of empathy (Carr et al. 2003; Preston et al. 2002; Wicker et al. 2003; Singer et al. 2004; de Gelder et al. 2004) lend support to or are at least consistent with the PAM.

This "bottom-up" view has been depicted as a Russian doll (de Waal 2008; Figure 3.5). Accordingly, empathy covers all forms of one individual's emotional state affecting another's, with simple mechanisms at its core and more complex mechanisms, cognitive filters, and perspective-taking abilities built on top. Autism may be reflected in deficient outer layers of the Russian doll, but such deficiencies most likely go back to deficient inner layers.

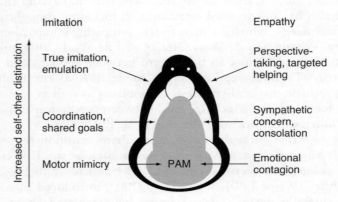

Figure 3.5   The Russian Doll model of empathy and imitation. Empathy (right) induces a similar emotional state in the subject as the object, with the perception-action mechanism (PAM) at its core. The doll's outer layers, such as sympathetic concern and perspective-taking, build upon this hard-wired socio-affective basis. Sharing the same mechanism, the doll's imitation side (left) correlates with the empathy side. Here, the PAM underlies motor mimicry, coordination, shared goals, and true imitation. Even though the doll's outer layers depend on prefrontal functioning and an increasing self-other distinction, they remain fundamentally linked to its inner core. (From de Waal, 2008)

Whereas monkeys (and many other social mammals) clearly seem to possess emotional contagion and some forms of targeted helping, the latter phenomenon is not nearly as robust as in the great apes. For example, at Jigokudani monkey park, in Japan, first-time mother macaques are kept out of the hot water springs by park wardens because of their experience that these females will accidentally drown their infants. They fail to pay attention to them when submerging themselves in the ponds (de Waal 1996b). This is something they apparently learn to do over time, showing that they do not automatically take their offspring's perspective. Ape mothers, in contrast, respond immediately and appropriately to the specific needs of their offspring and are very careful to keep them away from water (personal observation).

In conclusion, empathy is not an all-or-nothing phenomenon: it covers a wide range of emotional linkage patterns, from the very simple and automatic to the very sophisticated. It seems logical to first try to understand the more basic forms, which are widespread indeed, before addressing the interesting variations that cognitive evolution has constructed on top of this foundation.

Reciprocity

Chimpanzees and capuchin monkeys – the two species I work with the most – are special, because they are among the very few primates that share food outside the mother–offspring context. The capuchin is a small, easy animal to work with, as opposed to the chimpanzee, which is many times stronger than we are. But chimpanzees, too, are interested in each others' food and will share on occasion – sometimes even hand over a piece of food to another. Most sharing, however, is passive, where one individual will reach for food owned by another, who will let go (de Waal 1997b). But even such passive sharing is special compared to most animals, in which such a situation might result in a fight or assertion by the dominant, without sharing.

One series of experiments concerned the idea that monkeys cooperate on the basis of mental record-keeping of favors. We set up a situation to study tit-for-tat: I do something for you and, a while later, you do something for me. Inspired by a classic 1930s study at the Yerkes Primate Center and the theories of Trivers (1971), we presented a pair of capuchin monkeys with a tray with two pull bars attached to it (de Waal and Berger 2000). Both monkeys sat in a test chamber with mesh between them, so that they could see each other and share food through the mesh. The tray was counterweighted such that a single monkey couldn't pull it: they needed to work together. Only one side was baited, meaning that only one of the two monkeys would obtain a food reward.

After successful pulls we measured how much food the possessor shared with its helper. Possessors could easily keep the food by sitting in the corner and eating alone, but didn't do so. We found that food-sharing after cooperative efforts was higher than after solo efforts. That is, the possessor of food shared more with the monkey on the other side of the mesh if this partner had played a role in securing the food than if the possessor had acquired the food on its own. Capuchins thus seem to reward helpers for their efforts, which is of course also a way of keeping assistants motivated.

Fairness

The above relates to the distribution of pay-offs. How skewed can it be before cooperation disappears? According to a recent theory, the well-known human aversion to inequity relates to the need to maintain cooperation (Fehr and Schmidt 1999). Similarly, cooperative nonhuman species seem guided by a set of expectations about pay-off distribution. De Waal (1996a, 95) proposed a *sense of social regularity,* defined as: "A set of expectations about the way in which oneself (or others) should be treated and how resources should be divided. Whenever reality deviates from these expectations to one's (or the other's) disadvantage, a negative reaction ensues, most commonly protest by subordinate individuals and punishment by dominant individuals."

Note that the expectations have not been specified: they are species-typical. To explore expectations held by capuchin monkeys we made use of their ability to judge and respond to value. We knew from previous studies that capuchins easily learn to assign value to tokens. Furthermore they can use these assigned values to complete a simple barter. This allowed a test to elucidate inequity aversion by measuring the reactions of subjects to a partner receiving a superior reward for the same tokens.

We paired each monkey with a group mate and watched reactions if their partners got a better reward for doing the same bartering task. This consisted of an exchange in which the experimenter gave the subject a token that could immediately be returned for a reward. Each session consisted of 25 exchanges by each individual, and subjects always saw their partner's exchange immediately before their own (Figure 3.6). Food rewards varied from low-value rewards (a cucumber piece), which they are usually happy to work for, to high-value rewards (a grape), which were preferred by all

Figure 3.6 A capuchin monkey in the test chamber returns a token to the experimenter with her right hand while steadying the human hand with her left. Her partner looks on. (Drawing by Gwen Bragg and Frans de Waal after a video still)

individuals tested. All subjects were subjected to (a) an Equity Test, in which subject and partner did the same work for the same low-value food; (b) an Inequity Test, in which the partner received a superior reward (grape) for the same effort; (c) an Effort Control Test, designed to elucidate the role of effort, in which the partner received the higher-value grape for free; and (d) a Food Control Test, designed to elucidate the effect of the presence of the reward on subject behavior, in which grapes were visible but not given to another capuchin.

Individuals who received lower-value rewards showed both passive negative reactions (i.e., refusal to exchange the token, ignoring the reward) and active negative reactions (i.e., throwing out the token or reward). Compared to tests in which both received identical rewards, the capuchins were far less willing to complete the exchange or accept the reward if their partner received a better deal (Brosnan and de Waal 2003).

Of course, there is always the possibility that subjects were reacting to the mere presence of the higher-value food and that what the partner received (free or not) did not affect their reaction. However, in a recent replication of the study with more subjects and more control conditions it could be shown that the reaction is not due to available foods nor to what kind of food has been received previously. This new study confirmed that the reactions are due to what the partner is getting, and added effort as a factor, in the sense that the most negative reactions occurred when the own effort was large and the partner was nevertheless getting better rewards (van Wolkenten et al. 2007).

Capuchin monkeys thus seem to measure reward in relative terms, comparing their own rewards with those available and their own efforts with those of others. Although our data cannot elucidate the precise motivations underlying these responses, one possibility is that monkeys, like humans, are guided by social emotions. These emotions, known as "passions" by economists, guide human reactions to the efforts, gains, losses, and attitudes of others (Hirschleifer 1987; Frank 1988; Sanfey et al. 2003). As opposed to primates marked by despotic hierarchies, tolerant species with well-developed food-sharing and cooperation, such as capuchin monkeys, may hold emotionally charged expectations about reward distribution and social exchange that lead them to dislike inequity.

Morality and In-Group Loyalty

We have contrasted here two separate schools of thought on human morality. One sees people as essentially evil and selfish, and explains morality as a cultural overlay ungrounded in human nature or evolutionary theory. This dualistic school of thought, personified by T. H. Huxley, is still very much with us.

The second school, going back to David Hume and Charles Darwin (and ultimately Aristotle; Arnhart 1998), sees the moral sense naturally arising in our species. Apart from our obvious competitive tendencies, we are social to the core. The human species is what zoologists call *obligatorily social,* that is, its survival is closely tied to group life and cooperation. Obviously, the question of how we came to be this way can be answered only if we broaden the evolutionary horizon beyond the dog-eat-dog theories that have dominated science writing about human biology during the past three decades.

Morality is a group-oriented phenomenon born from the fact that we rely on a support system for survival (MacIntyre 1999). A solitary person would have no need for morality, nor would a person who lives with others without mutual dependency. Under such circumstances, each individual would go its own way. There would be no pressure to evolve moral tendencies or constraints.

In order to promote cooperation and harmony within the community, morality places boundaries on behavior, especially when interests collide. Moral rules create a *modus vivendi* among rich and poor, healthy and sick, old and young, married and unmarried, and so on. Since morality helps people get along and accomplish joint endeavors, it often places the common good above individual interests. It never denies the latter, but insists that we treat others the way we would like to be treated ourselves. More specifically, the moral domain of action is Helping or (not) Hurting others. The two H's are interconnected. If you are drowning and I withhold assistance, I am in effect hurting you. The decision to help, or not, is by all accounts a moral one.

Anything unrelated to the two H's falls outside of morality. Those who invoke morality in reference to, say, same-sex marriage or the visibility of a naked breast on primetime television are merely trying to couch social conventions in moral language. Since social conventions are not necessarily anchored in the needs of others and the community, the harm done by transgressions is debatable. Social conventions vary greatly: what shocks people in one culture (such as burping after a meal) may be recommended in another. Constrained by their impact on the well-being of others, moral rules are far more constant than social conventions. The golden rule is universal. The moral issues of our time – capital punishment, abortion, euthanasia, and taking care of the old, sick, or poor – all revolve around the eternal themes of life, death, resources, and caring.

Critical resources relating to the two H's are food and mates, which are both subject to rules of possession, division, and exchange. Food is most important for female primates, especially when they are pregnant or lactating (which they are much of the time), and mates are most important for males, whose reproduction depends on the number of fertilized females. This may explain the notorious "double standard" in favor of men when it comes to marital infidelity. Women, on the other hand, are favored in child custody cases, reflecting the primacy assigned to the mother–child bond. Thus, even if we strive for gender-neutral moral standards, real-life judgments are not immune to basic mammalian biology. A viable moral system rarely lets its rules get out of touch with the biological imperatives of survival and reproduction.

Given how well orientation toward the own group has served humanity for millions of years, and how well it serves us still, a moral system cannot possibly give equal attention to all life on earth. The system has to set priorities. As noted by Pierre-Joseph Proudhon over a century ago: "If everyone is my brother, I have no brothers" (Hardin 1982).

Morality evolved to deal with the own community first, and has only recently begun to include members of other groups, humanity in general, and nonhuman animals. While applauding the expansion of the circle, this expansion is constrained by affordability – that is, the circles are allowed to expand in times of abundance but will inevitably shrink when resources dwindle (Figure 3.7). This is so because the circles track levels of commitment: "The circle of morality reaches out farther and farther only if the health and survival of the innermost circles are secure" (de Waal 1996a, 213). Since we currently live under affluent circumstances, we can (and ought to) worry about those less fortunate than ourselves. Nevertheless, a level playing field, in which all circles count equally, clashes with ancient survival strategies.

It is not just that we are biased in favor of the innermost circles (ourselves, our family, our community, our species) – we *ought* to be.

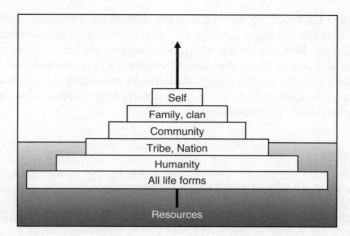

Figure 3.7 The expanding circle of human morality is actually a floating pyramid viewed from above. Loyalty and duty to immediate family, clan, or species serve as counterforce to moral inclusion. Altruism is spread thinner the further away we get from the center. The pyramid's buoyancy (i.e. available resources) determines how much of it will emerge from the water. The moral inclusion of outer circles is constrained by commitment to inner ones. (From de Waal 1996a)

Loyalty is a moral duty. If I were to come home empty-handed after a day of foraging during a general famine, and told my hungry family that I did find bread, yet gave it away to another family, they would be upset with me. It would be seen as a moral failure, as an injustice, not because the other family is not deserving of sustenance, but because of my duty to those close to me. The contrast becomes even starker during war, when solidarity with the own tribe or nation is compulsory: we find treason reprehensible.

All of this to say that morality is a human survival strategy. A child is not going against its own nature by developing a caring, moral attitude any more than that civil society is an out-of-control garden subdued by Huxley's sweating gardener. Moral attitudes have been with us from the start, and the gardener rather is, as John Dewey aptly put it, an organic grower. The successful gardener creates conditions and introduces plants that may not be normal for this particular plot of land "but fall within the wont and use of nature as a whole" (Dewey 1898, 109–10).

To deny the evolutionary roots of human morality and neglect the common ground with other primates would be like arriving at the top of a tower to declare that the rest of the building is irrelevant, that the precious concept of "tower" ought to be reserved for its summit. While making for good academic fights, semantics are mostly a waste of time. Are animals moral? Let us simply conclude that they occupy several floors of the tower of morality. Rejection of even this modest proposal can only result in an impoverished view of the structure as a whole.

References

Adolphs, R., L. Cahill, R. Schul, and R. Babinsky. 1997. Impaired declarative memory for emotional material following bilateral amygdala damage in humans. *Learning & Memory* 4:291–300.

Adolphs, R., H. Damasio, D. Tranel, G. Cooper, and A. R. Damasio. 2000. A role for somatosensory cortices in the visual recognition of emotion as revealed by three-dimensional lesion mapping. *Journal of Neuroscience* 20:2683–90.

Arnhart, L. 1998. *Darwinian Natural Right: The Biological Ethics of Human Nature*. Albany, NY: SUNY Press.

Aureli, F., and F. B. M. de Waal. 2000. *Natural Conflict Resolution*. Berkeley: University of California Press.

Aureli, F., M. Cords, and C. P. van Schaik. 2002. Conflict resolution following aggression in gregarious animals: A predictive framework. *Animal Behaviour* 64:325–43.

Badcock, C. R. 1986. *The Problem of Altruism: Freudian-Darwinian Solutions*. Oxford: Blackwell.

Baron-Cohen, S. 2000. Theory of mind and autism: A fifteen year review. In *Understanding Other Minds*, S. Baron-Cohen, H. Tager-Flusberg, and D. J. Cohen (Eds.), pp. 3–20. Oxford: Oxford University Press.

Baron-Cohen, S. 2004. Sex differences in social development: Lessons from autism. In *Social and Moral Development: Emerging Evidence on the Toddler Years*. L. A. Leavitt and D. M. B. Hall (Eds.), pp. 125–41. Johnson and Johnson Pediatric Institute.

Bischof-Köhler, D. 1988. Über den Zusammenhang von Empathie und der Fähigkeit sich im Spiegel zu erkennen. *Schweizerische Zeitschrift für Psychologie* 47:147–59.

Brosnan, S. F., and F. B. M. de Waal. 2003. Monkeys reject unequal pay. *Nature* 425:297–9.

Caldwell, M. C., and Caldwell, D. K. 1966. Epimeletic (care-giving) behavior in Cetacea. In *Whales, Dolphins, and Porpoises,* K. S. Norris (ed.), pp. 755–89. Berkeley: University of California Press.

Carr, L., M. Iacoboni, M. C. Dubeau, J. C. Mazziotta, and G. L. Lenzi. 2003. Neural mechanisms of empathy in humans: A relay from neural systems for imitation to limbic areas. *Proceedings from the National Academy of Sciences* 100:5497–502.

Church, R. M. 1959. Emotional reactions of rats to the pain of others. *Journal of Comparative & Physiological Psychology* 52:132–4.

Cords, M., and S. Thurnheer. 1993. Reconciliation with valuable partners by long-tailed macaques. *Ethology* 93:315–25.

Damasio, A. 1994. *Descartes' Error: Emotion, Reason, and the Human Brain.* New York: Putnam.

Darwin, C. 1981 [1871]. *The Descent of Man, and Selection in Relation to Sex.* Princeton, NJ: Princeton University Press.

Dawkins, R. 1996. No title. *Times Literary Supplement*, November 29:13.

de Gelder, B., J. Snyder, D. Greve, G. Gerard, and N. Hadjikhani. 2004. Fear fosters flight: A mechanism for fear contagion when perceiving emotion expressed by a whole body. *Proceedings from the National Academy of Sciences* 101:16701–6.

de Waal, F. B. M. 1996a. *Good Natured: The Origins of Right and Wrong in Humans and Other Animals.* Cambridge, MA: Harvard University Press.

de Waal, F. B. M. 1996b. Conflict as negotiation. In *Great Ape Societies*, W. C. McGrew, L. F. Marchant, and T. Nishida (Eds.), pp. 159–72. Cambridge: Cambridge University Press.

de Waal, F. B. M. 1997a. *Bonobo: The Forgotten Ape.* Berkeley: University of California Press.

de Waal, F. B. M. 1997b. The chimpanzee's service economy: Food for grooming. *Evolution & Human Behavior* 18:375–86.

de Waal, F. B. M. 1999. Anthropomorphism and anthropodenial: Consistency in our thinking about humans and other animals. *Philosophical Topics* 27:255–80.

de Waal, F. B. M. 2000. Primates – A natural heritage of conflict resolution. *Science* 289:586–90.

de Waal, F. B. M. 2006. *Primates and Philosophers.* Princeton, NJ: Princeton University Press.

de Waal, F. B. M. 2008. Putting the altruism back into altruism: The evolution of empathy. *Annual Review of Psychology* 59:279–300.

de Waal, F. B. M., and F. Aureli. 1996. Consolation, reconciliation, and a possible cognitive difference between macaque and chimpanzee. In *Reaching into Thought: The Minds of the Great Apes*, A. E. Russon, K. A. Bard, and S. T. Parker (Eds.), pp. 80–110. Cambridge: Cambridge University Press.

de Waal, F. B. M., and M. L. Berger. 2000. Payment for labour in monkeys. *Nature* 404:563.

de Waal, F. B. M., and R. Ren. 1988. Comparison of the reconciliation behavior of stumptail and rhesus macaques. *Ethology* 78:129–42.

de Waal, F. B. M., and A. van Roosmalen. 1979. Reconciliation and consolation among chimpanzees. *Behavioral Ecology & Sociobiology* 5:55–66.

de Waal, F. B. M., and D. Yoshihara. 1983. Reconciliation and re-directed affection in rhesus monkeys. *Behaviour* 85:224–41.

Desmond, A. 1994. *Huxley: From Devil's Disciple to Evolution's High Priest*. New York: Perseus.

Dewey, J. 1993 [orig. 1898]. Evolution and Ethics. Reprinted in *Evolutionary Ethics*, M. H. Nitecki and D. V. Nitecki (Eds.), pp. 95–110. Albany, NY: State University of New York Press.

di Pellegrino, G., L. Fadiga, L. Fogassi, V. Gallese, and G. Rizzolatti. 1992. Understanding motor events: A neurophysiological study. *Experimental Brain Research* 91:176–80.

Dimberg, U. 1982. Facial reactions to facial expressions. *Psychophysiology* 19:643–7.

Dimberg, U. 1990. Facial electromyographic reactions and autonomic activity to auditory stimuli. *Biological Psychology* 31:137–47.

Dimberg, U., M. Thunberg, and K. Elmehed. 2000. Unconscious facial reactions to emotional facial expressions. *Psychological Science* 11:86–9.

Eisenberg, N. 2000. Empathy and sympathy. In *Handbook of Emotion*, M. Lewis and J. M. Haviland-Jones (Eds.), 2nd edition, pp. 677–91. New York: Guilford Press.

Fehr, E., and K. M. Schmidt. 1999. A theory of fairness, competition, and cooperation. *Quarterly Journal of Economics* 114:817–68.

Flack, J. C., and de F. B. M. Waal. 2000. "Any animal whatever:" Darwinian building blocks of morality in monkeys and apes. *Journal of Consciousness Studies* 7(1–2):1–29.

Frank, R. H. 1988. *Passions Within Reason: The Strategic Role of the Emotions*. New York: Norton.

Freud, S. 1930. *Civilization and Its Discontents*. New York: Norton.

Gallese, V. 2001. The "shared manifold"' hypothesis: From mirror neurons to empathy. In *Between ourselves: Second-person issues in the study of consciousness*, E. Thompson (Eds.), 33–50. Thorverton, UK: Imprint Academic.

Gallup, G. G. 1982. Self-awareness and the emergence of mind in primates. *American Journal of Primatology* 2:237–48.

Ghiselin, M. 1974. *The Economy of Nature and the Evolution of Sex*. Berkeley: University of California Press.

Gould, S. J. 1980. So cleverly kind an animal. In *Ever Since Darwin*, pp. 260–7. Harmondsworth, UK: Penguin.

Greene, J., and J. Haidt. 2002. How (and Where) Does Moral Judgement Work? *Trends in Cognitive Sciences* 16:517–23.

Haidt, J. 2001. The emotional dog and its rational tail: A social intuitionist approach to moral judgment. *Psychological Review* 108:814–34.

Hamilton-Douglas, I., S. Bhalla, G. Wittemyer, and F. Vollrath. 2006. Behavioural reactions of elephants towards a dying and deceased matriarch. *Applied Animal Behaviour Science* 100:87–102.

Hardin, G. 1982. Discriminating altruisms. *Zygon* 17:163–86.

Hatfield, E., J. T. Cacioppo, and R. L. Rapson. 1993. Emotional contagion. *Current Directions in Psychological Science* 2:96–9.

Hauser, M. D. 2000. *Wild Minds: What Animals Really Think*. New York: Holt.

Hirschleifer, J. 1987. On the emotions as guarantors of threats and promises. In *The Latest on the Best: Essays in Evolution and Optimality*, J. Dupre (Ed.), pp. 307–26. Cambridge, MA: MIT Press.

Hobbes, T. 1991 [1651]. *Leviathan*. Cambridge: Cambridge University Press.

Hoffman, M. L. 1981. Perspectives on the Difference between Understanding People and Understanding Things: The Role of Affect. In *Social Cognitive Development,* edited by J. H. Flavell and L. Ross, 67–81. Cambridge: Cambridge University Press.

Hume, D. 1978 [1739]. *A Treatise of Human Nature*. Oxford: Oxford University Press.

Huxley, T. H. 1989 [1894]. *Evolution and Ethics*. Princeton, NJ: Princeton University Press.

Ladygina-Kohts, N. N. 1935 [2001]. *Infant Chimpanzee and Human Child: A Classic 1935 Comparative Study of Ape Emotions and Intelligence*. F. B. M. de Waal (Ed.). New York: Oxford University Press.

Levenson, R. W., and A. M. Reuf. 1992. Empathy: A physiological substrate. *Journal of Personality and Social Psychology* 63:234–46.

Lipps, T. 1903. Einfühlung, innere Nachahmung und Organempfindung. *Archiv für die gesamte Psychologie* 1:465–519.

Lorenz, K. Z. 1963 [1966]. *On Aggression*. London: Methuen.

Macintyre, A. 1999. *Dependent Rational Animals: Why Human Beings Need the Virtues*. Chicago: Open Court.

Masserman, J., M. S. Wechkin, and W. Terris. 1964. Altruistic behavior in rhesus monkeys. *Am. J. Psychiatry* 121:584–5.

Miller, R. E., J. V. Murphy, and I. A. Mirsky. 1959. Relevance of facial expression and posture as cues in communication of affect between monkeys. *AMA Archives of General Psychiatry* 1:480–8.

O'Connell, S. M. 1995. Empathy in chimpanzees: Evidence for theory of mind? *Primates* 36:397–410.

Plotnik, J., de F. B. M. Waal, and D. Reiss. 2006. Self-recognition in an Asian elephant. *Proceedings National Academy of Sciences* 103:17053–57.

Poole J. 1996. *Coming of Age with Elephants: A Memoir*. New York: Hyperion.

Povinelli, D. J. 1998. Can animals empathize? Maybe not. *Scientific American*: http://geowords.com/lostlinks/b36/7.htm

Preston, S. D., and F. B. M. de Waal. 2002a. Empathy: Its ultimate and proximate bases. *Behavioral & Brain Sciences* 25:1–72.

Preston, S. D., and F. B. M. de Waal. 2002b. The communication of emotions and the possibility of empathy in animals. In *Altruistic Love: Science,*

Philosophy, and Religion in Dialogue, edited by S. G. Post, L. G. Underwood, J. P. Schloss, and W. B. Hurlbut, 284–308. Oxford: Oxford University Press.

Preston, S. D., A. Bechara, T. J. Grabowski, H. Damasio, and A. R. Damasio. 2002. Functional anatomy of emotional imagery: Positron Emission Tomography of personal and hypothetical experiences. *Journal of Cognitive Neuroscience* 126.

Prinz, W., and B. Hommel. 2002. *Common Mechanisms in Perception and Action*. Oxford: Oxford University Press.

Reiss, D., and L. Marino. 2001. Mirror self-recognition in the bottlenose dolphin: A case of cognitive convergence. *Proceedings of the National Academy of Science* 98:5937–42.

Roes, F. 1997. An interview of Richard Dawkins. *Human Ethology Bulletin* 12(1):1–3.

Sanfey, A. G., J. K. Rilling, J. A. Aronson, L. E. Nystrom, and J. D. Cohen. 2003. The neural basis of economic decision-making in the Ultimatum game. *Science* 300:1755–8.

Schino, G. 2000. Beyond the primates: Expanding the reconciliation horizon. In *Natural Conflict Resolution,* edited by F. Aureli and F. B. M. de Waal, 225–42. Berkeley: University of California Press.

Singer, T., B. Seymour, J. O'Doherty, H. Kaube, R. J. Dolan, and C. D. Frith. 2004. Empathy for pain involves the affective but not sensory components of pain. *Science* 303:1157–62.

Smith, A. 1937 [1759]. *A Theory of Moral Sentiments*. New York: Modern Library.

Trivers, R. L. 1971. The evolution of reciprocal altruism. *Quarterly Review of Biology* 46:35–57.

van Wolkenten, M., S. F. Brosnan, F. B. M. de Waal. 2007. Inequity responses of monkeys modified by effort. *Proceedings of the National Academy of Sciences* 104:18854–9.

Verbeek, P., and de F. B. M. de Waal. 2001. Peacemaking among preschool children. *Peace and Conflict: Journal of Peace Psychology* 7:5–28.

Verbeek, P., W. W. Hartup, and W. C. Collins. 2000. Conflict management in children and adolescents. In *Natural Conflict Resolution*, edited by F. Aureli and F. B. M. de Waal), 34–53. Berkeley: University of California Press.

Watts, D. P., F. Colmenares, and K. Arnold. 2000. Redirection, consolation, and male policing: How targets of aggression interact with bystanders. In *Natural Conflict Resolution*, edited by F. Aureli and F. B. M. de Waal), 281–301. Berkeley: University of California Press.

Westermarck, E. 1912 [1906]. *The Origin and Development of the Moral Ideas,* Volume 1, 2nd Edition. London: Macmillan.

Westermarck, E. 1917 [1908]. *The Origin and Development of the Moral Ideas,* Volume 2, 2nd Edition. London: Macmillan.

Wicker, B., C. Keysers, J. Plailly, J. P. Royet, V. Gallese, and G. Rizzolatti. 2003. Both of Us Disgusted in My Insula: The Common Neural Basis of Seeing and Feeling Disgust. *Neuron* 40:655–64.

Williams, G. C. 1988. Reply to comments on "Huxley's evolution and ethics in sociobiological perspective." *Zygon* 23:437–8.

Williams, J. H. G., A. Whiten, T. Suddendorf, and D. I. Perrett. 2001. Imitation, mirror neurons and autism. *Neuroscience and Biobehavioral Reviews* 25:287–95.

Wispé, L. 1991. *The Psychology of Sympathy*. New York: Plenum.

Wolpert, D. M., Z. Ghahramani, and J. R. Flanagan. 2001. Perspectives and problems in motor learning. *Trends in Cognitive Sciences* 5:487–94.

Wright, R. 1994. *The Moral Animal: The New Science of Evolutionary Psychology*. New York: Pantheon.

Yerkes, R. M. 1925. *Almost Human*. New York: Century.

Zahn-Waxler, C., B. Hollenbeck, and M. Radke-Yarrow. 1984. The origins of empathy and altruism. In *Advances in Animal Welfare Science*, 21–39. M. W. Fox and L. D. Mickley (Eds.). Washington, DC: Humane Society of the United States.

Zahn-Waxler, C., M. Radke-Yarrow, E. Wagner, and M. Chapman. 1992. Development of concern for others. *Developmental Psychology* 28:126–36.

4

Why We Believe: Religion as a Human Universal

Ara Norenzayan

In a species with tremendous cultural diversity, the suite of propensities we call "religion" tops the list of species-specific human universals. Most people in most cultures throughout history are, and have been deeply religious, yet evolutionary science is only beginning to catch up with this phenomenon that is both a product and a shaper of the human mind. In this chapter, I argue that religion is not an evolutionary adaptation, but a recurring byproduct of the complex evolutionary landscape that canalizes the cultural transmission of religious beliefs and behaviors into convergent yet culturally distinct pathways. This means that religious beliefs are the product of cultural transmission constrained by evolutionary psychology. The core cognitive feature of religion – belief in supernatural agents, itself a byproduct of the naturally selected disposition for detecting agents – was further culturally transformed from counterintuitive agents to counterintuitive *and* morally concerned policing agents. This cultural innovation, along with costly commitment aided by ritual, made possible a novel social phenomenon – stable, large, cooperative moral communities of genetically unrelated individuals.

The Psychological Foundations of Religion

The evolutionary origins of religion continue to be vigorously debated. One view among evolutionary theorists of religion is that religion is a naturally selected adaptation. Although theorists do not agree as to what religion is an adaptation for, they share the idea that some aspects of religious behavior are the product of a genetically transmitted, modular trait complex, in the same way that the vertebrate eye, or ecolocution in bats, or possibly language, is an adaptation that has conferred a reproductive advantage to ancestral organisms. Some of these theorists highlight the adaptive value of religion for life in socially cohesive moral communities, either at the individual level (e.g., Alexander 1987; Bering 2003; Sosis and Alcorta 2003), or at the group level (Wilson 2002) Others maintain that religion's adaptive value springs from its capacity to provide hope and immortality in the face of debilitating existential anxieties, in particular the terror of contemplating one's own death (Becker 1973; Solomon et al. 2004). Strong adaptationist accounts of religion are in principle plausible, and they may lead to fruitful research on religion. Furthermore, there is indeed a large body of evidence supporting the idea that aspects of religion address the dual human problems of existential anxieties and social defection. However, I argue that these are social functions of religion that have been culturally evolved. The idea that religion is a naturally selected module must meet tests of adaptive design that is standard in evolutionary biology: compelling adaptive function in ancestral environments, unitary and complex design, efficiency, precision, specificity, economy, and reliability (see Williams 1966; Tooby and Cosmides 1992). A strong adaptationist model also needs to rule out the possibility that religion is a cultural byproduct of adaptive design (Atran and Norenzayan 2004; Atran 2002). In my view religion fails on all of these criteria (for similar views, see Boyer 2001; Kirkpatrick 1999; Bloom, December 2005) and is more likely an evolutionary byproduct. This does not render the evolutionary perspective any less relevant to religion, however.

Religion is not an evolutionary adaptation per se. In fact, I argue – with Guthrie (1993), Boyer (2001), Atran (2002), Bloom (December 2005), and others – that "religion" is not even a structure with unitary design and a specific function, like vertebrate vision, but simply points to a family resemblance category of converging set of cultural byproducts, rooted in innate psychological tendencies that constrain and channel, though do not wholly determine, the transmission and survival of certain beliefs and practices. The four Cs of religion – counterintuition (supernatural agents), commitment (costly sacrifice), compassion (relief from existential anxieties), and communion (emotion-arousing ritual) are themselves cultural manipulations of psychological adaptations. The hypersensitive tendency for detecting agents (basis of supernatural agency) and the motivation to commit to social groups (basis of sacrificial behavior) address panhuman existential concerns, in particular fear of death, loss of control, and the threat of social defection (Atran and Norenzayan 2004). In all societies there is an evolutionary canalization of these four features that tends toward what is commonly referred to as "religion"; passionate, ritualized communal displays of costly commitments to counterintuitive worlds governed by supernatural agents. These features of religion emerge in all known cultures and animate the majority of individual human beings in the world (Atran 2002). In this respect, the four Cs of religion are existential universals (Norenzayan and Heine 2005): they recruit psychological tendencies that are in principle available in the psychological repertoire of human beings everywhere, although the degree to which these tendencies are invoked can vary from culture to culture and across individuals, and the situations under which these tendencies are triggered can also vary.

These four conditions do not define the necessary and sufficient features of "religion." Rather, they provide a framework that delimits a causally interconnected set of phenomena. Thus, this canalization or convergence is not inevitable – it is simply the case that we point to "religion" when most or all of these features converge in a unified social and psychological configuration. We may or may not call the phenomena that fall under this set of conditions "religion." Nevertheless, this working framework offers an adequate conceptualization that roughly corresponds to what most social scientists consider religion (Atran and Norenzayan 2004). This framework, although takes its object of study from those features of religion that are pancultural, is not incompatible with the important task of examining how the culturally distinctive paths that religions take shape psychological tendencies (e.g., Weber 1946; for a recent exploration, see Cohen, Hall, Koenig, and Meador 2005). In fact, as I discuss later in this chapter, understanding exactly what are those features of religion that reliably occur across cultures will facilitate our understanding of the cultural transformations that have had a profound impact on the human mind, especially since the agricultural revolution.

Religion's conceptual foundations are given by task-specific, panhuman cognitive domains, including folkmechanics (object boundaries and movements), folkbiology (biological species configurations and relationships), and folkpsychology (intentional agents and goal-directed behavior) (Atran and Norenzayan 2004; Boyer 2001). God concepts are thus counterintuitive because they violate what studies in cognitive anthropology and developmental psychology indicate are expectations about the world's everyday structure, including such basic categories of "intuitive ontology" as *person*, *animal*, *plant* and *substance* (Atran 1989). They are generally inconsistent with fact-based knowledge, though not randomly. Beliefs about invisible creatures who transform themselves at will, or who perceive events that are distant in time or space, contradict factual assumptions about physical, biological and psychological phenomena. For example, ghosts are similar to human agents in most respects, having beliefs, desires, thirst, and hunger, yet they violate a few core assumptions of folk-physics and folkbiology, such as their ability to move through solid objects and often being immune to death.

Consequently, certain religious beliefs are more likely to be retained and transmitted in a population than random departures from common sense, and thus are culturally stabilized. Insofar as category violations shake basic notions of ontology, they are attention-arresting, hence resistant to memory degradation. But only if the resultant impossible worlds remain bridged to the everyday world can information be stored, evoked, and transmitted (Atran and Sperber 1991; Boyer 1996). Several lines of experiments support these assertions, indicating that minimally counterintuitive concepts (Boyer and Ramble 2001; Barrett and Nyhof 2001), as well as minimally counterintuitive narrative structures such as folktales (Norenzayan, Atran, Faulkner, and Schaller 2006), have a cognitive advantage over other cognitive templates (e.g., entirely intuitive, or maximally counterintuitive). Thus, minimally counterintuitive supernatural agents help people remember and presumably transmit the more numerous intuitive statements that comprise the bulk of any religious tradition (mundane happenings). Such beliefs, even if they were initially evolutionary byproducts, grab attention, activate intuition, and mobilize inference in ways that greatly facilitate their mnemonic retention, cultural transmission, and historical survival. Once cognitively selected, these beliefs are available to serve secondary social functions and undergo cultural selection and stabilization.

Supernatural Agents and the "Tragedy of Cognition"

One such social function relates to the emotionally eruptive existential anxieties (Malinowski 1922), particularly death (Becker 1973; Freud 1913; Solomon et al. 2004) common to all human lives in all societies. This is the "tragedy of cognition": the fact that human beings, like other animals, have an innate survival instinct. Yet higher-order cognitive abilities to imagine the future inevitably lead to the overwhelming inductive evidence of our own eventual death, and that of persons to whom we are emotionally connected, such as relatives, friends and leaders. Such inductions activate existential anxieties that may lead to terror and paralysis (Becker 1973). Reason alone is unequipped to address this tragedy. All religions propose some kind of a supernatural resolution to this quandary in some minimally counterfactual afterlife that is governed and guaranteed by one or several powerful supernatural agents (Atran and Norenzayan 2004).

Often anxieties that bring on the supernatural are purposely excited then assuaged (Durkheim 1915). Ethnographic accounts of initiation rituals illustrate this pattern, as these rituals invariably involve "rites of terror" (Whitehouse 1996), as observed in a wide range of cultures (Atran and Norenzayan 2004). Death-related anxieties have been linked to religious behavior in psychology as well. In a classic psychological study, Allport, Gillespie, and Young (1948) found that, among returning World War II frontline soldiers, memories for fear of death were associated with heightened faith in divine intervention. If supernatural agents are cognitively salient and possess some degree of omniscient and omnipotent powers, then they can be invoked to ease these existential anxieties, particularly the awareness of death that forever threatens human life everywhere. If so, then experimentally, heightened awareness of death should increase the propensity to interpret events in terms of supernatural agency. This is indeed the case.

In priming experiments, participants were randomly assigned to write about their death or about a neutral topic. Then their commitment to God and to supernatural explanations was measured. Results showed that strength of belief in God's existence and in the efficacy of supernatural intervention were reliably stronger after exposure to the death prime than after the neutral (Norenzayan and Hansen 2006).

Terror Management Theory (TMT) maintains that cultural worldviews which infuse our lives with order, meaning, and a symbolic immortality, are a principal buffer against the terror of death. Accordingly, TMT experiments show that thoughts of death encourage people to reinforce their cultural (including religious) beliefs and derogate alien cultural worldviews (Greenberg et al. 1990; Pyszczynski et al. 1999). According to this reasoning, awareness of death should enhance belief in a worldview-consistent deity, but diminish belief in a worldview-threatening deity. In contrast, my view suggests that the need for belief in supernatural agency is a buffer against the terror of death that is distinct from worldview-defense. To test this idea, North American (mostly Christian) participants were again primed with death or with a neutral topic. Then their commitment to a culturally alien supernatural agent, in this case a divine Buddha, was measured. The mostly Christian subjects who previously self-identified as believers in their own religion (none were Buddhists) were *more* likely to believe in the power of Buddhist prayer, but only when their awareness of mortality was heightened. Similarly, mostly Christian Canadian participants were *more* likely to believe in Shamanic spirits when their awareness of death was salient (Norenzayan and Hansen 2006).

In a cross-cultural extension, Yukatek-speaking Maya villagers were primed with death awareness, with our procedures modified to fit Maya cultural circumstances. We found no differences among primes for belief in the existence of God and forest spirits (near ceiling in this very religious society). However, belief in efficacy of prayer for invoking Maya deities (where there was more variability) was significantly greater with the death prime than with the neutral primes (Atran and Norenzayan 2004). These results encourage the idea that minimally counterintuitive supernatural agents achieve cultural success not only because of a memory advantage, but also because of powerful motivational reasons: they relieve existential anxieties that are not in principle resolvable by rational deliberation.

Moralizing Supernatural Agents and the "Tragedy of Social Defection"

Another social function of some aspects of what we call "religion" is to facilitate social cohesion. In one study, for example, religious kibbutz members were found to be more cooperative in a public goods game than secular members, and religious attendance predicted cooperative decision-making when controlling for a number of variables (Sosis and Ruffle 2003). Sosis and colleagues have focused on religious ritual as a costly signal that curbs the free-rider problem and as a result facilitate the stabilization of large cohesive groups (Sosis and Alcorta 2003). Here I examine what role, if any, supernatural agents have played in this co-evolutionary process. Specifically, I describe how supernatural agent beliefs were culturally exploited to solve the problem of defection in large groups of genetically unrelated individuals.

Social organisms can reap the benefits of group living only to the extent that the selfishness of each individual in the group does not threaten the very stability of the group. This is the "tragedy of social defection:" on one hand social organisms are motivated to engage in fitness-maximizing behaviors that are often detrimental to other conspecifics; on the other, group living collapses if enough individuals free-ride – that is, reap the benefits of group living without contributing to the group.

This is why several adaptations have evolved that make group living possible, under certain conditions. In kin selection, altruism overcomes selfishness, but only among those that are genetically related, such as parents and offspring (Hamilton 1964). Reciprocal altruism extended the benefits of group living to non-kin, but only if there is reliable recognition of conspecifics and repeated social interactions (Axelrod 1984). Indirect reciprocity expands the circle of altruism further, if reputations can be ascertained by third parties rather than only through personal interactions. But this mechanism is dependent on reputations being reliable signals of trust (Nowak and Sigmund 1998).

We know that each of these strategies has allowed for human social groups to flourish, but only to a certain extent. Extrapolating from neocortex size, Dunbar (2003) has estimated that human group sizes cannot exceed 150 individuals. While this specific number has been disputed (e.g., Smith 1996), it is apparent today from the size of modern human settlements that additional mechanisms must operate to explain the existence of super-large groups. So what made such large groups possible? The answer must be found in the human capacity for culture. The idea of supernatural agents, a byproduct of mundane cognitive capacities, was culturally transformed into *morally concerned supernatural policing agents*. This idea became culturally widespread, as it allowed for further expansion of human cooperation beyond the constraints that marked the old strategies of kin selection and various kinds of reciprocity (Shariff, Norenzayan, and Henrich 2010). The omniscience of supernatural agents greatly extended the social accountability of human beings to all times and all places. Moreover, these omniscient agents could track the transgressions of as many individuals as needed. The consequence is that the tragedy of social defection was contained: in a group committed to the existence of supernatural moral watchers, there is always someone watching you (see also Johnson and Bering, 2006). These agents also solve the problem of costly punishment (Henrich and Boyd 2001; Johnson and Bering, 2006). The costliness of punishing cheaters – both the act of punishing and the potential retribution for this act, itself creates a second order problem, as those who free ride on their punishing duties must also be punished. Belief in omniscient and powerful supernatural agents who can punish (in this lifetime or in another) is a marvelous cultural solution to this problem.

A growing body of empirical evidence supports this line of reasoning. Snarey (1996) examined the features of God concepts across cultures as a function of life-threatening water scarcity. Societies with high water scarcity were more likely to have high Gods – all-powerful, omniscient, and morally concerned deities who encouraged the pro-social use of natural resources. This finding held even when controlling for cultural diffusion of high Gods via missionary activities (Christian and Muslim). Thus, high Gods were culturally selected when freeloading was particularly detrimental to the cohesiveness of the social group.

In a different cross-cultural analysis, Roes and Raymond (2003) predicted, and found that, across cultures, large societies are more likely to invent and propagate high Gods – group size was correlated with the existence of high Gods, supernatural watchers who are omniscient and concerned about the morality of human interactions. This finding held controlling for the cultural diffusion of high Gods via missionary activity, as well as for societal inequality.

In societies with moralizing gods, a fear of supernatural agents among individuals can be evoked in order to enforce moral norms. In one study, children were explicitly told not to look inside a box, and then left alone in the room with it (Bering 2003). Those who were previously told that a fictional supernatural agent, Princess Alice, is watching were significantly less likely to peek inside the forbidden box. A later study (Bering 2006) found a similar effect among university students. Those who were casually told that the ghost of a dead student had been spotted in the experimental room were less willing to cheat on a rigged computer task.

Shariff and Norenzayan (2007) showed that this effect can occur even when thoughts of God are induced without explicit awareness, removing the possibility of demand characteristics leading to more pro-social behavior. Participants were randomly assigned to three groups. In the first group, participants unscrambled sentences that contained words like spirit, God, and divine. Another group played the game with words like court, civic, jury, and police – thereby priming them with thoughts of secular moral authority. Finally, the control group played the same word game, but with non-religious content. In an anonymous, non-iterated version of the "dictator" game, participants were then randomly assigned to be either the "giver" or the "receiver". Those assigned to the role of the giver were allotted ten dollars which they were given the opportunity to share – in any amount they saw fit – with the receiver, who would otherwise receive nothing. Assured anonymity, 38 percent of givers in the control conditions kept all the money for themselves. This figure fell to 14 percent for participants implicitly primed with God concepts. At the same time, the proportion offering five dollars to the receiver – an even half of the money – rose from 20 percent in the control conditions to 48 percent in the religiously primed condition. Importantly, the secular prime increased altruism as much the religious prime did, suggesting that religion is an important factor in motivating generosity, but certainly not the only factor.

These results suggest that, in addition to curbing cheating behavior, the imagined presence of supernatural policing agents can reduce selfishness and increase the adoption of fairness norms, even with anonymous strangers. The combination of reduced cheating and free-riding, and increased altruism and pro-sociality, would have led to cohesive societies, paving the way for the rapid increase in the size of stable social groups.

Psychological Mechanisms and a Possible Evolutionary Scenario

What specific psychological mechanisms account for the effect of religious thinking on pro-social behavior? Two possibilities present themselves. I discuss these two alternatives and the empirical evidence for each. I then discuss a possible evolutionary scenario which takes into account interactions between innate tendencies and cultural learning, suggesting how belief in moralizing gods spread in human populations.

A behavioral priming or ideomotor action account involves the fact that the activation of perceptual-conceptual representations increases the likelihood of goals, plans, and motor behavior consistent with these representations (Bargh et al. 1996). Supernatural concepts such as *God* and *prophet* are moral actors semantically and dynamically associated with acts of generosity and charitable giving. Irrespective of reputational concerns, participants may have automatically behaved more generously when these concepts were activated, similar to when participants are more likely to interrupt a conversation when the trait construct "rude" is primed, or when university students walk more slowly when the elderly stereotype is activated (Bargh et al. 1996).

Another plausible explanation, not necessarily incompatible with the first, is that the religious prime activated the perceived presence of supernatural watchers, which then increased pro-social behavior (for similar observations about supernatural agent concepts, see Bering 2006; Boyer 2001; Johnson and Bering, 2006). Generosity in cooperative games has been shown to be sensitive to even subtle changes that compromise anonymity and activate reputational concerns (Hoffman et al. 1994; Haley and Fessler 2005). Debates continue as to whether cooperative behaviors toward unrelated individuals, especially those driven by passionate commitment, exist independent of short-term self-interest (e.g., Gintis, Bowles, Boyd, and Fehr 2003). However, reputation management can go a long way in explaining the evolutionary stability of cooperative behavior between strangers, to the extent that selfish individuals are detected and subsequently excluded from future cooperative venture. If the mere presence of eyespots could increase generosity (Haley and Fessler 2005), it is very plausible that rousing belief in a supernatural watcher could produce similar effects. In a species as intensely social and reputation-conscious as humans, the activation of God concepts, even outside of reflective awareness, matches the input conditions of our ordinary agency detector and as a result triggers this hyperactive tendency to infer the presence of an intentional watcher. This sense of being watched then activates reputational concerns, undermines the anonymity of the situation, and as a result curbs selfish behavior. From this perspective, reputational sensitivity is a naturally selected tendency, a part of human brain evolution that might explain why supernatural watchers are especially likely to have culturally succeeded in social groups.

Finally, how did belief in these moralizing Gods evolve? One view invokes a natural selection account, such that genes that coded for such beliefs conferred reproductive benefits to group-living individuals by curbing selfishness and encouraging cooperation (e.g., Johnson and Bering, 2006). In contrast, I argue that cultural evolution is a more compelling explanation for the rise and persistence of these beliefs. In this view, once supernatural agency emerged as a byproduct of mundane cognitive processes such as agency detection and mindreading, cultural evolution favored the spread of a special type of supernatural agent –omniscient, moralizing supernatural watchers who facilitated cooperation and trust among strangers and contributed to the expansion of human group size (Norenzayan and Shariff, 2008). This latter evolutionary scenario is persuasive for at least two reasons. First, it accounts for an otherwise puzzling feature of religious pro-sociality – namely, the systematic cultural variability in the prevalence of moralizing Gods across societies that correlates with group size (e.g., Roes and Raymond, 2003). Many small-scale societies, which more closely approximate ancestral conditions, do not have omniscient and morally concerned deities. Belief in such Gods is ubiquitous in evolutionarily recent anonymous social groups, where reputational and kin selection mechanisms for cooperation are insufficient. Thus, beliefs in moralizing supernatural agents could be examples of culturally evolved variants that played a key historical role in the rise and stability of large cooperative communities since the agricultural revolution.

Second, mathematical modeling of cooperative behavior shows that reputation management as a strategy does not achieve evolutionary stability beyond dyadic relationships (Henrich and Henrich 2007). To the extent that these mathematical models provide a good fit to the empirical facts, widespread belief in God concepts cannot be explained by reputational sensitivity at the individual level. An alternative cultural evolutionary account would invoke cultural group selection, such that ancestral societies with moralizing God concepts would have outcompeted those without, given the cooperative advantage of believing groups (Wilson 2002). Unlike genetic group selectionist accounts of altruistic behavior, which face a number of well-known theoretical and empirical challenges (e.g., Atran 2002), cultural group selection is more plausible theoretically and substantiated empirically (see, e.g., Henrich and Henrich 2007).

Conclusion

Religion is a species-specific human universal. It is both the product of genetic and cultural evolution, a dual inheritance that characterizes the peculiar nature of human evolution (Richerson and Boyd 2005). There is universality of (1) belief in supernatural agents who (2) relieve existential anxieties such as death and deception, but (3) demand a passionate and self-sacrificing commitment that is (4) validated through emotional ritual. A rich array of culture-specific beliefs and practices has supplemented and influenced these features, leading to the vast and complex religious traditions that exist today. Over time, some cultural variants of supernatural agents emerged that facilitated the formation of large, cooperative societies of genetically unrelated individuals. Religions take culturally distinct but convergent paths that are constrained by a complex evolutionary landscape reflecting cognitive, emotional, and material conditions for social life.

References

Alexander, R. 1987 *The biology of moral systems*. New York: Aldine de Gruyter.

Allport, G., J. Gillespie, and J. Young. 1948. The religion of the post-war college student. *Journal of Psychology* 25:3–33.

Atran, S. 1989. Basic conceptual domains. *Mind and Language* 4:7–16.

Atran, S. 2002. *In gods we trust: The evolutionary landscape of religion*. Oxford: Oxford University Press.

Atran, S., and A. Norenzayan. 2004. Religion's evolutionary landscape: Counterintuition, commitment, compassion, communion. *Behavioral and Brain Sciences* 27:713–70.

Atran, S., and D. Sperber. 1991. Learning without teaching: Its place in culture. In *Culture, schooling, and psychological development*, edited by L. T. Landsmann, 39–55. Norwood, NJ: Ablex.

Axelrod, R. 1984. *The evolution of cooperation*. Basic Books.

Bargh, J. A., M. Chen, and L. Burrows. 1996. Automaticity of social behavior: Direct effects of trait construct and stereotype activation on action. *Journal of Personality and Social Psychology* 71:230–44.

Barrett, J. L. and M. A. Nyhof. 2001. Spreading non-natural concepts: The role of intuitive conceptual structures in memory and transmission of cultural materials. *Journal of Cognition and Culture* 1:69–100.

Becker, E. 1973. *The denial of death*. New York: Free Press.

Bering, J.M. 2003. *On reading symbolic random events. Children's causal reasoning about unexpected occurrences*. Paper presented at the Psychological and Cognitive Foundations of Religiosity Conference, Atlanta, GA, August 2003.

Bering, J. M. 2006. The folk psychology of souls. *Brain and Behavioral Sciences* 29:453–62.

Bloom, P. 2005. Is God an accident? *The Atlantic Monthly,* December: 105–12.

Boyer, P. 2001. *Religion explained: The evolutionary origins of religious thought*. New York: Basic Books.

Boyer, P. 1996. What makes anthropomorphism natural: Intuitive ontology and cultural representations. *The Journal of the Royal Anthropological Institute (N.S.)* 2:83–97.

Boyer, P. and C. Ramble. 2001. Cognitive templates for religious concepts: Crosscultural evidence for recall of counter-intuitive representations. *Cognitive Science* 25:535–64.

Cohen, A. B., D. E. Hall, H. G. Koenig, and K. G. Meador. 2005. Social versus individual motivation: Implications for normative definitions of religious orientation. *Personality and Social Psychology Review* 9:48–61.

Dunbar, R. I. M. 2003. The social brain: Mind, language, and society in evolutionary perspective. *Annual Review of Anthropology*, 32:163–81.

Durkheim, E. 1965 [1915]. *The elementary forms of the religious life*. New York: Free Press.

Freud, S. 1990 [1913]. *Totem and taboo*. New York: W. W. Norton & Co.

Gintis, H., S. Bowles, Boyd, and E. Fehr. 2003. Explaining altruistic behavior in humans. *Evolution and Human Behavior* 24:153–72.

Greenberg, J., T. Pyszczynski, S. Solomon, A. Rosenblatt, M. Veeder, S. Kirkland, and D. Lyon. 1990. Evidence for terror management theory II. *Journal of Personality and Social Psychology* 58:308–18.

Guthrie, S.G. 1993. *Faces in the clouds: a new theory of religion*. Oxford: Oxford University Press.

Haley, K. J. and D. M. T. Fessler. 2005. Nobody's watching? Subtle cues affect generosity in an anonymous economic game. *Evolution and Human Behavior* 26:245–56.

Hamilton, W. 1964. The genetical evolution of social behavior. *Journal of Theoretical Biology* 7:1–52.

Henrich, N. S. and J. Henrich, 2007. *Why humans cooperate: A cultural and evolutionary explanation*. Oxford: Oxford University Press.

Henrich, J. and R. Boyd. 2001. Why people punish defectors: Weak conformist transmission can stabilize costly enforcement of norms in cooperative dilemmas. *Journal of Theoretical Biology* 208:79–89.

Hoffman, E., K. McCabe, K. Shachat, V. Smith. 1994. Preferences, property rights and anonymity in bargaining games. *Games and Economic Behavior* 7:346.

Johnson, D. D. P., and J. M. Bering 2006. Hand of God, mind of man: Punishment and cognition in the evolution of cooperation. *Evolutionary Psychology*, 4, 219–33.

Kirkpatrick, L. 1999. Toward an evolutionary psychology of religion. *Journal of Personality* 67:921–52.

Malinowski, B. 1961 [1922]. *Argonauts of the Western Pacific*. E. P. Dutton.

Norenzayan, A. and A. F. Shariff 2008. The origin and evolution of religious prosociality. *Science* 322:58–62.

Norenzayan, A., and I. G. Hansen. 2006. Belief in supernatural agents in the face of death. *Personality and Social Psychology Bulletin* 32:174–87.

Norenzayan, A., and S. Heine. 2005. Psychological universals: What are they and how can we know? *Psychological Bulletin* 135:763–84.

Norenzayan, A., S. Atran, J. Faulkner, and M. Schaller. 2006. Memory and mystery: The cultural selection of minimally counterintuitive narratives. *Cognitive Science* 30:531–53.

Nowak, M. and K. Sigmund. 1998. Evolution of indirect reciprocity by image scoring. *Nature* 39:573–7.

Pyszczynski, T., J. Greenberg, S. Solomon. 1999. A dual process model of defense against conscious and unconscious death-related thoughts: An extension of terror management theory. *Psychological Review* 106:835–45.

Richerson, P.J., and R. Boyd. 2005. *Not by genes alone: How culture transformed human evolution.* Chicago: University of Chicago Press.

Roes, F. L., and M. Raymond, 2003. Belief in moralizing gods. *Evolution and Human Behavior* 24:126–35.

Shariff, A., A. Norenzayan, and Henrich, J. 2010. The birth of high gods. In *Evolution, Culture, and the Human Mind*, edited by M. Schaller, A. Norenzayan, S. Heine, T. Kameda, and T. Yamagishi. New York: Lawrence Erlbaum Associates.

Shariff, A.F. and A. Norenzayan. 2007. God is watching you: Priming God concepts increases prosocial behavior in an anonymous economic game. *Psychological Science* 18:803–9.

Solomon, S., J. Greenberg, J. Schimel, J. Arndt, and T. Pyszczynski. 2004. Human awareness of death and the evolution of culture. In *The psychological foundations of culture,* edited by M. Schaller and C. Crandall, 15–40. New York: Erlbaum.

Sosis, R., and C. Alcorta. 2003. Signaling, solidarity, and the sacred: The evolution of religious behavior. *Evolutionary Anthropology* 12:264–74.

Sosis, R. and B.J. Ruffle. 2003. Religious ritual and cooperation: Testing for a relationship on Israeli Religious and Secular Kibbutzim. *Current Anthropology* 44:713–22.

Smith, R.J. 1996. Biology and body size in human evolution: Statistical inference misapplied. *Current Anthropology* 37(3):451–81.

Snarey, J. 1996. The natural environment's impact upon religious ethics: A cross-cultural study. *Journal for the Scientific Study of Religion* 80:85–96.

Tooby, J., and L. Cosmides. 1992. The psychological foundations of culture. In *The adapted mind: Evolutionary psychology and the generation of culture,* edited by J. H. Barkow, Cosmides, L., and J. Tooby, 19–136. New York: Oxford University Press.

Weber, M. 1946. The Protestant sects and the spirit of capitalism. In *From Max Weber: Essays in sociology,* edited by C. Wright Mills and H. Gerth. Oxford: Oxford University Press.

Williams, G. 1966. *Adaptation and natural selection.* New Jersey: Princeton University Press.

Wilson, D. S. 2002. *Darwin's Cathedral.* Chicago: University of Chicago Press.

Whitehouse, H. 1996. Rites of terror. *Journal of the Royal Anthropological Institute (N.S.)* 2:703–15.

5

Evolutionary Psychology and Criminal Justice: A Recalibrational Theory of Punishment and Reconciliation

Michael Bang Petersen, Aaron Sell, John Tooby, and Leda Cosmides

Introduction

Exploitation – the imposition of costs on another for one's own benefit – was a major and ongoing adaptive problem during human evolution. What elements of the human mind evolved in response to the problems posed by exploitation? In this chapter, we analyze these problems, and derive predictions about the evolved design of psychological adaptations that allow us to detect, conceptualize, and respond adaptively to exploitation. We argue that our species-typical psychological architecture includes evolved programs whose function is to (1) evaluate the prospective return of continued association with the perpetrator of exploitive acts and, if the value is positive, (2) motivate actions that reduce the problems posed by the prospect of future exploitation. More specifically, the function of these actions is to recalibrate certain behavior-regulating variables in the minds of the perpetrator and other potential exploiters. Based on this argument, we analyze punitive and conciliatory strategies, outlining how each strategy targets different regulatory variables in the motivational systems of perpetrators. Evolutionary analysis and empirical evidence both suggest that the strategy deployed against an exploiter is governed by cues that were correlated during our evolutionary past with the future net value of the exploiter. As we will show, this framework has implications for understanding the political attitudes and moral intuitions that humans have toward issues and events involving criminal justice.

Evolution, Exploitation, and Crime

In a highly social species like ours, there are reasons to expect that exploitation will not take the form of a Hobbesian war of all against all: Biologists have identified a number of selection pressures that favor the evolution of mechanisms designed to restrain an organism (under some conditions) from imposing costs on conspecifics for its own benefit. These include kin selection (Hamilton 1964; Williams and Williams 1957), reciprocation and exchange (Trivers 1971; Cosmides and Tooby 1992), the existence of positive externalities (Tooby and Cosmides 1996) and the avoidance of aggressive countermeasures from the exploited organism or its allies (Maynard Smith and Parker 1976; Sell, Tooby, and Cosmides 2009, forthcoming). Nevertheless, these selection pressures only carve out exceptions to the general selective gradient. Outside of the scope of such exceptions, organisms are selected to benefit themselves, regardless of the consequences of such acts on others. Accordingly, throughout our evolution, the average person was situated in a world full of individuals poised to impose costs on him or her if such acts were self-beneficial (Cosmides and Tooby 1992; Duntley 2005; Trivers 1971).

As many researchers have recognized, the risk of being exploited poses a major, chronic family of adaptive problems for humans (Daly and Wilson 1988; Duntley and Buss 2004). Organisms equipped with adaptations to prevent, deter, or productively respond to the threat of exploitation by others would be favored by selection. As expected, humans appear to have evolved adaptations to mitigate at least some varieties of exploitation. For example, humans appear to have evolved reasoning specializations to detect cheaters in contexts of social exchange (Cosmides and Tooby 1992; 2005). Similarly, the existence of patterned responses to exploitation in collective action supports the view that a motivational specialization deploying punitive sentiment evolved as a defense against free riders (Price, Cosmides, and Tooby 2002).

In this chapter, we argue that intuitions, attitudes, sentiments, and moral discourse that spontaneously emerge when people confront crimes (whether directly or in the context of political questions about criminal justice) are, in part, the expressions of mechanisms that evolved to defend humans ancestrally against exploitative behavior. Here, we focus on the distinctive psychology that evolved to respond to the problems posed by acts of exploitation perpetrated by co-members of the small residential groups in which ancestral humans lived. Exploitation by members of outgroups typically activates a different suite of evolved defenses – coalitional psychology – that lies largely beyond the scope of this chapter. In short, as far as our evolved psychology goes, "crimes" are (certain) acts of exploitation by ingroup members, while the same acts by outgroup members (especially sets of outgroup members) will often be categorized as "attacks" – that is, represented and responded to using a different evolved psychology.[1]

In what follows, it is important to keep in mind that these mechanisms evolved to assume the causal and statistical structure of the ancestral world, and make functional sense in that context. Although our species-typical set of complex neurocomputational adaptations changes only very slowly (because species-wide gene substitution takes a great deal of time), our social environment has been changing rapidly since the rise of agriculture. Today, in an environment with nation-states comprising millions of people and sophisticated technology, we cannot assume that our evolved computational equipment is operating functionally. What we can assume, however, is that despite possible dysfunctionalities, our motivations, categories, intuitions, and moral concepts are still guided in part by evolved adaptations whose outputs would have been adaptive under ancestral conditions. In other words, we argue that modern crimes exhibit cues that satisfy the input conditions of the mechanisms in our evolved counter-exploitive psychology. We expect, therefore, that our opinions about crime should be guided by the evolved neural programs whose design we outline below. This allows us to test some of our hypotheses about the nature of these mechanisms by drawing upon the criminological literature involving attitudes toward crime.

One central theme in our argument is that the mind evolved to produce not only punitive responses to crime but also reconciliatory responses as well – a topic that has been overshadowed by treatments that focus on punishment. For example, the literature on cheating has mainly focused on cost-infliction, punishment, and exclusion (Price, Cosmides, and Tooby 2002; Frank 1988). But given the costs of inflicting punishment, practical limitations on its use in many contexts, and the availability of other avenues of social influence, we expect a variety of other counter-exploitive strategies to evolve in addition to punishment. Evidence suggesting that natural selection may have designed nonpunitive means of conflict resolution comes from primatologists who explore the role of reconciliatory behaviors in managing conflicts and aggressive encounters (Aureli and de Waal 2000; de Waal 1996; see also Trivers 1971 on reparative strategies in reciprocation). Similarly, anthropologists have documented restorative sanctions across diverse agricultural and small-scale societies (Braithwaite 2002; Fry 2000). Nevertheless, a position, which was most famously formulated by Freud (1961) but runs through large parts of twentieth century social science, depicts humankind as by nature punitive – only resorting to restorative reactions because of countervailing socialization processes that have emerged for culturally contingent reasons in "advanced" civilizations (Durkheim 1998; Elias 1994; Spierenburg 1984; Garland 1990). The renewed emphasis on punishment in recent evolutionary approaches leaves Freud's portrait of the inherent punitiveness of human nature relatively uncontested. Below, however, we will develop an alternative to the Freudian vision, in which we argue that the mind contains evolved programs that deploy both punitive and reparative strategies to deal with transgressors.

The dissection of exploitation and counter-exploitive strategies derives from new proposals about the computational architecture that evolved among humans to regulate social behavior (e.g., Tooby, Cosmides, Sell, Lieberman and Sznycer 2008). We will outline relevant features of the proposed architecture, and will then develop concepts of exploitation, punishment, and reconciliation anchored in this analysis. These proposals delimit the conditions under which punishment and reconciliation, respectively, should have been the best available responses to exploitive acts.

Internal Regulatory Variables

Given an evolutionary and computational approach, it is useful first to consider how certain evolved mental programs dissect human sociality, and then to locate exploitation, punishment, and reconciliation within this framework. One divergence from traditional approaches to psychology that we will review and then apply is the idea of *internal regulatory variables* and their relationship to emotion programs (Tooby and Cosmides 2005, 2008; Tooby, Cosmides, Sell et al. 2008). The claim is that the architecture of the human mind, by design, contains registers for evolved computational variables whose function is to store summary magnitudes that are necessary for regulating behavior and making inferences involving valuation. These are not traditional and familiar psychological constructs, such as concepts, representations, goal states, beliefs, or desires (although they may contribute to the emergence of any of these). Instead, they are underlying indices that acquire their meaning from the evolved behavior-controlling and information-processing procedures that access them. That is, each has a location embedded in the input-output relations of other evolved programs, and the function of the internal regulatory variables is to regulate the decision flow of those programs.

Easy examples include a variable tracking the intensity of hunger, and a different one tracking the intensity of fatigue. These are increased or decreased by various input systems, and, when integrated with other processes, regulate choice behavior. Regulatory variables that have more interesting properties seem required when one attempts to model in detail how the human psychological architecture must be designed to respond successfully to recurrent problems posed by the social world.

For example, in the recent mapping of the architecture of the human kin detection system, research identified a series of regulatory variables needed to make the system work functionally and to explain the data (Lieberman, Tooby, and Cosmides 2007). In this case, it appears that for each familiar individual i, the system computes and updates a continuous variable, the *kinship index* K_i, that corresponds to the system's pairwise estimate of genetic relatedness between self and i. When the kinship index is computed or updated for a given individual, the magnitude is taken as input to procedures that are designed to regulate kin-relevant behaviors in a fitness-promoting way. In the case of altruism, the kinship index is fed as one of many inputs to an estimator, whose function is to compute a magnitude that regulates the weight placed on the welfare of i (see next section). A high kinship index upregulates the weight put on i's welfare, while a low kinship index has little effect on the disposition to treat i altruistically. This is one element that upregulates the emotion of love, attachment, or caring.

In parallel, the kinship index is also fed into the sexual value estimator as one of many inputs. The function of the sexual value circuitry is to compute a magnitude, sexual value (SV_i), that regulates the extent to which the actor is motivated to value or disvalue sexual contact with individual i. As in the case of altruism, many factors (e.g., health, age, symmetry) affect sexual value. But a high kinship index renders sexual valuation strongly negative, making the idea of sex with individual i disgusting and aversive. In contrast, a low kinship index is expected to have no impact on the other factors leading to sexual valuation.

Empirical work (Lieberman, Tooby, and Cosmides 2007) has demonstrated that the kinship index is set by two cues: (1) whether an older sibling observes the mother caring for his or her younger sibling as an infant, and (2) the duration of coresidence between birth and the end of the period of parental investment. This system was designed by natural selection to detect which familiar others were close genetic relatives, create a magnitude corresponding to the degree of genetic relatedness, and then to deploy this information to motivate both a sexual aversion between brothers and sisters, and to motivate a disposition to behave altruistically toward siblings.

An internal regulatory variable – like the kinship index, the sexual value index, or the welfare trade-off ratio (see below) – acquires its meaning and functional properties by its relationship to the programs that compute it, and by the downstream decisions or processes that it regulates. It is clear from both research and introspection that such computations and their embedded variables are usually nonconscious or implicit, and express themselves as feelings, intuitions, and inclinations. Outputs of the nonconscious processes that access these variables may be consciously experienced, as (for example) disgust at the prospect of sex with a sibling, affection for, or indifference to, a sibling, fear on their behalf, grief at their loss, and so on.

Welfare Trade-Off Ratios in the Mind and in Behavior

Decisions involving welfare trade-offs are ubiquitous. Life in modern industrial societies involves innumerable daily dilemmas, such as, should I pick up trash that fell to the street? Should I let another car ahead of me? Should I accept the cost of babysitting my neighbors' children so that they can go out? Should I forego the benefit of playing loud music to avoid imposing the cost of it on my neighbor? Should I do the dishes, or let my spouse do them? In all such contexts trade-offs between one's own welfare and the welfare of others have to be made. The ancestral world of hunter-gatherers would also have been permeated with contexts in which our ancestors were forced to make trade-offs between the welfare of self and other. As an illustration drawn from modern foragers, Hill (2002) lists a range of contexts for cooperative behavior in the Ache of Paraguay, including everything from clearing camp spots for others, to feeding another's offspring, to entertaining others by singing. Equally, deciding when to be selfish or aggressive also requires making trade-offs. In short, making welfare trade-off decisions adaptively constituted an important and pervasive adaptive problem for our ancestors.

In making a choice that impacts another, in principle an individual could weight a specific other's welfare not at all, moderately, strongly, or could self-sacrificially place weight only on the other's welfare. It would be an odd human being who was completely indifferent to her own welfare, however. Obviously, natural selection favored the evolution of motivational systems that favored acting in one's own self-interest (i.e., to proximate cues that would have predicted fitness enhancement ancestrally). Selection also favored the evolution of motivational systems designed to modify the individual's behavior based on its effects on others (e.g., kin selection, reciprocation, fear of retaliation, fitness interdependence, changes in externalities, acquiescence to extortion). This is why it is also rare to find humans who uniformly act with total disregard for the impacts of their acts on the welfare of others. In short, our evolved decision-making architecture must have components designed to weight the welfare of self versus the welfare of others, and to balance them in ways that would have promoted fitness ancestrally.

How is this accomplished? It is our belief that a substantial proportion of human social interactions are regulated, in part, by evolved circuitry that includes a particularly important family of variables: welfare trade-off ratios, or WTRs (Tooby, Cosmides, Sell, et al. 2008). A WTR indexes the degree to which one's valuation of another's welfare is expressed in choices and behavior – i.e., the extent to which you are disposed to trade-off your own welfare against another person's welfare when you take action. According to recent research (Sell 2006b; Sell et al. 2009, forthcoming; Tooby, Cosmides, and Price 2006a; Tooby, Cosmides, Sell, et al. 2008), decisions that impact the welfare of others appear to reflect the operation of evolved circuitry that embeds an internal threshold magnitude, the WTR, and its associated welfare trade-off functions. The proposal is that these variables are magnitudes, instantiated in neural tissue, that function as control elements accessed during decision-making processes that impact welfare. Independent circuits – like the human kin detection system or the social exchange system – take in information about a person (e.g., cues of relatedness; or, did they reciprocate recently?) and use it over the life course to upregulate or downregulate the magnitude of the person-specific WTR – increasing or decreasing the disposition to help, for example.

During the decision-making process, the WTR variable between the self and the person impacted by the potential act is accessed to see whether the course of action being considered should be carried out, or whether it should not because it places too little value either on oneself or on the other, given the magnitudes of the costs and benefits to all affected parties (see Delton, Sznycer, Robertson, Lim, Cosmides, and Tooby, forthcoming). That is, emotions and decisions involving trade-offs exhibit a series of evolutionarily predicted, lawful patterns that parsimoniously implicate the existence of this family of variables. The WTR is a person-specific variable, which sets the threshold for acceptable cost-benefit transactions between the relevant person and the self – i.e., the threshold at which willingness becomes unwillingness with respect to the particular person. The level of my WTR toward another person thus guides how large a cost I will voluntarily incur in order to secure a benefit for the specific person; and, how large a cost I am willing to impose on that other to secure a benefit for myself. All else equal, the larger the WTR between myself and the specific other, the larger costs I am willing to incur and the smaller the costs I am willing to impose, respectively. Thus, if individual X has a welfare trade-off ratio of 1:1 toward individual J, that means that X values J's welfare equal to her own, while a WTR of 5:1 means that X would be willing to impose a cost of 4 on J to gain a benefit of 1, but not a cost of 6 to gain a benefit of 1. The welfare trade-off ratio constitutes the computational basis for the intuitive concept of the value of a particular person to oneself.

The circuitry within which welfare trade-off ratios are embedded is hypothesized to have several design features geared toward the problem of regulating cost-benefit transactions among individuals of differential value to the decision maker (see Sell, Tooby and Cosmides, forthcoming; Sell 2006b; Tooby, Cosmides, Sell, et al.

2008). First, our minds should intuitively and automatically assign a cost-benefit interpretation (including valuations from the perspective of self and other) to events and potential choices. For example, a formerly unacceptable cost might become acceptable to you if you receive new information about the increased benefit the other person might derive from an act or resource (i.e., their need has become greater). While we might not offer a person our newly bought sweater to clean his dirty hands, we might be willing to accept just the same cost (a ruined sweater) if the same person's child suffers a severe wound and the sweater could be used to stop the bleeding. The latter entails a far greater benefit to the recipient than the former.

Second, the agent parameter of the WTR system should be flexible enough to allow WTRs to be computed for a range of different types of agents, not just individual humans (Tooby, Cosmides, and Price 2006). There is no reason to expect that our ancestral social world was solely comprised by dyadic interactions. Triadic social exchange, as well as exchanges involving even larger numbers of individuals, would have been frequent (Tooby, Cosmides, and Price 2006). In order to engage in such n-person exchange and make decisions about allocating time and resources to collective action, we need to be able to, first, represent our own welfare and the welfare of the collective, and second, trade-off our own welfare relative to the welfare of the group. To the extent that our minds contain systems for representing multiple persons as a single entity (a group), the necessary computations can be performed by feeding this entity into the agent parameter of the regular WTR system – albeit with some specialized machinery regulating group trade-offs. Thus, we propose that the computational system that governs individual-level welfare trade-offs also enables us to form welfare trade-off ratios involving groups.

As is the case with other internal regulatory variables, the psychological architecture in which the WTR is embedded will contain information-processing mechanisms that continuously scan situations for the existence of relevant ancestral cues, which in the environment of evolutionary adaptedness were reliably correlated with either increases or decreases in welfare. Upon encountering such information, these mechanisms recalibrate the WTR. But to understand what precise kinds of information are responsible for setting the level of a person's WTR toward another, we need to dissect the concept of WTRs further.

Monitored and Intrinsic WTRs

There are two adaptively distinct contexts in which we trade-off our welfare relative to the welfare of others. First, there are situations in which our behavior is either directly monitored by the person whose welfare is affected, or where it is highly probable that the person (or their allies) will become aware of our agency. Second, there are situations in which the affected individuals are not present or capable of defending their interests, as when the choices we make are private. In the former context it is necessary to assess the potential responses from other persons and to factor in these responses in making our decisions. When decisions are not likely to be public, then only intrinsic reasons for weighting the other person's welfare need to be integrated into the decision. Hence, there are at least two parallel, independent WTRs: (1) the intrinsic WTR ($_{intrinsic}$WTR), which sets an altruistic floor in the weighting of the other party's welfare, even when the actor's choices are not being observed; and (2) the public or monitored WTR ($_{monitored}$WTR) that guides an individual's behavior when the recipient (or others) can observe the behavior (Sell et al. 2009; Sell, Cosmides, and Tooby, forthcoming, a, b; Tooby and Cosmides 2008). Some altruism is motivated through love (involving a high intrinsic WTR), and some through fear, shame, or hope of reward – and the mechanisms involved are different. Kin-selected mechanisms produce intrinsic WTRs – these make you want to help your brother (at least in part) for his own sake. In contrast, threats from powerful others select for low intrinsic WTRs toward them (better for you if they did not exist), but significant monitored WTRs toward them (as when societies are organized around catering toward powerful and oppressive elites). Of course, monitored WTRs occur not just in such dramatic conditions, but ubiquitously through life (as when a person does something to win approval from a friend, spouse, or coworker).

Accordingly, for each individual J with whom individual X interacts, we should expect the mind to compute both an intrinsic $WTR_{x,j}$ and a monitored $WTR_{x,j}$. The level of the intrinsic $WTR_{x,j}$ governs how X trade-offs his or her welfare relative to the welfare of J when J's responses to the act do not need to be considered (when they do not know about the act; when they have no power to respond, etc.). The level of the intrinsic $WTR_{x,j}$ should be set by computations of the basic interdependence of X's own welfare and the welfare of J. That is, it can be reproductively advantageous for X to benefit J regardless of whether or not she finds out, if she is his sister, best friend, or someone else whose existence, health, and capacity to act are valuable to him (Tooby and Cosmides 1996).

In contrast, the level of the monitored $WTR_{x,j}$ should be influenced not only by all of the same parameters as the intrinsic $WTR_{x,j}$, but also by a range of other cues which would have correlated with J's ability to inflict costs on or generate benefits for X upon detecting his or her actions. In general, examples of evolutionarily recurrent cues to J's ability to affect our welfare are (cf. Sell 2006b; Sell, Tooby, and Cosmides 2009):

- J's physical strength
- the size and degree of coordination of J's coalition
- J's social status, J's skills and competences
- J's access to resources.

This theoretical analysis predicts that, other things being equal, the human mind should be designed to place less weight on another person's welfare and more on one's own to the extent the other party is physically weaker. Sell and colleagues demonstrated that this relationship not only exists but is robust (Sell et al. 2009; Sell, Tooby, and Cosmides 2009).

Anger and WTRs

The usefulness of these tools in the analysis of human sociality can be seen, for example, in the analysis of anger (Sell 2006b; Sell, Tooby, and Cosmides 2009, forthcoming). In this view, anger (in addition to being an experienced psychological state) is the expression of an evolutionarily organized neurocomputational system whose design features evolved to regulate thinking, motivation, and behavior adaptively in the context of resolving conflicts of interest in favor of the angry individual. Two negotiating tools regulated by this system are the threat of inflicting costs (e.g., aggression, punishment) and the threat of withdrawing benefits (e.g., the downregulation of cooperation, relationship termination, ostracism). Humans differ from nearly all other species in the number, intensity, and duration of close cooperative relationships, so traditional models of animal conflict must be modified to more fully integrate this cooperative dimension.

If the human mind really contains welfare trade-off ratios as regulatory variables that control how well one individual treats another, then evolution can build emotions whose function is to alter welfare trade-off ratios in others toward oneself. Anger is conceptualized as a mechanism whose functional product is the recalibration in the mind of another of this other person's welfare trade-off ratio with respect to oneself. That is, the goal of the system (its evolutionarily designed product, not its conscious intention) is to change the targeted persons' disposition to make welfare trade-offs so that they more strongly favor the angered individual in the present and the future. As in animal contests, the target of anger may relinquish a contested resource, or may simply be more careful to help or to avoid harming the angered individual in the future.

In human cooperative relationships, there is the expectation that the cooperative partner will spontaneously take the welfare of the individual into account. Hence, in cooperative relationships, the primary threat from the angered person is the signaled possibility that the angry individual will withdraw future benefits if the unsatisfactory welfare trade-off ratio is not remedied. If the withdrawal of this cooperation would be more costly to the target of the anger than the burden of placing greater weight on the welfare of the angry individual, then the motivational system in the target should be induced to recalibrate – that is, to increase her welfare trade-off ratio toward the angry individual, and so treat her better in the future.

The anger program is designed to recalibrate the angry individual's own WTR toward the target of the anger for two functional reasons. The first is that it curtails the wasteful investment of cooperative effort in individuals who do not respond with a sufficient level of cooperation in return. The second is that the potential for this downward recalibration functions as leverage to increase the WTR of the target toward the angry individual. In the absence of a cooperative relationship, the primary threat is the infliction of damage. In the presence of cooperation, the primary threat is the withdrawal of cooperation. Concepts that are anchored in the internal regulatory variable $_{monitored}$WTR include respect, consideration, deference, status, rank, and so on.

We call the ability to inflict costs to enforce welfare trade-off ratios in one's favor *formidability*, and brains should have evolved a set of programs that (1) evaluates one's own and others' formidabilities, (2) transforms each of these evaluations into a magnitude (a *formidability index*) associated with the person, and, in situations where cooperation is not presumed, (3) implicitly expect or accord some level of deference based on relative formidability. Among our ancestors (see above), one major cue that an individual would have been able to inflict costs was his/her physical strength. Furthermore, in the human social world, the ability to inflict costs should correlate with social status, position in a hierarchy, economic resources, social allies. The programs estimating formidability should assess all such cues.

The approach briefly sketched above can be unpacked into a large number of empirical predictions about anger. For example, it was predicted that physical strength in men would be a partial cause of individual differences in the likelihood of experiencing and expressing anger. Other things being equal, stronger men are predicted to be more likely to experience anger and express anger; they should feel more entitled; they should expect others to give greater weight to their welfare, and become angrier when they do not. Furthermore, arguments precipitated by anger should reflect the underlying logic of the welfare trade-off ratio: The complainant will emphasize the cost of the other's transgression to her/him and the value of one's cooperation to the transgressor, and will feel more aggrieved if the benefit the transgressor received (the justification) is small compared to the cost inflicted. A series of empirical studies support both sets of predictions of this theory about the design of anger (Sell 2006b; Sell, Tooby and Cosmides 2009, forthcoming).

In the next section, we will describe how the more general notion of a WTR allows us to outline an evolutionary and computational concept of exploitation. After this examination, we use the distinction between monitored and intrinsic WTRs to analyze punishment and reconciliation as different evolved strategies to deal with exploitive persons and crimes.

Exploitation as a Display of a Low WTR

With this approach in mind, it is possible to examine exploitation more generally, as well as some possible adaptations to it. To begin with, fitness benefits flow from being with people who care about your welfare and attend to the welfare consequences of their actions. For this reason, selection should favor motivations to increase the degree to which you surround yourself with people who express a high WTR toward you in their actions. Conversely, there are potentially large fitness costs related to being around people who do not attend to or care about your welfare. An individual J with a sufficiently low WTR toward another individual X will not hesitate to use X as nothing more than a means to realize J's own ends (as evidenced by rape, murder, slavery, the subjugation of women, economic exploitation, etc.).

Ancestrally, therefore, there was selection for avoiding engaging in social interactions with people with a low WTR toward oneself, and/or for limiting the power of such individuals to make trade-offs unfavorable to you (and your family and friends). To achieve this, one must be able to gauge the WTR that others express in their actions, especially toward you and those you most value. Relevant information will in part come from behaviour directed against third parties. Hence, to the extent that their WTRs toward third parties predict their dispositions to act toward those you value (including yourself), then indeed the mind should in general track the WTR in the interactions it is exposed to. In general, we should be interested in behavior that reveals WTRs. That is, in addition to whatever else we note and remember, behavior should be interpreted and remembered in terms of the WTR relationships it reveals. Whenever an action affects the welfare of both the actor and someone else, the act expresses (some) information about how much the actor values herself versus the impacted person – how much they are willing to trade off their own welfare to increase the welfare of someone else.

Accordingly, across cultures, acts that indicate a low welfare trade-off ratio toward oneself or a group to which one belongs (family, coalition, band, ethnicity) ought to be distinguished from other kinds of actions by our psychology, and should be viewed as problematic or *wrong* (an evolved conceptual primitive). Exploitative acts – those in which one party imposes large costs on another to gain a much smaller benefit – fulfill these criteria. Indeed, empirical studies provide evidence that an intuitive concept of exploitation exists as a cross-culturally universal feature of human social life. That is, low WTR acts by others toward ourselves or toward others we are positively involved with are viewed as morally wrong. Stylianou (2003) thus summarizes the current criminological data by arguing that there is consensus both within and between cultures about how to rank different harmful crimes. Of course, crimes do not exhaust acts that indicate a low WTR. Cues to low WTRs include inattention, failure to be aware of another's interests, lack of empathy when another experiences a gain or loss, a failure to remember the person, an unwillingness to listen to their statements about their welfare, ridicule, insults, emotional expressions of hostility, and so forth (for discussion, see Sell 2006b).

The Computation of Baselines and a Definition of Exploitation

Before a definition of exploitation can be reached, it is necessary to reflect on a final complexity with regards to the computational processes that tag acts as 'exploitive'. It is important to recognize that it is cognitively impossible for an individual to anticipate the impact of every act on the welfare of every local individual. The computational scope of such an evaluation is unbounded. For this reason, we did not evolve to respond to behavioral choices as if they were the product of unbounded computation. Instead, humans implicitly accept scope limitations on their definitions of acceptable versus wrong conduct, and do so because we evolved mutually consistent cognitive procedures for framing situations.

For one thing, this means that an act of exploitation cannot simply be defined as acting with a low WTR toward another. This is because most of our acts do not and could not take into account the cacophony of mutually irreconcilable needs of everyone in our social universe. Instead, our minds evolved the automatic practice of setting the starting point (baseline) from which welfare is viewed as having been increased or decreased at the level that would have existed prior to or in the absence of the act. For instance, if I have gathered food, I might feed myself instead of feeding a random stranger without this being regarded as an instance in which I exploited the stranger. This is because, given this cognitive system for implicitly generating baselines, by eating food I have gathered I have not lowered the stranger's pre-existing welfare. Rather, I have chosen to not increase it. It is important to recognize that this is not a fact about the world, but the one framing out of many that evolution has caused our minds to adopt. From a physicist's perspective, this case is similar to a case in which I eat food that someone gave to the stranger: in both cases, my eating the food reduces the stranger's welfare by the same amount when compared to other acts I might have committed. However, the mind evolved to compute baselines in a way that leads these two cases to be treated differently.[2] Consequently, in one case the welfare of the other is seen as unchanged (an absence of exploitation – and an absence of charity), and in the other case the mind computes that the welfare of the other person is lowered (an act of exploitation). Additional rules for setting baselines exist as well, as in social exchange and collective actions (in which a failure to act can be reframed as imposing a cost below a baseline that is computed by considering the state of affairs if expected or required cooperative acts had been mutually carried out). The key point is that what counts as an exploitive transgression is defined with respect to these computed welfare baselines.

Hence, to a first approximation, exploitation can be defined as an act that (1) expresses a welfare trade-off ratio that is either too low or negative toward an individual or group, and (2) imposes a cost that reduces the welfare of the impacted individual or group below the baseline they were entitled to. Infliction of minor costs to gain major benefits (for someone within one's cooperative sphere) is less often viewed as exploitation because it clashes with the input conditions for recognizing low WTRs. A situation that would render such behavior more problematic is if one attempts to conceal it – thereby covertly removing it from the reciprocity system.

Crime as Exploitation

There is a substantial body of evidence indicating that natural selection has fashioned anti-exploitive psychological mechanisms (on cheater detection, Cosmides and Tooby 1992 and 2005: on punitive sentiment as an anti-free-riding device, Price et al 2002 and Tooby et al. 2006a). More relevant to criminal justice is evidence about possible evolved psychological responses and defenses to the infliction of costs outside of the context of defection in cooperative endeavors (for an overview, see Duntley 2005; for empirical studies on rape avoidance mechanisms, see Chavanne and Gallup 1998; Petralia and Gallup 2002; Thornhill and Palmer 2000). The adoption of a WTR-oriented approach enables us to specify adaptive problems that cut across such types of cost-infliction. Despite their differences, theft, rape, hit and run driving, assault, and synagogue, church, or mosque desecration are all reliable signals of low WTRs, and therefore probabilistic signals that their perpetrators are more likely to inflict future damage than others who have not committed these acts. In this section, we will review a number of ways in which different crimes can be viewed as acts of exploitation in this sense.

Essential to exploitation is the imposition of high costs on a person or group, or the imposition of costs outside of a cooperative relationship (Duntley and Buss 2004; Sell 2006b; Tooby, Thrall, and Cosmides 2006). Harmful acts cross-culturally perceived as anti-social or crimes (see Ellis and Hoffman 1990), such as rape, theft, assault, and murder, all satisfy this requirement. Modern criminology has repeatedly documented that the perceived seriousness of such acts are highly influenced by the degree of damage done to the victim's welfare (Stylianou 2003; Warr 1989). This is in line with the evolutionary concept of exploitation as expressing a low WTR by means of imposing a cost.

However, from an evolutionary perspective, the perception of an act as exploitive is not just governed by the magnitude of the cost, but also by the relationship between the imposed cost and the benefit gained by the perpetrator. Thus, keeping the costs constant, we should also expect the level of benefits generated for the perpetrator to negatively influence the degree to which acts are perceived as exploitive. Sell et al. predicted and found this relationship in the degree to which anger is provoked by a situation (Sell, Tooby and Cosmides, forthcoming). Rossi, Simpson, and Miller (1985) found that people rate the crime of theft more mildly when it is motivated by an attempt to provide food for the perpetrator's family in need. Such intuitions are ubiquitous, as when, for example, they are scathingly invoked by Anatole France when he remarked that "The law, in its majestic equality, forbids the rich as well as the poor to sleep under bridges, to beg in the streets, and to steal bread." (France 1894).

The majority of crimes we are confronted with (e.g., in the mass media) are directed against others than ourselves. Importantly, acts expressing low welfare trade-off ratios among third parties are also adaptively significant, and so it is expected that our evolved machinery respond to (some of) them as well. Harmful acts committed by a perpetrator P and directed against a victim V can be consequential for a third individual T in at least two ways. First, to the extent that the victim is a genetic relative or valuable social partner, T suffers directly by the lowering of the fitness of the relative or the capacity to act of the social partner. Second, the exploitive acts might raise the threat that T will be a future direct victim of the perpetrator. The adaptive problems associated with each scenario contain specific computational problems, which a third party witnessing some kind of cost-infliction needs to solve.

The estimation of the direct costs requires an assessment of the value of the victim V to the observer T. In line with this, Hembroff (1987) finds that people react more strongly to crimes directed against well-integrated members of the community. (Such acts might also provoke a stronger response because the collective reputation of the community for deterrence is more strongly threatened when central figures are attacked.) Landsheer and Hart (2000) found similar effects among adolescents, who react more strongly to an offense when they know the victim than when they do not.

Having observed an act of exploitation, estimating whether the same perpetrator is likely to victimize oneself is a more cognitively complex task. As Panchanathan and Boyd (2003) have pointed out, it requires the observer to assess whether the perpetrator's infliction of costs on the victim was motivated by a general exploitive disposition or whether the specific act was part of a more local conflict between the perpetrator and the victim. In terms of WTRs, it requires the observer to assess whether the act expresses a low WTR solely toward the victim, or a low group-WTR toward a set that includes both the observer and the victim as members. If it expresses the latter, the observer is confronted with a potentially severe adaptive problem even if she is not intrinsically invested in or otherwise allied with the victim.

Moreover, such an act of exploitation can have another important negative consequence: Other parties are observing the act. Some of these parties express acceptable WTRs purely for prudential reasons, restraining themselves because of the potential consequences to them if they attempted exploitation. If acts toward members of a set or coalition are not responded to, this invites these others to exploit members of the set (Tooby, Cosmides, and Price 2006). Deterrence is an evolved function of revenge, and operates in a parallel fashion for individuals and groups. It is important to note that coalitional identities are automatically categorized by the mind (Kurzban et al. 2001). It is this automatic categorization and generalization that makes victimization of one member of a coalition an advertisement of the vulnerability to exploitation of other members of the coalition. Therefore, other members of a coalition (or their social allies) have an interest in advertising that victimizations of its members will not go unpunished (Tooby, Cosmides, and Price 2006). It strikes the mind as intuitively reasonable to recognize so-called hate crimes as a category, and to treat them more punitively; this reaction makes sense given that observers can use acts committed against a single group member to infer that other members of the group are now vulnerable to exploitation.

Due to these selection pressures, we should expect our minds to (1) be able to navigate adaptively between individual- and group-WTRs, (2) assess whether specific behaviors are guided by one or the other, and (3) be highly sensitive to cues that, under ancestral conditions, reliably predicted a low WTR toward groups, coalitions, or social categories that we either belong to or intrinsically value. For example: If a harmful act occurs randomly without prior provocation, it could constitute one important cue that the threat the perpetrator poses generalizes to others beyond the victim. In line with this, Rossi, Waite, Bose, and Berk (1974) show that violence between people who have not interacted prior to the incident is seen as more serious than violence between individuals who knew each other beforehand. Similarly, classical studies in the anthropology of law indicate that, in some societies, collective reactions against violent persons are carried out only when these are seen as a potential danger to all community members (Hoebel 1964).

Criminological research strongly suggests that acts do not need to be physically harmful to be perceived as seriously offensive (Warr 1989). To the extent that an otherwise harmless act violates some locally accepted moral norm, it can generate strong indignation and punitive sentiment (Tooby, Thrall, and Cosmides 2006; Tooby, Cosmides, and Price 2006). Flag burning or naming a stuffed animal "Mohammed" are modern examples, but the anthropological literature contains numerous other accounts of strong disapproval or punitive responses to norm violations (Hoebel 1964). In general, showing intense disregard for those symbolic markers or emblems that function as indices of the status of the group is cross-culturally viewed as an "outrage" (Tooby, Thrall, and Cosmides 2006). Mistreatment of a group status index powerfully communicates that the perpetrator does not value the group and its members, and does not believe that members of that group have sufficient collective support or formidability to defend their interests. It presages future exploitation. This can mobilize a collective response to advertise the group's strength and vigilance in defending their status and their members. In a similar vein, symbolic transgression directed against a specific individual should be viewed as exploitive by that individual and others valuing her, because it involves the public devaluation of this person's status (and an advertisement of her low formidability).

Summing up, the theory that the human motivational system contains welfare trade-off ratios, which are embedded as control elements in decision-making systems, enables us to understand crime as exploitation and, hence, as acts expressing a low WTR by means of the imposition of a cost. From the victim's perspective, the harmful act's degree of seriousness or perceived wrongness should, to a large extent, be determined by the ratio between the harm caused and the benefits generated. From a third-party perspective, the seriousness should be also influenced by the value of the victim to the observer, the extent to which the exploitive act was motivated by exploitive tendencies that can be generalized to the observer or the observer's group, and the precedent the act sets for the future if it is not responded to. If the tendency to act exploitatively is clearly limited to a specific perpetrator–victim pair (e.g., a husband and wife), then responses of others are expected to be more limited. In contrast, a general disregard for the welfare of the members of a group can be displayed by publicly exploiting an individual bearing a coalitional marker or having a widely-known coalitional identity. Table 5.1 displays an overview of these varieties of exploitation, which intuitively are perceived as "wrong."

Based on these and other cues, we expect the mind to automatically compute an index of the seriousness of exploitive acts; i.e., to calculate the degree to which the expressed WTR of an individual is discrepant from an acceptable WTR, given the parameters outlined above. This index is one element that underlies the intuitive reaction that a particular action is wrong. The function of the feeling of wrongness is to motivate individual or collective action to redress the fitness threat posed by those who commit certain acts. For this reason, we are designed to feel that something is more intensely wrong if it happens to us, our family, our friends, or our group; that it is more wrong to the extent that it predicts or invites bad future outcomes (even if the actual damage, as with status outrages, is minor); that it is more wrong if the benefit gained was small in proportion to the cost inflicted; and so on.

Table 5.1 A partial list of factors setting WTRs and indicating low WTRs.

Factors inducing X to "value" Y (Factors that set WTRs)	Acts intuitively perceived as "wrong" by person X (Indicators of a low WTR relevant to person X)
X's and Y's relative fighting ability	Intentional imposition of a large cost for small benefit on X
Size and "strength" of X's and Y's coalitions	Direct challenge to X's status or authority
Y's social skills and competences	Lack of empathy for X
Y's access to resources	Symbolic transgressions against X or X's group
Degree of relatedness between X and Y	Acts imposing large costs on someone valuable to X
Y's mate value	Costly acts motivated by low-group WTRs toward a group in which X is member
...	...

Evolved Strategies for Responding to Exploitation: An Overview

Because our ancestors were continuously subject to threats of exploitation during their evolutionary history, we expect that selection favored the evolution of neurocognitive programs to respond adaptively to exploitation. In other words, the relevant adaptive problem is the existence in the local social world of individuals who hold low WTRs – a state that reliably predicts future cost-infliction. How should humans be designed to respond to this problem? Responses (each of which is reflected in the formal or informal criminal justice systems of various cultures) include:

1. killing the perpetrator, which permanently removes the threat
2. expelling the perpetrator from the social world through ostracism or confinement; or, on an individual basis, not engaging in future cooperative endeavors with those who have cheated
3. punishing the perpetrator through infliction of costs or withdrawal of benefits
4. reconciling with the perpetrator.

There are two major kinds of benefits that result from active responses targeting the perpetrator: (1) the direct benefit that arises from a response's impact on the perpetrator (e.g., the perpetrator is deterred from misbehaving in the future), and (2) the indirect benefit that arises from the impact of the response on third parties (i.e., others are deterred from behavior that is exploitive). Importantly, these responses largely presume a sufficient nucleus of like-minded individuals to enforce them, compared to a sufficiently low number of individuals who would oppose them. We will only touch briefly on the effects of such populational characteristics. If, however, there is not the collective strength to actively operate on the perpetrator, remaining responses are: (1) do nothing and put up with it; (2) avoid the perpetrator, to the extent possible; or (3) leave the social group (hunter-gatherers frequently settle long-simmering conflicts by group fission; Lee and DeVore 1968). The rest of the chapter is oriented toward discussing each of the four categories of responses listed above. While we begin by discussing killing and ostracism, our main focus is on punishment and reconciliation. Killing and ostracism as evolved responses to exploitation will only be dealt with on a more cursory level.

If, over evolutionary time, individuals frequently encountered others whose prospective existence was a net fitness cost (as exploiters, competitors, or impediments to realizing fitness gains), then evolution should plausibly have favored circuits that motivate killing, when the costs and risks are not too great (Buss, and Duntley 2003; Daly and Wilson 1988). Collective action reduces the per individual costs of killing as a tool to remove social threats, and so sentiments favoring the social deployment of killing (execution) are expected to be a widespread feature of the ethnography of the collective treatment of exploiters (i.e., criminal justice). One important element that moderates such motivational outputs is the connection that some community members (such as family members, friends, or sympathizers) may have with the perpetrators. To the extent that perpetrators are connected, social conflict is engendered over inflicting such serious and irremediable harm on individuals who are valued by at least some others in the community.

Ostracism (as with group expulsion or confinement) is another way of limiting the costs inflicted by exploitive individuals. One benefit is that the potential malefactor is physically prevented from reaching potential victims during the enforced absence – like execution, it incapacitates them, but only for the duration of the confinement. It also has significance as an act of punishment, which brings us to the recalibrational theory of punishment and reconciliation as evolved responses to social exploitation, which continue to shape attitudes toward criminal justice. Our next objective is to outline this theory.

A Recalibrational Theory of Punishment and Reconciliation

If the problem is exploitation, and the threat of future exploitation is exhibited in acts that express low welfare trade-off ratios, then what does this imply for how our minds ought to be structured to respond to this threat? One strategic component acts by solving the problem physically or spatially. This creates the basis for the above-discussed responses such as capital punishment, the physical restraint of potential malefactors (e.g., confinement), and the ejection of the malefactor from the social group. Another strategic component acts by solving (or mitigating) the problem motivationally. In this case, our evolved responses should constitute strategies that are organized to act through the evolved computational architecture of the malefactor's motivational system. If the problem is that the WTRs in the malefactor's minds are too low, then the solution should be to take actions that recalibrate the WTRs in the malefactor upward. Hence, we expect reactions to displays of cost-imposition guided by low WTRs, i.e., exploitation, to be strategies with the goal of upregulating the level of the exploitive person's WTR toward relevant potential victims (Sell 2006b; Sell et al. 2009, forthcoming; Tooby et al 2006a). Below, we will outline punishment and reconciliation from this recalibrational perspective. Although both strategies seek to upregulate the exploitive person's WTRs, punishment primarily targets the monitored WTRs, while reconciliation targets intrinsic WTRs (sometimes along with the recalibration of monitored WTRs by positive incentives).

Punishment and the Recalibration of Monitored WTRs

In general, punishment can be defined as the conditional imposition of costs on an agent who has committed an act because the agent has committed that act. Punitive strategies emerge from the logic of conflict, and so are not recent cultural inventions. A range of nonhuman animals (including higher primates) display punitive tendencies against exploiters or antagonists (Clutton-Brock and Parker 1995; de Waal 1992), suggesting that this form of interaction has been with our evolutionary lineage for tens of millions of years. Similarly, accounts of revenge as a motivation are cross-culturally and historically ubiquitous (Daly and Wilson 1988; Jacoby 1983).

More specifically, circuits that motivate revenge evolved as part of a system for defending the organism's interests against acts of exploitation that would occur in the absence of revenge circuitry. There are a number of elements to the revenge system:

- an element that computes baselines
- an element that detects cost-imposition with respect to those baselines and implicated WTRs
- an element that generates a calibrated intensity of punitive sentiment – specifically, with goals (1) to cause the experience of suffering in the malefactor and (2) to pair the inflicted suffering with the communication to the malefactor of what acts the delivered suffering is repayment for
- an element that modulates the intensity and expression of the infliction of suffering in light of the relative formidabilities of the potential punishers and the potential targets of revenge.

The latter elements relate to the fact that, on the one hand, the system must provide its own strong and distinct motivational imperative, because carrying out punishment is often costly and painful, lowering the achievement of other competing goals and motivations. Hence, the core of this system is the generation of punitive sentiment (i.e., the motivation to inflict suffering as a response to a prior bad action). This core, we argue, evolved specifically to recalibrate the WTR in the psychological architecture of the malefactor (although, when the net value of the perpetrator is negative, then the revenge system may generate the motivation to kill rather than to recalibrate). On the other hand, the link between felt punitive sentiment and actual punitive behavior is affected by several social contingencies (cf. the final element in the above list). As the social scale gets larger, for example, one complication is the negotiation of the transfer of the agency of revenge from harmed families to the community – many of whom may be allies and supporters of the perpetrator. The fluid and contentious concept of "fairness" emerges from the dynamics of integrating the voices of other community members, in proportion to their power and influence in the community.

There is now a sizeable experimental literature documenting that individuals are indeed sometimes punitively motivated and, hence, are willing to incur costs to punish others, including (at least in experimental games) the impulse to punish those who treat third parties unfairly (Cameron 1999; Fehr and Fischbacher 2004; Fehr and Gächter 2002). This also holds true to a greater or lesser extent for games conducted in a range of nonindustrial small-scale societies (Henrich et al. 2004). Neuroscience results suggest that the motivation for punishing cheaters is in part created by a heightened activation in the brain's reward centers – rewards that (under certain conditions) can outweigh financial disincentives to punish (de Quervain et al. 2004). Furthermore, experimental studies indicate that punitive sentiments appear to be specifically designed to be elicited by exploitive acts (Price et al. 2002; Tooby, Cosmides, and Price 2006).

This punitive sentiment has been explored from a number of theoretical evolutionary standpoints (Boyd and Richerson 1992; Boyd, Gintis, Bowles, and Richerson 2003; Frank 1988; Trivers 1971; Price et al. 2002; Tooby, Cosmides, and Price 2006). However, it seems worthwhile to explore whether analyses applying the WTR framework might offer additional clarity. How can we make sense of punishment in the light of the theory of welfare trade-off ratios? Given that exploitive acts are the result of low WTRs, punitive counterstrategies can be interpreted as efforts designed to recalibrate the decision variables in the minds of the targets of punishment – that is, the goal of punishment is the upregulation of the exploitive person's WTR toward prospective victims.

In this regard, we can conceptualize actual punitive cost-infliction or credible threats about it as (1) signals about a socially created contingency ("engage in prohibited behavior, and your welfare will be lowered"), and (2) signals about formidability, which makes this contingency real ("we have the ability to inflict costs, if you don't defer") (Sell 2006a; Sell, Tooby, and Cosmides 2009). Therefore, punishment taps directly into the input conditions of the systems that function to calibrate the target's monitored WTR toward the punisher(s).

Notice the consequentialist nature of the recalibration, if indeed successful: The adverse consequences of not caring about the welfare of the punisher (or those the punisher is acting to protect) are fully contingent on the punisher's ability to monitor the exploiter's behavior. Accordingly, we should expect the effects of cost-infliction to be confined to recalibrating the monitored WTR, to the extent that targets can confidently distinguish when they are being monitored or not. At the level of conscious experience, the successful punitive strategy should instill fear of the consequences of future exploitation in the perpetrator.

Experimental economic games do show that punishment powerfully reduces free-riding in a way consistent with the recalibrational perspective (Fehr and Gächter 2000; Ostrom, Gardner, and Walker 1994). The set-up of these repeated games lets players have full information about the behavior of other players, whereby any punishment-induced recalibrations of monitored WTRs can take full effect on the punished player's subsequent behavior (as he or she will in fact be monitored). Importantly, if the possibility of punishment is later removed in these games, we see rapid increases in free-riding (Fehr and Gächter 2000; 2002). Consistent with the claim that punishment recalibrates monitored WTRs, the effects of past punishment on social behavior are, thus, contingent on the possibility of future punishment. Similarly, both experimental studies and criminological macro-studies of crime trends seem to indicate that the effectiveness of deterrence is primarily conditioned by the certainty of detection and punishment (Klepper and Nagin 1989; Hirsch et al. 1999). This seems to indicate that punishment-induced recalibrations only guide behavior to the extent that this behavior is experienced as being monitored by punitive agencies.

The socially replicated elements (rituals) of punishment in formal and informal criminal justice contexts should in important ways be deducible from the input conditions of the evolved motivational and cognitive architecture responsible for resetting monitored WTRs (especially the revenge subsystem). The structure of the architecture suggests that punishment ought to have the following characteristics:

- The act that is being punished needs to be specified to the perpetrator – that is, it is not sufficient to harm the individual. The individual must know why he is being made to suffer.
- The harm inflicted must be communicated as having been caused by the perpetrator's prior exploitive act – that is what defines it as fitting the evolved mental category *punishment*. You are punished for what you did. (In modern societies, there is a judicial indictment that specifies the act. The absence in some contexts of this communicative step can make justice appear Kafkaesque.)
- The perpetrator is confronted with why the act was harmful to other persons or to some other entity (the group, deities, etc.), why the perpetrator's justification (if any) is insufficient to excuse it, and the guilty finding is often accompanied by a description about what was "outrageously" exploitive about the crime.
- The process of punishment is communicated as being "right" or legitimate. That is, that there is an agreement among enough social actors to define this social reality as the proper outcome. This agreement is recognized to reset baselines about what is legitimate, so that the punishment itself is not something that properly could provoke a retaliatory response from the punished individual. (Ordinarily, a person might reasonably attempt to nullify the confiscation of his property, or to retaliate against someone who has inflicted pain. But punishment resets the baselines after the punishing act, so that everything is then viewed as being at a new equilibrium that replaces previous arrangements).
- There is an attempt to communicate that the agencies of punishment are formidable – powerful and to be feared. Thus, another important element of punishment is that it requires a power differential that allows the punishers to inflict greater costs than they incur in the effort. This is why collective punishment looms larger than individual revenge. Hence, the infliction of punishment signals a dominance-subordination relationship, and the acceptance of punishment by the target signals the target's ratification that the subordination is legitimate, along with the punishment's new baselines.
- The punishers expect the punished individual to signal his or her social subordination to (deference to, respect for) the punishing entity.
- There is the attempt to communicate that the agencies of punishment will remain vigilant about future behavior (i.e., monitoring will continue).

- Finally, the magnitude of the inflicted cost used as punishment is modulated by the magnitude of the exploitation. Intuitions should set the magnitude of the punishment so that it is sufficient to reset the perpetrator's
WTR system, so that future exploitation would no longer be considered
as worthwhile by the perpetrator. If previous punishment was discovered
to be insufficient to reset a repeat offender's WTR system, the collective or individual punisher feels the impulse to increase the intensity of
punishment until it does work. If this process is a persistent failure, then
this may activate sentiments favoring return to the physical strategies of
incapacitation, such as execution or permanent confinement.

In short, there is an organized communicative component to the
process of punishment derived from the structure of the punisher's motivational system. This communication goes from the parties enacting the punishment toward both detected perpetrators of
exploitation, and toward undetected potential perpetrators. Both
common experience and the philosophy of punishment support the
view that punishment has an expressive or communicative aspect,
which takes it beyond simple cost-infliction (see, for example, Duff
1996; Nozick 1981).

It is important to recognize that this system works if the target of
punishment can correctly interpret the full range of future behavior
that the punishers intend to proscribe. Computationally, this is an
important issue, because possible behaviors are infinite. Moreover,
the contents of lengthy legal codes are largely unknown to citizens
in modern societies, and in small-scale societies legal systems are
generally not codified. We suggest that what allows this system to
work is that the minds of perpetrators and punishers alike intuitively grasp that what is most commonly at issue are welfare trade-
off ratios expressed in actions outside of converged upon baselines.
This is experienced as implicit and self-evident, and encapsulates
(but does not exhaust) many widely shared intuitions about what is
right and wrong.

Reconciliation and the Recalibration of Intrinsic WTRs

Punitive sentiments evolved because punishment works – but only
within certain limits. If punishment is effective because it upregulates monitored WTRs, then punishment should leave unaffected
behavior that potential exploiters confidently believe is unmonitored
by punitive agencies. Because a great deal of behavior is potentially
unobserved, pure reliance on punitive strategies leaves exploitation

that takes place in a broad range of conditions uncountered. That is, resetting only monitored WTRs is the grave defect of punitive strategies, because it only works for acts likely to be monitored. (Indeed, the actual decision function in potential exploiters ought to approximate the probability of being monitored, scaled by the magnitude of the costs inflicted if detected, compared to the benefit to the perpetrator of exploitation.) Viewed this way, the core of the problem of exploitation is that potential exploiters have too low an intrinsic welfare trade-off ratio toward potential victims. If they had high intrinsic WTRs toward others, they would not be motivated to injure them in pursuing their own interests, and there would be no problem.

This raises the possibility that another family of evolved strategies, complementary to punishment, could be designed to manipulate and upregulate the intrinsic WTRs of potential exploiters toward their victims (or groups and communities). If intrinsic WTRs could be generally increased, this would prevent exploitation, even during situations that punitive agencies could not monitor at sufficient frequencies. Here we will outline how nonpunitive strategies against exploitation might operate, and how their properties derive from the computational architecture of the intrinsic WTR motivational subsystem. This set of strategies can be subsumed under the heading "reparative strategies". A virtue of reparative strategies is they maintain and uphold deep social relationships, while punitive strategies rupture them. The limitation on this family of strategies is, however, that the long-term nature of payoffs over evolutionary time should make the upregulation of intrinsic WTRs difficult to achieve. The difficulty is especially aggravated in mass societies where people routinely interact with large numbers of socially distant individuals who they have little reason to have an intrinsic interest in.

Theoretically, an intrinsic WTR from X to J should be set to reflect how much changes in the welfare of J affect the fitness of X. Biologists recognize that genetic relatedness selects for an evolved system of family sentiments that makes humans have high intrinsic WTRs toward their children, and other close relatives (Hamilton 1964; Lieberman et al. 2007). Kin selection places some limits on exploitation toward kin, but not on the far larger category of non-kin. However, individuals who share interests or who broadcast positive externalities to others are commonly also bound together in relationships of fitness interdependence — indeed, often more strongly than kin are (Tooby and Cosmides 1996). These relationships — termed deep engagement relationships – are an important feature of human sociality, and are believed to underlie friendship, romantic love, several added components of family sentiment (over what kin selection explains), and a general appetite to cultivate relationships in which one is valued in a way that makes the self difficult to replace to engaged others. Ideally, the well-situated ancestral human was best off when enmeshed in a network of relationships in which he was valued as irreplaceable by others (i.e., had low substitutability). Such relationships often provoke mirroring: that is, one of the things that make individuals value others is the fact that these others value them in the first place. Information signaling this kind of friend-, mate-, family-, coalition-, or community enmeshment ought to set intrinsic WTRs upwards toward other individuals in those relationships.

Humans are intensely social and cooperative, and throughout our evolution it was critically important to have reliable associates who valued you strongly enough to assist you when you were in dire need. This appetite for others who can be relied on is powerful. Exploitative behavior reduces the degree to which others value the exploiter, making highly exploitive individuals particularly vulnerable to risks raised by a lack of sufficient intrinsic social support. When individuals who rely on exploitive formidability in their dealings get sick, or find themselves outnumbered or ambushed, their fortunes can reverse rapidly. This leads to the expectation that such individuals will be (1) more paranoid or suspicious of the motives and support of others; and (2) hungry for evidence that they are valued. (Individuals who are unusually antisocial may have become that way because they (1) received signals throughout their life history that no one intrinsically valued them, (2) chose to pursue exploitive benefits that accrue to differential formidability over the gains of cooperation, or (3) have an impaired ability to detect or respond to signals designed to regulate the intrinsic WTR system – perhaps from developmental anomalies or genetic noise.)

If the emotion program of anger is triggered by the recognition that another has engaged in an act that expresses too low a WTR toward you, there is a reciprocal emotion program that is triggered by the converse: guilt. Guilt is an emotion program that is triggered when you receive information that you have engaged in an act that expresses too low a WTR toward another, given their value to you In this view, guilt is a recalibrational emotion program whose function is to upregulate your intrinsic WTR toward an individual (and/or your monitored WTR toward an individual, if the action is detected). This recalibrational process is triggered when the inter-pretive system in your brain detects that your prior WTR (or its expression in action–decisions) has been too low, given the value of the victim to you. If you carelessly back your car into your mother, breaking her legs and rendering her amnesic, you feel guilt, even if no one but you knows what happened and, therefore, there is no punishment to fear.

Hence, we should expect that reparative strategies should involve conveying information to the exploitive person that he or she has underestimated the true magnitude of the harm inflicted; or underesti-mated the true value of the relationships jeopardized; or overestimated the gain to the exploiter of acting selfishly, when compared to the mag-nitude of the loss inflicted on the other party. If the intervention is suc-cessful, the target should realize how his or her own welfare is causally connected to the welfare of the person the target has been damaging (Tooby and Cosmides 1996). Guilt provides data formats in which rec-alibrational upregulations of intrinsic WTRs are made accessible to other behavior-regulating algorithms (Tooby, Cosmides, Sell, et al. 2008; Sznycer, Price, Tooby, and Cosmides 2007). In other words, strategies to upregulate intrinsic WTRs should be guilt-inducing strat-egies. (Of course, if the "debt" or guilt is too great ever to be dis-charged, and the net future payoff of the relationship will be negative, then guilt-inducement may sever rather than repair social ties.)

Because the level of X's intrinsic WTR toward J is set in part by the degree to which J values X in return (Tooby and Cosmides 1996), we should expect guilt-inducing strategies to make the perpetrator's stake in the exploited person more salient. Provoking guilt in the face of a transgression through confronting or reminding is a common repara-tive strategy. Participants should emphasize the high costs inflicted by the transgressor and the paltry or transient benefits reaped. Most important of all, the value of the victim to the transgressor can be stressed. This might be done by dwelling on the history of benefits the transgressor has received from the victim (she is your mother, after all), or by stressing the previous commitment of the victim to the rela-tionship (see, Sell et al., forthcoming, a, for discussion of WTRs in arguments). In line with this, empirical analyses of verbal strategies to elicit guilt show that the predominant strategy is to remind the other how his or her behavior violates obligations central to a relationship (Vanglesti, Daly, and Rudnick 1991). Another possibility is to signal that the exploitive path threatens to terminate the relationship (in a small social group, this can mean ostracism). These signals should motivate the exploitive person to reconsider the benefits associated with the relationship, and to act on that appreciation.

Reciprocally, the emotional display accompanying the emotion of guilt – the expression of suffering by the perpetrator at the contemplation of the harm he has inflicted – is a form of evidence that is relevant to computing how much recalibration is required by the transgression. Indeed, if the remorse is both genuine and great enough, this may indicate that the intrinsic WTR may be high enough after all. That is, it may not need recalibration to prevent the perpetrator from transgressing again. This would occur, for example, if the transgression reflected a lack of understanding or forethought, and was not a reflection of permanent comfort with imposing costs on others. In contrast, punitiveness by judges and juries is intensified if the perpetrator expresses no remorse – a situation indicating that values of regulatory variables in the perpetrator's cognitive architecture are set to commit the same act again, should the opportunity arise.

One component of the reparative approach focuses on facilitating recalibration in the perpetrator by emphasizing neglected value information about the victims, while another component focuses on generating new information by changing the external situation the malefactor is embedded in. For example, a direct provision of added benefits from victims to the malefactor advertises a change in the value of the victim-malefactor relationship to the malefactor. Under the right circumstances, this can trigger reparative guilt, revising the malefactor's intrinsic WTR upwards. This may be the moral intuition behind the Biblical Sermon on the Plain, where the following strategy against exploitation is suggested: "Love your enemies, do good to them that hate you. Bless them that curse you, and pray for them that despitefully use you." (Luke 6:27–36; see also the parallel Sermon on the Mount, Matthew 5–7). The benefits could take a wide variety of forms from actual material benefits to immaterial ones such as providing comfort, help or support. For example gift giving, the sharing of resources and physical contact are cross-culturally recurrent elements of reconciliation rituals (Fry 2000). Marriages create a confluence of fitness interests, and are commonly used to end feuds; similarly, if more rarely, there are a variety of ethnographic cases of reparative cross-adoptions. Observations of children similarly indicate that transferring benefits indeed facilitates reconciliation (see Fujisawa, Kutsukake, and Hasegawa 2005; Ljungberg, Horowitz, Jansson,

Westlund, and Clarke 2005). Finally, there is evidence suggesting that this kind of strategy may be used among nonhuman primates. Thus, grooming – a benefit normally exchanged among social partners – plays an important role in conciliatory practices in certain species (de Waal 1996). It is important to recognize, however, that the actual function of primate conciliatory practices may be quite limited (Silk 2000; 2002); that is, the signal may be restricted to: "The fight is over for now", rather than reflecting the start of a more expansive social repair process.

This latter component underscores some of the inherent evolutionary problems of reparative strategies. Thus, if increasing the delivery of benefits to exploiters were an unconstrained general strategy, it would be a failing strategy, since it would simply provide another incentive for exploiters to exploit. Consequently, this strategy is deployed only under narrow circumstances, when the goal is to re-enmesh the target into a more pro-social relationship or relationships. If, for example, the victim is too weak to be punitive, attempts to increase how much the exploiter values the victim may be the best of a poor set of options. Such a response is on a continuum with appeasement, the psychological phenomenon of "identification with the aggressor," and Stockholm Syndrome – responses elicited by the relative weakness of the victim compared to the perpetrator. It is a high-risk strategy, prone to failure. Accordingly, we predict that when individuals favor reparative strategies they should do so less confidently than when individuals favor punishment.

That conciliatory strategies are risky is revealed (for example) in feuding, which is ethnographically ubiquitous. Thus, feuding and many exploitive interactions are more symmetric than asymmetric and involve patterns of adversarial interaction in which both parties have been negatively impacting the other, leading to chronic losses for both sides. Attempts to change such a dynamic are often hampered, because pro-social acts from one side can be mistaken for weakness, and hence invite heightened extortive efforts. Indeed, the enactment of punitive strategies signals a dominance relationship, and so the acceptance of the punishment may be resisted because it signals acquiescence to social subordination (the underlying theme acted out when defendants refuse to recognize the authority of a court to try them). To overcome such deadlocks, third parties may attempt to organize reconciliatory events in which the acts are designed to heighten *mutual* valuation of the parties to each other, leading to mutual changes in WTRs.

Reconciliation and Recalibration of Monitored WTRs

We have now discussed how reparative strategies might recalibrate intrinsic WTRs. However, it is important to recognize that the term "reconciliation" may refer to two distinct, if related, phenomena, which the recalibrational framework may help to clarify, and which reveal how reconciliation also might affect monitored WTRs. In general, the evolved organization of recalibration involves acts or signals that are designed to initiate a process of recalibration in a target. When the function of recalibration is finished, the process of recalibration should terminate. Thus, the social process triggered by transgression moves through sequential phases: (1) recalibrational efforts (in the senders) linked to processes of WTR recalibration in the target; (2) termination of recalibrational efforts and return to normal relations once recalibration has occurred (or is presumed to have occurred). One temporal boundary that might get referred to as "reconciliation" is the signal that the recalibration effort is finished – a termination point that is more clearly recognized if the target gives signals of successful recalibration, such as remorse, subordination, or an intention to act with higher WTRs in the future. This kind of reconciliation forms the endpoint of a reparative process that, as discussed, attempts to recalibrate someone's intrinsic WTRs.

A second, related meaning of reconciliation is the attempt to lower someone's disposition to inflict costs by embedding them in conditional cooperative relationships from which the target has the potential to either derive large benefits or to lose them. Being subject to new conditional cooperative relationships revises monitored WTRs, not intrinsic WTRs, because subsequent exploitation will lead to the withdrawal of conditionally delivered benefits if it is detected. It is important to recognize that efforts to domesticate a transgressor by embedding him in conditional cooperative relationships are not themselves punishment – the transgressor is better off. Both reparative strategies are closely related to each other, and are often found together because they mutually reinforce each other, and often depend on bringing about the same types of social arrangements.

To Punish or to Reconcile?

It is important to recognize that punitive and reparative strategies exist in tension with each other. The infliction of costs – even when those costs are inflicted as retaliation for prior exploitive acts – sends a signal that the punishers do not feel inhibited in inflicting costs on the target of punishment. In other words, severe punishment is itself a signal of a low intrinsic WTR. This information should be picked up by the representational systems responsible for calibrating reciprocal intrinsic WTRs in the punished individual. Thus, while punishment might productively upregulate monitored WTRs, and hold the threat of future inflictions, they might at the same time lower intrinsic WTRs in the target of punishment – an outcome that at least partly offsets its advantages. While experimental economic games show that punishment indeed increase cooperation in environments with perfect opportunities for monitoring behavior (cf. above), other studies indicate that fear of punishment might in fact lower more general pro-social tendencies (Caprara, Barbaranelli, Pastorelli, Cermak, and Rosza 2001). The distinction between different kinds of WTRs explains such otherwise conflicting observations.

Based on the preceding discussion, it is clear that certain factors increase the probability a punitive strategy will be used, and others increase the probability that a reparative strategy will be used. Punitive strategies are more favored when (1) monitoring is possible and not too costly; (2) the actors are formidable enough with respect to the exploiter (or can withhold valuable enough future cooperation) that they can punish successfully and without too much cost; and/or (3) the exploiter has little potential for intrinsically valuing the set of potential victims (because of personality, or a lack of connections). Reparative strategies are more favored when (1) monitoring is impossible, or too costly and unreliable; (2) the actors are not formidable enough with respect to the exploiter and/or his allies (or have no bargaining power deriving from benefits that might be withheld), so that attempted punishment is too costly and/or insufficiently injurious; (3) the exploiter has substantial potential to intrinsically value the set of potential victims; and (4) the exploiter shows evidence of remorse – that is, shows some intrinsic valuation of the victims. If the malefactor's remorse is great enough, or opposition to punishment by his allies is too strong, then malefactors may be subject only to reparative acts. In sum, these factors revolve around the value of maintaining interactions with or a relationship with the malefactor, and we expect this to be the critical factor when a decision maker is to assess whether punishment or reparation are to be deployed. Table 5.2 provides an overview of some of the factors being processed in such assessments.

Table 5.2 A partial list of hypothesized (interrelated) factors used by the punishment and reconciliation systems.

Factors favoring reconciliation between X and Y	Factors favoring punishment of Y by X	Factors favoring execution/expulsion of Y by X
Y has a high Association Value to X	Y has a low Association Value to X	Y has a negative Association Value toward X
Monitoring Y is difficult or costly	Monitoring Y is possible and low cost	X's previous recalibrational strategies against Y have failed
Y is relatively high in formidability	Y is relatively low in formidability	Y has no or relatively weak coalitional allies
X and Y are related	X's previous conciliatory strategies against Y have failed	...
Y shows signs of remorse	...	...
...	...	...

The Evolutionary Benefits of Being Punitive Versus being Reparative

Upon detection of an exploitive individual whose acts express low WTRs toward others, our minds need to solve the problem of choosing the best of the two types of response. Of course, all else equal, it is more adaptive to be valued intrinsically rather than extrinsically, because intrinsic valuation will result in benefits even in one's absence or temporary states of ineffectiveness. Also, reparative strategies leave the productive relationships of a selective exploiter intact. While reparative strategies potentially yield more benefits, such strategies may often be less effective by themselves, because it is hard to upregulate intrinsic WTRs broadly to all potential victims. Such strategies may also involve subjecting people to more potential exploitation, because attempted repair involves continued social contact with, and exposure to, an individual who knowingly has caused harm in the past. In contrast, punitive strategies can revise monitored WTRs easily, protecting broad classes of potential victims – but only so long as monitoring is effective.

To solve the problem of choosing between reconciliation, punishment, execution, or ostracism/confinement, our minds evolved to weigh a number of factors against each other. These factors include the relative formidability of the punishers compared to the punished, the likelihood of recidivism and future harm, and the future benefits of continued interactions with the malefactor – including the malefactor's enmeshment with others in deep and productive social relationships. The key decision element is the malefactor's value as an associate: the estimated net lifetime value of maintaining interactions or a relationship with the malefactor from the point of view of the decision maker. We will refer to this as the malefactor's *Association Value* (Tooby and Cosmides 1996). Hence, we suggest that the human evolved psychological architecture contains subcomponents that are designed to spontaneously compute this index – an *Association Value index*, together with accompanying implicit representations of the degree of uncertainty about the true magnitude of the Association Value. Within a community, there will of course be a distribution of Association Values of members of the community toward an individual. In making collective decisions about the fate of a transgressor, each individual will be accessing the distinct Association Value she puts on the transgressor, with interactive negotiation within the community about a collective judgment.

Ancestrally, groups were small, and ingroup members in general could be presumed to have a positive Association Value to many co-members (family, friends, allies, etc.). We expect that this led to an elaborate evolved psychology of reparation – one that can be eclipsed in large-scale societies where strangers swamp closely networked social actors. In a small-scale society, an individual may be productive in many of his relationships, and exploitive only in a few. Under these circumstances, repair may appeal to many social actors, who would not want to lose an individual they value because of that individual's acts toward third parties they may not value as highly.

If the value of ongoing relationships with the malefactor is high enough (as it often is in small-scale societies, and sometimes is in large-scale societies), then reparative strategies may be all that are used. To the extent, however, that a transgressor's Association Value is negative, sentiments may spontaneously move toward execution or permanent ostracism (in the developed world, life in prison). Confinement is a combination of ostracism and punishment. It incapacitates by physically restraining the malefactor from having contact with potential victims, and at the same time such restrictions on movement are aversive. If the value of the malefactor to those empowered to act is low but positive, then temporary confinement (which prevents exploitation for its duration, and functions as a punishment) may be chosen. In line with this, recent research in dyadic cooperation suggests that when subjects have available as one response the opportunity to avoid cooperative interactions with exploitive individuals, their choice to punish has a modestly hopeful meaning: They punish those who they anticipate will cooperate with them in the future – as a bargaining move – and simply avoid those they have decided not to cooperate with (Krasnow, Cosmides, and Tooby, forthcoming). Hence reparation signals the highest valuation, punishment a lower but still positive valuation, and expulsion or execution signals the lowest intrinsic valuation. The point is, that sentiments about what to do are not usually rationally arrived at, but rather are intuitively and spontaneously felt in individuals – we would suggest as the result of the interaction between individuals' evolved species-typical computational systems and the availability of relevant cues.

This constellation of selection pressures leads us to expect that reconciliation is a wary process. The offended parties should approach reconciliation with caution, and the activation of reparative motivations should coincide with the activation of attention-allocation mechanisms that motivate the offended parties to scrutinize the situation for cues of whether the strategy is indeed successful. Due to the role of guilt in the upregulation of intrinsic WTRs, these mechanisms should make us especially sensitive to the lack of remorse and repentance. In line with this, appeasement postures and expressions of apology and remorse do indeed seem to be cross-cultural elements of reconciliation rituals (Fry 2000). Reciprocally, the absence of remorse signals the ineffectiveness of reparative attempts, and intensifies punitive sentiments. Where punishment is not codified, punishers often proceed until they provoke a sufficiently intense signal of recalibration from the target of punishment. Reconciliation can be thought of as a reciprocal strategy, which starts cautiously and unfolds as coordinated signals are exchanged between the two parties. In contrast, the execution of punishment might be conceived of as a more one-sided event, in which the punisher induces recalibration in the punished without the punished necessarily acquiescing (see Tooby, Cosmides, Sell, et al. 2008).

Punishment and Reconciliation as a Sequential Process

Although punishment and reconciliation as two strategy-types exist in some tension with each other if executed at the same time, employing them in sequence – first punishment, then repair– may help each compensate for the defects of the other. With punitive sentiment, humans have a desire to have the target experience a period of suffering. This derives from the evolutionary logic of recalibration and deterrence. An initial punishment phase creates deterrence (by setting a price)—deterrence would not be present if reparative strategies were used only by themselves. However, people may intuitively sense that punishment alone will leave the target more hostile, that is, with a lower intrinsic WTR toward social members than before. This may be exacerbated by the fact that the preferred form of punishment in developed societies – confinement – itself isolates the malefactor. Isolation, in turn, weakens or eliminates the kinds of social relationships of mutual valuation that lead individuals to harbor high intrinsic WTRs toward others – the psychological factor that functions as one primary inhibitor of exploitation.

Implicit or explicit recognition of this problem may motivate a policy of ordering punishment first, followed by repair. That is, there may be a life-cycle to recalibration because the strategies conflict with each other if carried out at the same time. Between punishment and repair, there is the "reconciliatory" signal of the termination of recalibrational efforts – we are now no longer adversarially attempting to make you suffer, and expect to return to a "normal" pro-social relationship. We mutually acknowledge that new baselines have been established, which are new starting points (i.e., you are not entitled to punish us for punishing you). People often use phrases like "paid their debt to society" – where the "debt" that is discharged is the obligation to experience an amount of recalibrational suffering commensurate with the magnitude of the crime.

When an individual leaves confinement, incapacitation is over, and repair may be seen as an important follow-up strategy as the malefactor has renewed access to potential victims. Once the malefactor is about to become free to move about in the community, and has opportunities to exploit again, the salience of adding reparative strategies should increase, with the goal of upregulating default intrinsic WTRs, and the potential for positive sum cooperative interactions (with conditional WTRs). That is, once the punitive phase is ended and the repair phase begins, the target may become the object of pro-social efforts to embed him in beneficial social relationships that will recalibrate his intrinsic WTRs, his monitored WTRs, or both. The distribution of suspended sentences or parole is expected to track this logic: It should seem intuitively appropriate that individuals who give out stronger cues that their tendency to exploit can be dealt with more easily by reparative strategies should have shorter sentences (or suspended sentences), or should be let out on parole earlier. Factors like family, valued skills, a job, a supportive living situation, productivity, community connections, remorse, efforts at restitution, low formidability, an absence of attempts to advertise a hostile or exploitive orientation – all play into these decisions. Similarly, the intuitions underlying social work within criminal justice systems should seek to build on these factors, and establish relationships of interdependence and mutual valuation.

The Choice between Punishment and Reconciliation: An Overview

Based on the preceding arguments, Figure 5.1 provides an overview of the role of one critical factor (Association Values) in the psychological processes regulating the choice between punishment and reconciliation. These processes are initiated by an external cost-imposing event caused by an individual Y. This event activates computational programs assessing the expressed WTR and compares the costs imposed with the given baseline. If appropriate, these programs tag the act as "wrong" and the malefactor as an "exploiter." This tag sets other processes in motion. Most importantly, a suit of computational systems assesses the malefactor's Association Value and triggers the appropriate motives. In this computational process, the Association Value estimator extracts a number of cues from the environment relating to the costs of losing the individual as a social partner. A high Association Value triggers reparative motivations; a lower Association Value triggers punitive motivations, and motivations leading to expulsion or execution are triggered by a very low or negative Value. Whether these motivations in fact trigger the corresponding behaviors will depend on an assessment of the broader social situation. As argued, we expect punitive reactions to be inhibited if the malefactor Y is part of a relatively formidable coalition that is likely to retaliate with cost-infliction. In reverse, this could increase the estimated payoffs associated with a reparative strategy. If such a strategy is unsuccessful, however, the exploited individual could be forced to migrate out of the group. Hence, ancestrally, the latter strategy could have been the only option available in the face of formidable and well-connected exploiters.

To the extent that behavioral reactions are unleashed, varying degrees of attention are allocated toward scrutinizing the effects of the chosen strategy. For example, high-risk strategies such as reparation

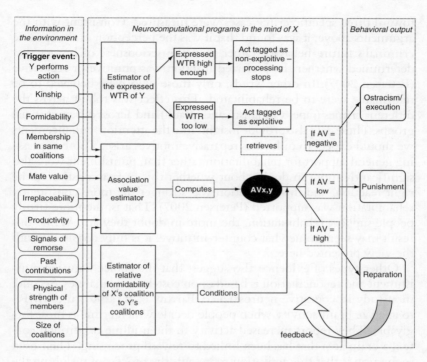

Figure 5.1 The psychological process regulating the choice between punitive and reparative responses to exploitation

should entail higher levels of attentiveness. This scrutiny creates feedback loops, where the malefactors' Association Value is recomputed and potentially new strategies are deployed. Thus, we might expect a successful use of punishment to subsequently trigger a reparative strategy. In reverse, failed reparation (i.e., Y does not show signs of remorse in response to the reparative gestures) could lead to punishment or eventually to the deployment of strategies of ostracism or execution.

Discussion about the Evidence Supporting the Argument

Several lines of evidence on human behavior suggest that Association Values play an important role in anti-exploitation decisions. First, a large-scale survey designed to test aspects of the arguments presented here suggests that humans do engage in cost-benefit analysis when choosing whether to punish or to reconcile. In the survey, attitudes toward three specific crime cases were measured. Consistent with the arguments above, it was found that it was the perception of the specific criminal's future behavior rather than the seriousness of his act that determined whether the preferred reaction was punitive or reparative (Petersen 2007). In other words, only those who were believed to be reformable were to be rehabilitated. This effect was robust across the different crimes (rape, vandalism and assault) and across different social groups. These data also provide insights into the attention-enhancements we should expect to unlock as reparative motives arise. Those expressing general support for rehabilitation rather than punishment were also significantly more in doubt about whether this in fact constituted the right reaction, and this association was stronger the more consistently rehabilitation was supported (Petersen 2007). That is, the more firmly people support rehabilitation, the more in doubt they are. While this result may seem somewhat counter-intuitive, it is fully consistent with the view presented here.

Other types of evidence also suggest that the choice between punishment and reconciliation is based upon cost-benefit analyses. Second, in a study in cognitive neuroscience, Farrow et al. (2001) uses fMRI to analyze brain activity when people decide which crime is most forgivable. They report increased activity in the midline orbifrontal cortex, a brain area that has been linked to reward processing. Their own suggestion is that this activation represents the process of weighing the relative merits of two options against each other (presumably, to forgive one individual versus another). Third, Fry (2000) sums up the anthropological observations on reconciliation by arguing that reconciliation, cross-culturally, seems most likely to occur when relationships are important and difficult to replace – just what one would expect from the framework presented here. Finally, some evidence from studies of children's conciliatory behavior suggests that the frequency of reconciliation is higher among friends than acquaintances (Cords and Killen 1998). There is also evidence to the contrary (Butovskaya et al. 2000), but a more recent study indicates that these contrasting observations occur because friends reconcile using more implicit strategies such as simply being friendly instead of explicitly offering gifts etc. (Fujisawa, Kutsukake, and Hasegawa 2005). This last observation is not at odds with the recalibrational theory. Presumably, friends have hitherto engaged in mutual beneficial activities. An individual P's intrinsic WTR toward a friend V can probably be upregulated by V reminding P of these benefits. It might not be necessary to explicitly display the worth of the relationship by transferring new benefits.

Reconciliation has also been studied among nonhuman primates. In many ways, the argument presented here constitutes a computationally specific parallel to the way in which the primatologist de Waal (1996) makes sense of nonhuman primate conciliatory behavior (it should be noted, though, that the adaptive problem is phrased a bit differently in the primate literature, as will be discussed below). Both experimental work and observations in primate groups suggest that the likelihood of reconciliation following hostile encounters is correlated with the social value of the relationship (Aureli and de Waal 2000; although, see Silk 2002). An imaginative experimental study by Cords and Thurnheer (1993) illustrates the argument. In this study, conflicts between two long-tailed macaques were induced using food. Baseline ratings for the frequencies of reconciliation following these conflicts were obtained. Afterwards, a popcorn dispenser was installed in the macaques' cage with the unique feature that it had to be cooperatively handled to produce the reward. Conflicts were induced but this time the experimentally heightened value of the Macaques to each other increased the frequency of reconciliation by a factor of three. Furthermore, while social value seems to predict the likelihood of reconciling among nonhuman primates, data shows that the severity of an aggressive encounter has little consistent effect on the likelihood of reconciling afterwards (Silk 2002). This is consistent with the above-mentioned results on human attitudes. Finally, primate observations indicate that reconciliation is indeed a wary process, which slowly unfolds as the former antagonists exchange certain kinds of signals, presumably indicating their good faith (de Waal 2000).

Yet, the primate data needs to be viewed cautiously. In the primate literature, it is common to view reconciliation as attempts to transform adversarial relationships into pro-social relationships. Based on observations indicating that frequencies of reconciliation following aggressive encounters are correlated with degree of kinship, Silk (2000; 2002) questions this argument. Kinship-based relations are more pro-social than other types of relations, and are less likely to be enduringly disrupted by momentary conflicts (Cords 1988); in other words, they should not need reparation. Hence, another view of the function of reconciliation in nonhuman primates is as a signal that the present aggressive encounter is now terminated, and other activities can be pursued without fear of its continuation.

In the human case, however, even if reconciliation among humans is more frequent between kin than between unrelated persons following acts of exploitation (and we expect it to be), this is not inconsistent with the WTR-derived argument. Thus, in our perspective, the adaptive problem posed by exploitation is the existence of individuals with low WTRs toward valued others (or the self), or low group-directed WTRs. These predict a likelihood of future and ongoing exploitation. This problem is real whether or not the perpetrator is related to the observer. The adaptive solution can involve upregulations of the kin's monitored or intrinsic WTR, but all else equal, the fact that kin are intrinsically valuable (Hamilton 1964) should make reparative strategies preferable (when proximity is not inherently negative sum).

Finally, it is possible to assess the predicted importance of malefactors' estimated Associational Value and related cues in the light of the historical development of modern criminal justice systems. In small-scale societies, perpetrators generally have strong ties to most members of the social group, making reparative strategies potentially effective. Moreover, the greater number of supporters an exploiter has, the more opposition there will be to punishment by the target's allies – also limiting the use of punishment. In large-scale societies, the class of potential victims falling outside of the circle of enmeshment is very large, monitoring is more difficult, and punitive agencies can become far more powerful than individual malefactors. These factors predict cross-cultural trends toward increasing use of punishment in larger scale societies. This might partly explain the rise of relatively ruthless punitive systems widely deployed in mass societies after the emergence of agriculture (Spierenburg 1984).

Yet, this development only holds until the seventeenth century, and for the last three hundred years criminal justice in the Western world has grown milder (Garland 1990).[3] This turn toward a modest use of reparative strategies can be explained by the interaction between the psychological architecture regulating the choice between punishment and reconciliation, and at least two cultural developments. First, it is possible that the rise of the printing press and, subsequently, newspapers, photography, television and film (with more direct psychophysical representations of the treatment of individuals inside criminal justice systems) causes ordinary experience in industrial societies to more closely mimic the greater engagement found among individuals in smaller scale societies. Especially, the distribution of information made possible by the printing press seems to have played an important role in establishing a sense of collective identity in large-scale societies (Anderson 1991). Second, these processes might have been fuelled by the institutional developments of capitalist market society and later welfare state institutions. Capitalist society breeds more inclusive coalitional identities as extensive labor divisions facilitate experiences of successful social exchange with people highly dissimilar from oneself. Similarly, the establishment of social welfare schemes in the twentieth century has facilitated more equal levels of living standards, as well as a reduction in class and ethnic differentiation through clothing, and other aspects of appearance. Arguably this reinforces the perception by individuals that the nation-state is their coalition. This mental representation is no longer constantly challenged by direct observations of others in their community who appear extremely different (see, for example, Larsen 2006; Rothstein 1998). In line with this, research shows that punitiveness is lower in economically developed countries (Mayhew and van Kesteren 2002) and in countries with large welfare states (Christie 2004).

This final analysis also underscores the point that it is important not to generalize attitudes among elites in developed countries to all cultures. This is especially true in relation to the ideology that it is proper to treat all individuals "equally"; an ideology seemingly produced by perspective-taking alliance formation within democratic political processes. In general, we expect baselines with regard to acceptable levels of differential treatment to be defined by within a group, based on its internal distribution of alliances and power. In many social settings, for example, exploitive or even lethal acts against outgroup members are not viewed as crimes at all, but often as laudable. Even acts against ingroup members without social allies may be viewed similarly. Stable entrenched power differentials lead to social concepts of legitimate status-based entitlement, such as the emergence of aristocracies with prerogatives that would be viewed as criminal in democratic nations.

The Seriousness of the Act and the Quantitative Modulation of the Reaction

In the modern criminal justice system, the harmfulness and seriousness of a crime is of fundamental importance when specific sentences are measured out. One interesting feature of the argument presented here is that we should not expect our species-typical psychology to place the same weight on the seriousness of the exploitive act (i.e., the discrepancy between the revealed and the acceptable WTR) when choosing between punishment and reconciliation. Rather, this choice is expected to be determined by a prospective estimation of the transgressor's Association Value – that is, the future value of maintaining a relationship with the exploitive person. As will be argued below, this estimate is based on numerous cues, of which the seriousness of the act is only one. Thus, in a nutshell, the argument is that we fit our reaction to the exploitive person rather than to his or her act. Even in the face of serious exploitation, we can opt for a reparative strategy. Contrasted with formalized and codified sanctioning systems found in developed countries (which are hampered by an imperative to be consistent), public opinion on criminal justice issues is expected to be more flexible, and more oriented to individualized forms of sanctioning that are specifically tailored to the criminal at hand. Studies of public opinion in different countries confirm this (Finkel et al. 1996; Petersen forthcoming).

At the same time, the recalibrational framework suggests that the perceived seriousness of the offense does play an important role in anti-exploitation decisions. While punishment and reconciliation are two qualitatively distinct reactions, both types of reactions can also be modulated quantitatively with respect to their intensity. An aggressive strategy can entail both high and low cost-infliction. Similarly, conciliatory guilt-induction and enmeshment can be aimed at inducing high or low guilt, high or low interdependence, and relationships can be curtailed or ended outright. When the evaluation of the net future value of a continued relationship with the perpetrator has inclined the actors toward either punitive or reparative strategies, the seriousness of the perpetrators' exploitation is expected to modulate the intensity of the strategy.

Within this framework, the problem posed by exploitation is that it indicates that the perpetrator does not value the victim or other members of our group sufficiently – predicting future exploitation. The costliness of the act to the victim, together with the benefit of the act to the perpetrator, gives a reliable indication of the offender's current WTR toward the target – i.e., how low the perpetrator's interest in our welfare is. Our intuitive grasp of the seriousness of a transgression reflects the discrepancy between the revealed and the acceptable WTR. Thus, the seriousness of an offense – and indirectly its costliness – tells us how much the perpetrator's WTR (whether monitored or intrinsic) toward us needs to be upregulated before it is deemed to be sufficiently high. This information should necessarily be reflected in the intensity of the reaction by which we seek to achieve this objective. The survey data referred to above supports this role of the seriousness of the act. Thus, while the perceived seriousness of crimes does not directly influence whether punishment or restoration is preferred, it does influence the length of the preferred sentences (Petersen 2007). Similarly, other studies have consistently shown that preferred sentence lengths are determined by the seriousness of the act (Darley and Pittman 2003; Darley, Carlsmith, and Robinson 2000).

The Computational Architecture of Our Anti-Exploitation Motivational System

In deciding how to respond to exploitation, our evolved circuits need to know the net future value of remaining associated with the perpetrator. However, events in the future are inherently unobservable. Accordingly, to the extent that exploitation has been an ancestrally recurrent adaptive problem, natural selection should have selected for circuits designed to monitor cues that predict Association Value. These circuits should influence behavior by regulating the activation of motivational programs producing felt emotions (Tooby, Cosmides and Barrett 2005; Tooby and Cosmides 2008; Tooby, Cosmides, Sell et al. 2008).

Ancestral Cues to the Net Future Value of Interacting with Exploitive Persons

We propose that our evolved psychological architecture is designed to compute an Association Value index for a potentially exploitive person based on at least four analytically distinct types of cues: (1) cues relating to potential benefits of association; (2) cues relating to the likelihood of future exploitative acts; (3) cues relating to the potential harm if the act is indeed repeated; and (4) cues predicting changes in these variables if either reparative or punitive strategies are deployed.

Important cues to the potential benefits of engaging in close future social interaction with an individual would be:

- kinship (Hamilton 1964);
- the expectation of future benefits based on the history of benefit delivery from this individual in the past;
- the individual's general level of resources or productivity (status, access to resources, skills and competences, leadership abilities, positive externalities, etc.);

- whether the individual is a member of own's coalition or a rival one (because ingroup members are (all else equal) more willing cooperative partners; see Cosmides, Tooby and Kurzban 2003; Tooby, Cosmides and Price 2006);
- the attractiveness of the individual as a sexual partner;
- the general irreplaceability or value of the individual (e.g., the co-parent to one's child would serve an irreplaceable function due to his or her unique interest in the child's welfare; see Tooby and Cosmides 1996).

As matter of fact, criminological studies of the public's attitudes provide evidence that outgroup members (as defined by ethnicity, race or accent) are seen as more eligible for punishment (Dixon, Mahoney, and Cocks 2002; Hurwitz and Peffley 1997; Petersen 2007; Ugwuegbu 1979), that well-integrated ingroup members are punished less (Hembroff 1987; Goul Andersen, 1998), and that the physically attractive are treated more mildly (Mazella and Feingold 1994).

When estimating the magnitude of potential future costs of reconciling, two cues seem to be especially important. First, the costliness of the initial exploitive act (to ingroup members) should provide some estimate of how harmful potential future exploitive acts would be to decision makers. This is because it sets an upper limit on the individual's maximum intrinsic WTR toward community members. Hence, we expect the seriousness of the act to (indirectly) influence the decision about whether to punish or reconcile by having an effect on the estimate of the net prospective social value of the exploitive person to the decision makers. Second, the mind should be sensitive to cues about the exploitive person's ability to evaluate costs and benefits accurately: those who consistently misperceive the harm associated with their acts will be more prone to harm us greatly. When deciding whether to punish or conciliate, we should accordingly be motivated to look for cues that indicate whether the exploitive person indeed understands the harm he has caused.

Furthermore, we should expect our mind to monitor cues that predict how likely repeated exploitation is. We expect the following cues to be important:

- the past behavior of the exploitive person (is it a first time offense?);
- the degree to which the exploitive person expresses remorse;
- the person's degree of impulse control;
- the degree of intentionality behind the exploitive act.

At a computationally specific level, "intentional acts" can be thought of as acts resulting from decision making processes in the perpetrator that accessed information about the magnitude of the costs imposed, the magnitude of the benefits received, and on whom the costs were imposed (Sell 2006b). Compared to unintentional exploitation, intentional acts will more reliably reveal the true level of the under-lying WTR and will better predict future cost-imposition.

Opinion studies have documented the cross-cultural importance of all such cues: Restorative sanctions are less preferred against repeated criminal activity (Finkel et al 1996; Petersen 2007); the more inten-tional exploitive acts are (e.g., from accidental to negligent to fully intentional), the more punitive sanctions are viewed as legitimate compared to restorative sanctions (Hamilton and Sanders 1992); and remorse significantly increases the perceived degree to which exploitive acts can be forgiven and the degree to which rehabilitation is viewed as the appropriate goal of the criminal sanction (Petersen 2007; Robinson, Smith-Lovin and Tsoudis 1994).

When an exploitive act is observed, our mind should be pro-grammed to detect and process all these cues and compute an index of the net future value of the exploitive person. To the extent this Association Value is estimated as high, conciliatory motives should be activated. In contrast, punitive motives should be elicited if the value is perceived as low. Differences in this assessment to different members of the community (e.g., victim's family vs. perpetrator's family) often lead to conflicts about what course of action to take. Finally, the intensity of these motives and the behavior they give rise to should be regulated by the seriousness of the exploitive act.

The Emotional Side of Punishment and Reconciliation

It is easy to confuse scientific claims about the evolved function of a computational mechanism with claims about conscious events. However, the proposal here is about the circuit logic of evolved pro-grams that were built into our neurocomputational architecture by natural selection, and not about conscious deliberation. This circuitry and its logic operate outside of consciousness, although it may occa-sionally place some of its products into conscious awareness, where we experience them as feelings, inclinations, intuitions or ways of thinking. From an evolutionary psychological perspective, emo-tions such as anger are simply one kind of evolved program – each with a functional problem-solving logic that deals with its respective adaptive problem, imposed by natural selection. As discussed above, anger is the primary emotion program that evolved to deal with the recurrent adaptive problem posed by encounters with people who place too little weight on one's welfare. One of its primary outputs is the motivation to signal why the target should upregulate her WTR, through either the punitive infliction of costs, or the withdrawal of cooperative benefits, depending (speaking approximately) on the target's Association Value to the angry individual.

Since the punitive infliction of costs (driven by angry punitive sentiment) appears as a leading option when provoked by exploitation, it would be enacted as the response unless the mind's "arguments" against inflicting harm could counterbalance it. Aside from the power of the perpetrator or the community support he or she enjoys, the main factor that should diminish the impulse to harm the perpetrator is his or her Association Valuation to the person experiencing the response. If the Association Value is high enough, the prospect of inflicting costs on the perpetrator calls up a countervailing evaluative emotional subsystem – compassion. These two sets of circuits will be outputting their unique forms of value information and motivational tendencies – to injure, and to refrain from injuring, the perpetrator. Hence, the circumstances of the transgression, the characteristics of the perpetrator, and the perpetrator's relationship to supporters and detractors in the community are processed by these mechanisms, which then produce an emotional configuration representing the mind's best guess of an adaptive behavioral response. We therefore expect anger and (potentially) compassion to be key ingredients in an emotional mix elicited by exploitation (Petersen 2010).

As we sketched out, punitive and conciliatory strategies exist in tension as alternatives, because cost-infliction works against conciliatory attempts to upregulate the exploitive person's intrinsic WTR toward the punitive. Yet despite their differences, both kinds of strategies should be heavily regulated by the anger program and anger should be a key part of the emotional side of both. Anger is the data format by which the perceived seriousness of the injury is broadcast into consciousness and to other computational systems (Sell et al., forthcoming; Tooby, Cosmides, Sell et al. 2008). The felt magnitude of anger should be directly related to the displayed level of the WTR, for example, the seriousness of the exploitive act, and will play an important role in the motivation of recalibrational responses (Sell 2006b; Sell et al. 2009, forthcoming). Accordingly, we expect anger to be a central regulator of the intensity of not only punitive strategies but also of restorative strategies. For example, someone could act in a way that did not weight another person's values sufficiently either because (1) they did not value the person's welfare (in which case punishment is a useful recalibrator), or (2) they had an incorrect model of the victim's values but a sufficiently high WTR (in which case re-education might serve as well). That is, if the perpetrator had only known what it meant to the victim, he would not have committed the act. This gives a definition of remorse: recalibrational suffering based on re-education about the victim's values. Anger not only incites behaviors designed to increase the weight the target places on the angry individual's welfare; it also motivates communication designed to educate the transgressor so that she has a correct model of the values of the angry individual – values that the exploitive act violated, and values that the malefactor should respect in the future, to the extent that he places weight on others' welfare.

In support of this claim, empirical studies show that forgiveness and reconciliation both operate within a background of anger (Averill 1982; Walker and Gorsuch 2004). Thus, while reconciliatory strategies do not impose costs on the exploitive person, they do involve an anger-motivated condemnation and denunciation, which conveys to the exploitive person the magnitude and the nature of the harm.

While anger strongly predominates when punitive strategies are induced, this is not necessarily the case in conciliatory strategies. Where the Association Value of the transgressor is high enough, signals from the compassion subsystem emerge as factors that countervail against anger. Empirical studies show that emotions of compassion or sympathy toward the exploitive person play an important motivational role when engaging in reconciliation (Gault and Sabini 2000; Petersen 2010). In general, compassion seems to be involved in abstaining from harming others and providing benefits for individuals in need (Haidt 2003; Wispé 1991).

Thus, the motivational role of compassion in reconciliation is expected within the recalibrational theory outlined here. Compassion inhibits punitive sentiments that might end the relationship, or reduce the Association Value of the transgressor by injuring or killing them. Moreover, compassion (gated by valuation) should orchestrate responses that embody the conciliatory strategy – that is, it organizes behavior that could potentially feed into the system that revises intrinsic WTRs in the target. Someone motivated by compassion acts with forbearance and kindness, advertising the degree to which the compassionate person values the transgressor. This signal of valuation by the victim for the transgressor shows the transgressor that this is one of a limited number of persons in the world who do value them, making the victim more intrinsically valuable to the transgressor. Where Association Value is high and conciliatory strategies are emerging, the resulting conflicting emotions of anger and compassion correspond to the folk concept of feeling "hurt."

An Overview

The following is a possible interpretation of the interplay between the systems dissecting the dimensions of exploitive acts, and the motivational systems producing anger and compassion, which are triggered when harm is imposed on the self or an ingroup member. First, the act's seriousness is assessed to evaluate whether the cost-imposition reflects a welfare trade-off ratio that is too low. Second, to the extent that the act is recognized as an exploitive act, feelings of anger proportional with the seriousness are produced. Third, the release of anger – which is the data format in which the detection of a person with a low WTR is broadcasted to other mechanisms (Tooby, Cosmides, Sell et al. 2008) – serves as a vehicle for the activation of other computational systems. These systems will access the Association Value index for the transgressor – the motivational variable that reflects the mind's estimate of the net future value of associating with the exploitive person. Fourth, to the extent that this value is estimated to be high, reparative emotions toward the exploitive persons are triggered and will co-exist with anger. While anger will foster condemnation, reparative sentiments (such as compassion) should moderate cost-infliction on the exploitive person and potentially invite a restorative strategy. However, if the Association Value index is low, no checks on anger are produced and a punitive strategy will be deployed. Fifth, to the extent that reparative emotions are elicited, attention-allocating mechanisms should be activated that search for cues of remorse and guilt in the exploitive person to consolidate or abort adoption of a conciliatory strategy.

This is an individual-level description, without taking into account either how individuals and larger groups influence each other in this process, or the larger dynamics by which a community negotiates a coordinated response (if any). Obviously, there will be a distribution of different behavioral inclinations in different members of the social group based on their relationships (real or vicarious) to the victim and the exploiter, their social distances, their vulnerability to the precedent set by the transgression, their evaluations of the relevant baselines, their formidabilities (power or lack of power) compared to the victim and malefactor, and so on. Nevertheless, based on these variables, one can use this analysis to predict systematic patterns in the responses of individuals to exploitation. Hence, we expect this architecture to regulate how we react to harmful acts at all levels of social interaction: in the family, between friends, at the workplace, and when we are confronted with crime in the media. Indeed, a number of studies of attitudes toward crime depicted in the media have concluded that, if those surveyed believe that criminals are dispositionally "good" – that they wish to behave lawfully, but are driven into criminality because of poverty or problems in their upbringing, then they favor rehabilitative strategies. If they, on the other hand, believe that criminals are dispositionally "bad," and that their criminality is the result of rational calculations or stable anti-social desires, then they support harsh punishments (see Claster 1992; Lakoff 1996; Sasson 1995; Wilson and Herrnstein 1985; the terminology of "good" and "bad: is taken from Claster [1992]). Such stereotypes seem to satisfy the input conditions of the computational systems eliciting punitive and conciliatory strategies, respectively.

Conclusion

In this chapter, we have developed an evolutionarily informed computational sketch of some of the evolved programs that are deployed when individuals deal with exploitation, crime, punishment, and reconciliation. We think that this approach might illuminate certain recurrent phenomena in formal and informal criminal justice systems, such as spontaneous political attitudes concerning crime (Petersen, forthcoming). We argue that the acts that we perceive as exploitive are acts that reveal the low value of welfare trade-off variables in the minds' of perpetrators (provided we have a pro-social orientation toward the victims). Punishment and reconciliation are two evolved strategies to remedy this adaptive problem, targeting different aspects of the exploitive person's computational architecture to upregulate the value he places on potential victims. From a more phenomenological perspective these strategies are designed to induce fear and guilt, respectively. Due to the structure of the relevant selection pressures, punitive strategies will be elicited when the net future Association Value of the criminal is estimated as low. In contrast, when this value is estimated as high, conciliatory strategies are more likely to be favored.

This perspective, then, provides an alternative to the Freudian idea of nonpunitive orientations merely as a product of culture's sublimation of aggressive drives.[4] According to the recalibrational view, both restorative and punitive orientations emerge from the interplay between the valuation that members of the community place on the criminal or transgressor and a set of evolved programs embodying alternative defenses against exploitation. Punishment and reconciliation are both natural counterstrategies, endogenous to the human mind.

Notes

1. For example, at present there is a discourse in the United States about whether to treat certain individuals as enemy combatants or as criminals—each one involving a different set of laws and expectations. We suggest that these different sets originate in different evolved mental categories and motivational circuits corresponding to different kinds of ancestral threat. Different voices in this debate (including people of different nationalities and religious groups) might be spontaneously drawn to one side of the debate or another based on where their minds draw the boundary "ingroup member."

2. Our minds evolved to compute baselines according to this and other cognitive principles based on the net long term evolutionary payoffs of adopting one versus another. Some of the payoffs driving our species convergence include: (1) endless and inconclusive conflict emerges if different players interpret the world using different ways of establishing baselines, so there is strong selection for convergence; (2) many other ways of establishing baselines are selected against, in that they discourage convergence on benefit-benefit interactions; (3) this rule for defining baselines does not involve computing over a combinatorial explosion of counterfactual possibilities; (4) this rule is consistent with presocial ways of interpreting causation and evaluating choices when planning. These evolved principles for setting baselines underlie cross-cultural commonalities in such concepts as property, and the recognition that transgressions of commission (baseline change) are more recognizable and worse than transgressions of omission (leaving baselines unchanged).

3. At least, until quite recently. Within the last two decades countries across the Western world have thus experienced increased sentencing lengths and rising numbers of inmates (Kury and Ferdinand 1999; Prat et al., 2005).

4. Furthermore, this theory might explain why the Freudian argument might seem phenomenologically convincing. In tandem with the elicitation of conciliatory motivations, attention-allocating mechanisms will motivate ongoing scrutiny of the success of the strategy, with punitive motivations inhibited to the extent the strategy appears to be working. Accordingly, the confidence that punishment is the right choice when it is being inflicted might systematically be higher relative to the confidence that reconciliation is the proper strategy. But this typically smaller confidence in reparative strategies is not a sign that only punitiveness is endogenous. Rather this difference is the expression of functional design.

References

Anderson, B. 1991. *Imagined communities*. London and New York: Verso.

Aureli, F., and F. de Waal. (Eds.) 2000. *Natural conflict resolution*. Berkeley and Los Angeles: University of California Press.

Averill, J. 1982. *Anger and aggression*. New York: Springer-Verlag.

Boyd, R., and P. Richersen. 1992. Punishment allows the evolution of cooperation (or anything else) in sizable groups. *Ethology and Sociobiology* 13(3):171–95.

Boyd, R., H. Gintis, S. Bowles, and P. Richerson. 2003. The evolution of altruistic punishment *PNAS* 100(6):3531–5.

Braithwaite, J. 2002. *Restorative justice and responsive regulation*. New York: Oxford University Press.

Buss, D. M., and J. D. Duntley. 2003. Homicide: An evolutionary perspective and implications for public policy. In *Violence and Public Policy*, edited by N. Dess, 115–28. Westport, CT: Greenwood Publishing Group, Inc.

Butovskaya, M., P. Verbeek, T. Ljungberg, and A. Lunardini. 2000. A multicultural view of peacemaking among young children. In *Natural Conflict Resolution*, edited by F. Aureli and F. de Waal, 243–62. Berkeley and Los Angeles: University of California Press.

Cameron, L. 1999. Raising the stakes in the ultimatum game: Experimental evidence from Indonesia. *Economic Inquiry* 37(1):47–59.

Caprara, G. V., C. Barbaranelli, C. Pastorelli, I. Cermak, and S. Rosza. 2001. Facing guilt: Role of negative affectivity, need for reparation, and fear of punishment in leading to prosocial behaviour and aggression. *European Journal of Personality* 15(3):219–37.

Chavanne, T. J., and G. G. Gallup. 1998. Variation in risk taking behavior among female college students as a function of the menstrual cycle. *Evolution and Human Behavior* 19:27–32.

Christie, N. 2004. *A suitable amount of crime*. London and New York: Routledge.

Claster, D. S. 1992. *Bad guys and good guys: Moral polarization and crime.* Westport, CT: Greenwood Press.

Clutton-Brock, T. H., and G. A. Parker. 1995. Punishment in animal societies. *Nature* 373:209–16.

Cords, M. 1988. Resolution of aggressive conflicts by immature long-tailed macaques. *Animal Behavior* 36:1124–35.

Cords, M., and M. Killen. 1998. Conflict resolution in human and non-human primates. In *Piaget, Evolution, and Development*, edited by J. Langer and M. Killen, 193–217. Hillsdale, NJ: Lawrence Erlbaum Associates.

Cords, M., and S. Thurnheer. 1993. Reconciling with valuable partners by long-tailed macaques. *Ethology* 93(4):315–25.

Cosmides, L., and J. Tooby. 1992. Cognitive adaptations for social exchange. In *The Adapted Mind*, edited by J. H. Barkow, L. Cosmides, and J. Tooby, 163–228. Oxford: Oxford University Press.

Cosmides, L., and J. Tooby. 2005. Neurocognitive adaptations designed for social exchange. In *The Handbook of Evolutionary Psychology*, edited by D. M. Buss, 584–627. Hoboken, NJ: Wiley.

Cosmides, L., J. Tooby, and R. Kurzban. 2003. Perceptions of race. *Trends in Cognitive Sciences* 7(4):173–9.

Daly, M., and M. Wilson. 1988. *Homicide.* Hawthorne, NY: Aldine.

Darley, J. M., and T. S. Pittman. 2003. The psychology of compensatory and retributive justice. *Personality and Social Psychology Review* 7(4):324–36.

Darley, J. M., K. M. Carlsmith, and P. H. Robinson. 2000. Incapacitation and Just Deserts as Motives for Punishment. *Law and Human Behavior* 24(6):659–83.

Delton, A., D. Sznycer, T. Robertson, J. Lim, L. Cosmides, and J. Tooby. (forthcoming). *An evolved internal regulatory variable for making welfare tradeoffs.*

de Quervain, D., U. Fischbacher, V. Treyer, M. Schellhammer, S. Ulrich, A. Buck, A. and E. Fehr. 2004. The neural basis of altruistic punishment. *Science* 305:1254–8.

de Waal, F. 1992. Aggression as a well-integrated part of primate social relationships: A critique of the seville statement on violence. In *Aggression and Peacefulness in Humans and Other Primates*, edited by J. Silverberg and P. J. Gray. New York: Oxford University Press.

de Waal, F. 1996. *Good natured: The origins of right and wrong in humans and other animals.* Cambridge, MA: Harvard University Press.

de Waal, F. 2000. Primates – A natural heritage of conflict resolution. *Science* 289:586–90.

Dixon, J. A., B. Mahoney, and R. Cocks. 2002. Accents of guilt? Effects of regional accent, race, and crime type on attributions of guilt. *Journal of Language and Social Psychology* 21(3):162–8.

Duff, A. 1996. Penal communications: Recent work in the philosophy of punishment. *Crime and Justice,* 20:1–97.

Duntley, J. D. 2005. Adaptations to dangers from humans. In *The Handbook of Evolutionary Psychology*, edited by D. M. Buss, 224–49. Hoboken, NJ: J. Wiley and Sons, Inc.

Duntley, J. D., and D. M. Buss. 2004. The evolution of evil. In *The Social Psychology of Good and Evil*, edited by A. Miller, 102–23. New York: Guilford.

Durkheim, E. 1998. Two laws of penal evolution. In *Sociology of Punishment*, edited by D. Melossi. Aldershot, UK: Ashgate.

Elias, N. 1994. *The civilizing process*. Oxford and Cambridge: Blackwell.

Ellis, L., and H. Hoffman. (Eds.) 1990. *Crime in biological, social, and moral contexts*. New York: Praeger.

Farrow, T., Y. Zheng, I. D. Wilkinson, S. A. Spence, J. F. W. Deakin, N. Tarrier, P. D. Griffiths, and P. W. R. Woodruff. 2001. Investigating the functional anatomy of empathy and forgiveness. *NeuroReport* 12(11):2433–38.

Fehr, E., and U. Fischbacher. 2004. Third-party punishment and social norms. *Evolution and Human Behavior* 25:63–87.

Fehr, E., and S. Gächter. 2000. Cooperation and punishment in public goods experiments. *The American Economic Review* 90:980–94.

Fehr, E., and S. Gächter. 2002. Altruistic punishment in humans. *Nature* 415:137–40.

Finkel, N. J., S. T. Maloney, M. Z. Valbuena, and J. Groscup. 1996. Recidivism, proportionalism, and individualized punishment. *American Behavioral Scientist* 39(5):474–87.

France, A. 2002 [1894]. *The Red Lily*. McLean, VA: IndyPublish.

Frank, R. H. 1988. *Passions within reason: The strategic role of the emotions*. New York: W. W. Norton & Company.

Freud, S. 1961 [1929]. *Civilization and its discontents*. New York: W. W. Norton & Company.

Fry, D. P. 2000. Conflict management in cross-cultural perspective. In *Natural Conflict Resolution*, F. Aureli and F. de Waal, 334–51. Berkeley and Los Angeles: University of California Press.

Fujisawa, K. K., N. Kutsukake, and T. Hasegawa. 2005. Reconciliation pattern after aggression among Japanese preschool children. *Aggressive Behavior* 31(2):138–52.

Garland, D. 1990. *Punishment and modern society. A study in social theory*. Oxford: Clarendon Press.

Gault, B. A., and J. Sabini. 2000. The roles of empathy, anger, and gender in predicting attitudes toward punitive, reparative, and preventative public policies. *Cognition and Emotion* 14(4):495–520.

Goul Andersen, J. 1998. *Borgerne og lovene [Citizens and the law]*. Aarhus: Aarhus University Press.

Haidt, J. 2003. The Moral Emotions. In *Handbook of Affective Sciences*, edited by R. Davidson, K. Scherer, and H. Goldsmith, 852–70. Oxford: Oxford University Press.

Hamilton, L., and J. Sanders. 1992. *Everyday justice: Responsibility and the individual in Japan and the United States.* New Haven: Yale University Press.

Hamilton, W. D. 1964. The genetic evolution of social behavior, I and II. *Journal of Theoretical Biology* 7:1–16, 17–52.

Hembroff, L. A. 1987. The seriousness of acts and social contexts: A test of Black's Theory of the Behavior of Law. *The American Journal of Sociology* 93(2):322–47.

Henrich, J., R. Boyd, S. Bowles, C. Camerer, E. Fehr, and H. Gintis (Eds.). 2004. *Foundations of Human Sociality: Economic Experiments and Ethnographic Evidence from Fifteen Small-Scale Societies.* Cambridge: Oxford University Press.

Hill, K. 2002. Cooperative food acquisition by Ache foragers. *Human Nature*, 13(1):105–28.

Hirsch, A., A. E. Bottoms, E. Burney, and P.-O. Wikstrom. 1999. *Criminal deterrence and sentence severity: An analysis of recent research.* Oxford: Hart Publishing.

Hoebel, E. A. 1964. *The law of primitive man.* Cambridge, MA: Harvard University Press.

Hurwitz, J., and M. Peffley. 1997. Public perceptions of race and crime: The role of racial stereotypes. *American Journal of Political Science* 41:375–401.

Jacoby, S. 1983. *Wild justice: The evolution of revenge.* New York: Harper & Row.

Kelly, R. L. 1995. *The foraging spectrum: Diversity in hunter-gatherer lifeways.* Washington: Smithsonian Institution Press.

Klepper, S., and D. Nagin. 1989. The deterrent effect of perceived certainty and severity of punishment revisited. *Criminology* 27(4):721–46.

Krasnow, M., L. Cosmides, and J. Tooby. (forthcoming). *Trust, Reciprocity and Punishment: Adaptations for Small Scale Cooperation.*

Kurzban, R., J. Tooby, and L. Cosmides. 2001. Can race be erased? Coalitional computation and social categorization. *PNAS* 98(26):15387–92.

Lakoff, G. 1987. *Women, fire, and dangerous things.* Chicago: Chicago University Press.

Landsheer, J. A., and H. Hart. 2000. Punishments adolescents find justified: An examination of attitudes toward delinquency. *Adolescence* 35(140):683–93.

Larsen, C. A. 2006. *The Institutional Logic of Welfare Attitudes.* Aldershot, UK: Ashgate.

Lee, R., and I. DeVore. 1968. Problems in the study of hunters and gatherers. In *Man the Hunter*, edited by R. Lee and I. DeVore, 3–29. Chicago: Aldine.

Lieberman, D., J. Tooby, and L. Cosmides. 2007. The architecture of human kin detection. *Nature* 445:727–31.

Ljungberg, T., L. Horowitz, L. Jansson, K. Westlund, and C. Clarke. 2005. Communicative factors, conflict progression, and use of reconciliatory strategies in pre-school boys – A series of random events or a sequential process? *Aggressive Behavior,* 31(4):303–23.

Lowie, R. 1961. *Primitive society.* New York: Harper Torchbooks.

Mayhew, P., and J. van Kesteren. 2002. Cross-national attitudes to punishment. In *Changing Attitudes to Punishment,* edited by J. V. Roberts and M. Hough, 63–92. Portland, OR: Willan Publishing.

Maynard Smith, J. and G. Parker. 1976. The logic of asymmetric contests. *Animal Behavior* 24:169–75.

Mazella, R., and A. Feingold. 1994. The effects of physical attractiveness, race, socioeconomic status, and gender of defendants and victims on judgments of mock jurors: A meta-analysis. *Journal of Applied Social Psychology* 24:1315–44.

Nozick, R. (1981). *Philosophical explanations.* Cambridge, MA: Harvard University Press.

Ostrom, E., R. Gardner, and J. Walker. 1994. *Rules, games and common pool resources.* Ann Arbor, MI: The University of Michigan Press.

Panchanathan, K., and R. Boyd. 2003. A tale of two defectors: The importance of standing for evolution of indirect reciprocity. *Journal of Theoretical Biology* 224(1):115–25.

Petersen, M. B. 2007. *Straf eller rehabilitering? Evolutionspsykologi, følelser og politisk holdningsdannelse [Punishment or rehabilitation? Evolutionary psychology, emotions, and political opinion formation].* Aarhus: Politica.

Petersen, M. B. 2010. Distinct Emotions, Distinct Domains: Anger, Anxiety and Perceptions of Intentionality. *Journal of Politics,* 72(2).

Petersen, M. B. (forthcoming). Public Opinion and Evolved Heuristics. Forthcoming in the *Journal of Cognition and Culture,* 9(3–4):315–37.

Petralia, S. M., and G. G. Gallup. 2002. Effects of a sexual assault scenario on handgrip strength across the menstrual cycle. *Evolution and Human Behavior* 23:3–10.

Price, M. E., L. Cosmides, and J. Tooby. 2002. Punitive sentiment as an anti-free rider psychological device. *Evolution and Human Behavior* 23:203–31.

Robinson, D. T., L. Smith-Lovin, and O. Tsoudis. 1994. The effects of remorse on mock criminal confessions. *Social Forces* 73(1):175–90.

Rossi, P. H., J. E. Simpson, and J. L. Miller. 1985. Beyond crime seriousness: Fitting the punishment to the crime. *Journal of Quantitative Criminology* 1(1):59–90.

Rossi, P. H., E. Waite, C. E. Bose, and R. E. Berk. 1974. The seriousness of crimes: Normative structure and individual differences. *American Sociological Review* 39(2):224–37.

Rothstein, B. 1998. *Just institutions matter.* Cambridge, UK: Cambridge University Press.

Sasson, T. 1995. *Crime talk.* New York: Aldine de Gruyter.

Sell, A. 2006a. Anger expressions dissected: Why does his face look like that? Paper presented at 18th annual meeting of the Human Behavior and Evolution Society, HBES, University of Pennsylvania, June 7–11, 2006.

Sell, A. 2006b. Regulating welfare tradeoff ratios: Three tests of an evolutionary-computational model of human anger. Doctoral Dissertation. Santa Barbara: Center for Evolutionary Psychology, University of California.

Sell, A., L. Cosmides, J. Tooby, D. Sznycer, C. von Rueden, and M. Gurven. 2009. Human adaptations for the visual assessment of strength and fighting ability from the body and face. *Proceedings of the Royal Society B*, 276:575–84.

Sell, A., J. Tooby, and L. Cosmides. (forthcoming a) *Anger and welfare trade-off ratios: Mapping the computational architecture of a recalibrational emotion system.*

Sell, A., J. Tooby, and L. Cosmides. 2009. Formidability and the logic of human anger. *Proceedings of the National Academy of Science,* in press.

Silk, J. B. 2000. The function of peaceful post-conflict interactions: An alternate view. In *Natural Conflict Resolution*, edited by F. Aureli, and F. de Waal, 179–81. Berkeley and Los Angeles: University of California Press.

Silk, J. B. 2002. The form and function of reconciliation in primates. *Annual Review of Anthropology* 31:21–44.

Spierenburg, P. 1984. *The spectacle of suffering.* Cambridge: Cambridge University Press.

Stylianou, S. 2003. Measuring crime seriousness perceptions: What have we learned and what else do we want to know. *Journal of Criminal Justice* 31:37–56.

Sznycer, D., J. Price, J. Tooby, and L. Cosmides. 2007. Recalibrational emotions and welfare trade-off ratios: Cooperation in anger, guilt, gratitude, pride, and shame. Paper presented at 19th annual meeting of the Human Behavior and Evolution Society, HBES, College of William & Mary, Virginia, May 30–June 3, 2007.

The Bible, 21st Century King James Version, www.biblegateway.com

Thornhill, R., and C. Palmer. 2000. *A natural history of rape: Biological bases of sexual coercion.* Cambridge: MIT Press.

Tooby, J., and L. Cosmides. 1992. The psychological foundations of culture. In *The Adapted Mind*, edited by J. H. Barkow, L. Cosmides, and J. Tooby, 19–135. Oxford: Oxford University Press.

Tooby, J., and L. Cosmides. 1996. Friendship and the bankers paradox: Other pathways to the evolution of adaptations for altruism. *Proceedings of the British Academy* 88:119–43.

Tooby, J., and L. Cosmides. 2005. Conceptual foundations of evolutionary psychology. In *The Handbook of Evolutionary Psychology*, edited by D. M. Buss, 5–67. Hoboken, NJ: J. Wiley & Sons, Inc.

Tooby, J., and L. Cosmides. 2008. The evolutionary psychology of the emotions and their relationship to internal regulatory variables. In

Handbook of Emotions, edited by M. Lewis, J. M. Haviland-Jones, and L. F. Barrett, 3rd edition, 114–37. New York: Guilford.

Tooby, J., L. Cosmides, and H. C. Barrett. 2005. Resolving the debate on innate ideas. In *The Innate Mind: Structure and Content*, edited by P. Carruthers, S. Laurence, and S. Stich, 305–37. New York: Oxford University Press.

Tooby, J., L. Cosmides, and M. E. Price. 2006. Cognitive adaptations for n-person exchange: The evolutionary roots of organizational behavior. *Managerial and Decision Economics* 27:103–29.

Tooby, J., L. Cosmides, A. Sell, D. Lieberman, and D. Sznycer. 2008. Internal regulatory variables and the design of human motivation: A computational and evolutionary approach. In *Handbook of approach and avoidance motivation*, edited by A. J. Elliot, 251–71. Mahwah, NJ: Lawrence Erlbaum Associates.

Tooby, J., N. Thrall, and L. Cosmides. 2006. The role of 'outrages' in the evolved psychology of intergroup conflict. Paper presented at 18th annual meeting of the Human Behavior and Evolution Society, HBES, University of Pennsylvania, June 7–11, 2006.

Trivers, R. 1971. The evolution of reciprocal altruism. *The Quarterly Review of Biology* 46:35–57.

Ugwuegbu, D. 1979. Racial and evidential factors in juror attribution of legal responsibility. *Journal of Experimental Social Psychology* 15:133–46.

Vangelisti, A. L., J. A. Daly, and J. R. Rudnick. 1991. Making people feel guilty in conversations: Techniques and correlates. *Human Communication Research*, 18:3–39.

Walker, D., and R. Gorsuch. 2004. Dimensions underlying sixteen models of forgiveness and reconciliation. *Journal of Psychology and Theology* 32:21–5.

Warr, M. 1989. What is the perceived seriousness of crime? *Criminology* 27(4):795–822.

Williams, G. C., and D. Williams. 1957. Natural selection of individually harmful social adaptations among sibs with special reference to social insects. *Evolution* 11(1):32–9.

Wilson, J. Q., and R. J. Herrnstein. 1985. *Crime and human nature*. New York: Simon and Schuster.

Wispé, L. 1991. *The psychology of sympathy*. New York: Plenum Press.

6

Patterns of Chimpanzee's Intergroup Violence

Christophe Boesch

Taï National Park, Côte d'Ivoire

October 3rd 1987: A large party, including Brutus, and five males, was resting under a group of red colobus monkeys to the far east of the territory. At 2:25 pm, when they heard strangers drum further far off to the east, they all jumped to their feet. Rapidly, a seventh male and eight females, most of them with babies, joined. All were in a tight group advancing silently and rapidly for 5 minutes in a straight line toward the direction of the earlier drumming. Then, Brutus changed slightly more toward north-east leading them away from the possible main group of strangers, and all the females with Kendo and Ulysse lagged now behind. Typical to such a situation, the females follow a while as support but avoid the last, often physical, part of the attack. Brutus, old Falstaff, Macho, powerful Schubert, Rousseau, one juvenile male, and a young immigrant female now progressed in a line more slowly and were carefully listening for any signs of the strangers. They also looked regularly to the south-east from where a few calls of the strangers could be heard. Fifteen minutes after the first signs of the strangers, Brutus, the leader seemed to notice something ahead and started a quick and silent run followed by the six others. I followed as I could without making too much noise. Some 100 meters ahead, the attackers found some strangers, as I heard violent barking and anxious screams of two chimpanzees. The pursuit lasted for a minute, eventually all the barking concentrated on one point. I joined them just as Kendo was overtaking me, full speed and barking aggressively. A stranger female with a 3- to 4-year-old infant had been trapped and was surrounded now by Brutus and his team of males, while the adolescent female was drumming nearby. Holding her back by a foot and one hand, they prevented the victim, with an infant clinging to her belly, from making any move. She screamed and barked at the males. They hit and bit her on head, shoulders, and legs, she face the ground, covering the infant with her body. I did not see any blood on her or on the ground. They did not torment her for more than a minute in a row, and then let her rest for a moment, but pulled at her leg whenever she tried to move away. The hands and feet of the infant remained visible throughout the whole attack, but I never saw any of the males grab or bite the infant. Five minutes after her capture, the stranger males arrived to rescue her, aggressively barking and screaming. Immediately, Brutus, Rousseau, Kendo and Snoopy faced them in a line. In no time, the female rushed toward her males. For some seconds, the two parties faced one another, the strangers being 3 or 4, all males. Then, Brutus and his crew attacked and the strangers disappeared without a sound. The chase unfolded over about 200 meters. While Brutus and Rousseau returned quickly toward the west, the younger males with the adolescent female remained in the east drumming and barking for another 25 minutes before heading back as well.

Elaborate team work, leadership in the attack, coordinated attack by waves, intentional searching for enemies in a weak position, taking of prisoners, support by teams, systematic territorial defense, patrols with deep incursions into foreign territory.... All this sounds very war-like! Could it be that chimpanzees were already practicing some kind of warfare which is then after all of much older origin than if humans were the innovators? It would not be the first time that a claimed "human uniqueness" would have been dethroned by an earlier origin, as it is the case for example for tool use and hunting, sets of behavior shared uniquely between chimpanzee and man.

Introduction

On her "Life and Death at Gombe," Jane Goodall (1979) reported for the first time in a dramatic way the war-like fight that occur between chimpanzee communities in her study site, the Gombe National Park in Tanzania. The impression left on the general public was so great that William Boyd largely inspired himself from this report in his worldwide bestseller "Brazzaville Beach" (1990). Such accounts of high levels of violence were rapidly labeled by some as abnormalities resulting from increased level of stress, either due to artificial food provisioning – which was provided to the Gombe and Mahale chimpanzees – or resulting from increased human encroachment on their ranges, including the presence of human observers (Power 1991; Clark 2002; Hart and Sussman 2005). Power (1991) proposed that reports of possible peaceful encounters between groups from early studies on chimpanzees were more representative of the species, such as those of the Budongo Forest (Reynolds 1965) and the observations from Taï chimpanzees. However, evidence contradicting such an explanation includes new lethal incidents in additional non-provisioned populations like the chimpanzees of the Kibale National Park (Wilson and Wrangham 2003; Watts et al. 2006), and an apparent intergroup killing in a non-habituated chimpanzee population in Loango National Park, Gabon (Boesch et al. 2007). We therefore ask ourselves if such violence is really exceptional and how it might differ in different populations of chimpanzees.

In general, animals should initiate intergroup contests when the benefit appears to outweigh the costs. This is especially true if said benefits are closely correlated to fitness through access to food resources or territorial enlargement that increases access to resources. Direct aggression between groups has been observed in many social animal species, whereby group members physically confront members of neighboring groups or total strangers with levels of aggression at least similar to, if not exceeding, those observed within groups. (For lions, see Packer et al. 1988; Grinnell et al. 1995. For African wild dogs, Creel and Creel 2002. Wolves: Mech and Boitani 2003. White faced capuchins: Gros–Louis et al. 2003. Red colobus monkey: Starin 1994. Black and white colobus: Harris 2006. Spider monkey: Aureli et al. 2006. Chimpanzees: Boesch and Boesch–Achermann 2000; Goodall et al. 1979; Watts et al. 2006; Wilson and Wrangham 2003).

Chimpanzees live in social groups or 'communities' occupying specific territories and containing multiple adult males and females and their offspring (Nishida 1968; Goodall 1986; Boesch and Boesch–Achermann 1990). Chimpanzee males spend their entire lives in their natal groups and display remarkable levels of cooperation with other group males, including joint participation in intergroup encounters (Goodall 1986; Boesch and Boesch–Acherman 2000; Mitani et al. 2002). Large coalitions of males have regularly been observed to patrol the boundaries of their territory, sometimes violently fighting intrusions by neighboring chimpanzees and making deep incursions into neighboring territories (Goodall et al 1979; Goodall 1986; Kawanaka and Nishida 1974; Nishida et al. 1985; Boesch and Boesch-Achermann 2000; Watts and Mitani 2000; Watts et al. 2006; Mitani and Watts 2005; Wilson et al. 2004). Transfer between groups is mostly limited to young nulliparous estrus females, who are readily accepted by the resident males and can be rapidly integrated into new groups (Goodall 1986; Nishida 1989; Boesch and Boesch-Achermann 2000). Under some specific circumstances, however, parous females have been seen to be incorporated in new communities with their offspring (Nishida et al. 1985; Emery Thompson et al. 2006). In contrast, adult males and sometimes mothers with infants have been subject to extreme violence leading, in some cases, to the death of the attacked individuals (Goodall et al. 1979; Wilson et al. 2004; Nishida and Kawanaka 1985; Watts et al. 2006). The killing of adult males from neighboring groups can be particularly violent, with prolonged and vicious gang attacks leading to numerous injuries including emasculation by amputation of testes and penis followed sometimes by very rapid killing (Goodall et al. 1979; Watts et al. 2006). In cases of stranger parous females with dependant infants, many instances of infanticide, often followed by cannibalism, have been documented (Goodall et al. 1979; Suzuki 1971; Wilson et al. 2004). In one instance, intergroup violence has been observed to lead to the complete dissolution of whole social groups with the deaths of all the males in Gombe National Park, Tanzania (Goodall 1986) and it was suspected but not observed in another case in Mahale Mountains National Park, Tanzania (Nishida et al. 1985).

Lethal intergroup aggression in chimpanzees has been proposed to present similarities with primitive warfare in human populations, based mainly on observations that both species regularly use large male coalitions, systematic patrolling of territory boundaries, and violent killing of adults from neighboring groups that can lead to the annihilation of a whole group (Goodall 1986; Alexander 1989; Manson and Wrangham 1991; Dennen 1995; Wrangham and Peterson 1996; Gat 1999; Boesch and Boesch-Achermann 2000; Otterbein 2004). This view has been criticized by others who highlight dissimilarities between the two species, mainly that sexual, marital, and social friendly contacts persist over extended periods of time between opponent groups in humans (Knauft 1991; Kelly 2005).

However, the sometimes dramatic nature of intergroup aggression in chimpanzees has led to under appreciation of the fact that such lethal violence represents only the minority of the encounters between communities in wild chimpanzees (Kawanaka and Nishida 1974; Goodall 1986; Watts et al. 2006). Most notably, after more than 18 years of observation of the chimpanzees of the Taï National Park, Côte d'Ivoire, initially of one community and then of three neighboring ones, no lethal violence was observed despite regular aggressive interactions between communities and the systematic employment of macro-coalitions by the males (Boesch and Boesch-Achermann 2000). Especially striking is the fact that observers had not seen infants of stranger mothers to be killed nor to be subject to intense aggressions by the attacking males, and the injuries suffered by the females were minor compared to the reports provided from other chimpanzee populations (Boesch and Boesch-Achermann 2000). Therefore, a key to understanding the evolution of intergroup violence is to ask why we observe such differences between chimpanzee populations.

Intergroup violence seems to be a typical aspect of chimpanzee sociality. However, no consensus has emerged about the evolutionary basis of such intergroup violence. The killings of infants of stranger females suggests that males may use such violence to gain access to more females, as in infanticide by males in species such as lions, gorillas and langurs (Packer et al 1988; 1991; Hrdy 1977; Robbins 1995; Watts 1996). In chimpanzees, however, there is as yet no convincing evidence that females are more likely to immigrate into the group of the infanticidal males. On the other hand, it has been proposed that the main function of such violence is to physically eliminate male competitors (Manson and Wrangham 1991; Wrangham 1999; van der Dennen 1995; Knauft 1991). Even though this would seem to explain the dramatic cases of adult males killed by coalitions of neighboring attackers that have been observed first in Gombe chimpanzees and then in other East African populations, we still need to explain what the male attackers would gain from this. A complementary explanation posits that, as fitness would increase with territory size, different level of violence might be expected depending on feeding competition, as land gain results in access to more resources (Williams et al. 2004).

Until now, intergroup violence in chimpanzees has been largely considered from the perspective of the gains or losses to the males (but see Williams et al. 2004 for considering more the female perspective). Females in chimpanzees have, however, been shown under some demographic conditions to implement much of their preference when it comes to sexual partners (Stumpf and Boesch 2005; 2006). This may go as far as females producing infants with males who are not members of their own group; ~10 percent of the offspring in Taï result from extra-group paternities (Vigilant et al. 2001; Boesch et al. 2006), and a similar proportion of extra-group paternity was inferred from Gombe and Bossou (Constable et al. 2001; Sugiyama et al. 1993). Moreover most females transfer between communities before maturity and seem to select communities with large numbers of adult males (Nishida et al. 1985; Boesch and Boesch-Achermann 2000). Therefore, females may have more reasons to interact with neighboring community than has hitherto been realized.

Here, we describe 485 intergroup encounters involving four communities of chimpanzees of known composition from 1982 to 2005 in the Taï National Park, Côte d'Ivoire (Boesch et al. in press). We present new evidence of lethal violence in this population, but confirm that fatal violence is less common than documented for other chimpanzee populations. We discuss these findings in relation to the importance of mating strategies in intergroup relationships and stress the importance of considering female strategies for a complete perspective on intergroup conflicts.

Methods

We observed four neighboring chimpanzee communities in the Taï National Park, Côte d'Ivoire (for more details, see Boesch and Boesch-Achermann 2000; Boesch et al. in press). Observations started with the North Group in 1979, with habituation to human observers achieved by 1982 (see Figure 6.1 for the demographic data of the four communities). The Middle Group was fully habituated in 1995 and was under daily observation until summer 2004. The Middle Group shares a territory limit in the north with the North Group and in the south with the South Group (see map in Herbinger et al. 2001). This South Group was fully habituated in 1993 and has since been under constant observation by field assistants and students (see Figure 6.1). Habituation of the East Group started in 2000 and, by February 2005, 11 adult males had been identified and at least 2 more males were suspected to be present; similarly, 12 females have been identified, but the total number of females is still unknown. (See Figure 6.1. Note that numbers for the East Group are provisional; community size was estimated by assuming that the age

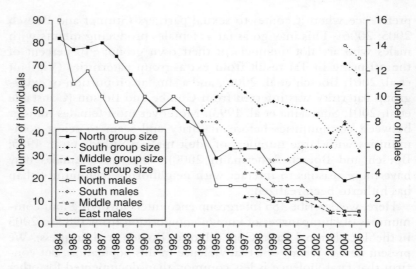

Figure 6.1 Demographic data of the four chimpanzee communities observed

structure and sex ratio were the same as in the three other communities.) The intergroup interactions reported here come from 25, 12 and 9 years of observations on the North, South, and Middle Groups, respectively.

Intercommunity encounters take many forms: target individuals can discover neighbors by surprise, be surprised by them, or be involved in intentional searches for them during patrols of territory boundaries. We considered only situations in which neighboring chimpanzees were seen or heard as intercommunity encounters.

Human presence influences interactions with non-habituated chimpanzees. Typically, naïve chimpanzees immediately run away when seeing humans independently of the intensity of the intergroup conflict, although human presence only marginally affects the frequency of encounters.

Because not all community members can be observed at all times, ascertaining why apparently healthy individuals sometimes disappear is a challenge, and some authors have suggested that intergroup violence is the most likely explanation for the sudden disappearance of healthy full-grown adult individuals (Nishida et al. 1985; Wrangham and Peterson 1999). For example, the disappearance of seven males of K-group in the Mahale chimpanzees during an 8-year period without any direct observation or corpse remains found has been suggested to be due to intergroup violence (Nishida et al. 1985). However, sudden disappearances of healthy individuals could have many causes beside chimpanzee violence, such as predation by lions or leopards (Boesch 1991; Tsukahara 1993), human poaching (Boesch pers. obs.; Reynolds 2005), and disease (Boesch and Boesch-Achermann 2000; Leendertz et al. 2004; 2006). Although predation by big cats can sometimes be excluded due to their rarity or known absence, such as in Gombe and Kibale National Parks, and poaching by humans can sometimes be excluded, such as possibly in Mahale and Gombe National Parks, disease affects all chimpanzee populations (Goodall 1986; Nishida 1990; Boesch and Boesch Achermann 2000). Chimpanzees rarely show disease symptoms before disappearing (Leendertz et al. 2006; Boesch and Boesch-Achermann 2000), and some diseases, such as anthrax or Ebola, can lead to startlingly rapid deaths of adult chimpanzees (Boesch and Boesch-Achermann 2000; Formenty et al. 1999; Leendertz et al. 2004). For example, the alpha male of the Middle Group died from anthrax within three hours of showing the first symptoms of weakness (Leendertz et al. 2004). Therefore, the assumption that the disappearance of a healthy adult individual is a sign of violent death through intergroup hostility is tenuous, and will lead to an over-estimation of the frequency of intergroup killings. However, contrary to Hart and Sussman (2005), we think the fieldworkers' judgments about the causes of death should be trusted when they find fresh chimpanzee corpses.

Results

From 1982 to 2005, 485 intergroup encounters were recorded. After the habituation of both the South and Middle Groups, we could collect data on encounters between neighboring groups of known demographic compositions. Of all encounters, 42 percent (146 out of 348) occurred between two of the study groups. Human presence did not affect these encounters, so detailed observation was possible. Three main types of encounters were observed. The most frequent type was encounters that were auditory only; the second type was aggressive encounters, and the third was affiliative encounters that involved parous adult females. Table 6.1 presents observations of visual encounters classified according to whether they were mainly

Table 6.1 Summary of intergroup encounters observed in three chimpanzee communities in the Taï forest.

Community	Observation time	Contact auditory	visual	Prisoner	Kill	Support	Sexual interaction (♀ visit)
North Group	12–82 to 4–05	224	70	9	0	20	13(1)
Middle Group	9–99 to 2–04	64	22	5	0	2	14(9)
South Group	11–96 to 12–05	64	41	4	2	11	18(16)

violent, resulted in death, or included sexual interactions. In what follows, we present an example for each type of encounter.

Lethal Violence between Communities

For the first 23 years of the Taï chimpanzee project, no lethal attacks were witnessed. However, in the past 3 years, two cases of fatal inter-community attacks have been observed, both perpetrated by South Group males.

Case 1: 8 September 2002: Infanticide (observers: Nicaise Oulaï and Camille Bolé)

A large party that included five adult males and nine adult females of the South Group was moving north into the western part of the territory of the Middle Group, when they heard neighbors from the West drum (16:06). At 16:27, they surprised a party of the neighbors in a fruiting tree. The neighbors ran west, pursued by some of the South Group males. A young adult male, Sagu, realized that an infant male has been left in the tree and is whimpering. He climbed the tree, seized the infant, and descended, then hit the infant against the ground. Responding to the screams of the infant, the neighbors made loud calls, but only one adult female, who was immediately chased away by some South Group chimpanzees, came into view. Sagu climbed in the tree with the infant and hit it against the branches. At 16:39, Sagu started to bite the infant and the sound of breaking bones could be heard, then he twisted one foot of the infant, who screamed loudly. In response, the two groups exchanged calls. At 16:50, Sagu let the infant fall to the ground and seven adults of the South Group looked carefully at him for 12 minutes. At 17:12, Gogol bit the infant in the throat, probably killing him, then broke the infant's fingers, feet and some articulations and extracted some foot bones without eating anything. After 11 minutes, Gogol left the corpse on the ground with others.

This attack took place in an area where the Middle Group and its Westerner neighbor Group overlap, and since no Middle Group infants disappeared at that time, we assume that the killed infant belonged to a female of an unhabituated group in the West. The chimpanzees showed no interest in cannibalizing their victim.

Case 2: 1 March 2005: Adult male killed (observer: Emmanuelle Normand)

A party of the South Group, including the four adult males of the community, two adolescent males and four adult females, heard the East neighbors and all ran silently toward them. When the observer caught up with them, all the South Group individuals, including three females, Sumatra, Zora, and Wapi, had gathered around a young adult male chimpanzee of the East Group. The observer could see the victim clearly in the mass of the aggressors, and saw that all, except Taboo, bite and hit him violently. At one point, Sumatra is ejected from the group, and hit by Kaos who jumped on her back. After this, they both rejoined the attacker mass. All individuals present were very excited and screamed. Twenty-two minutes after the beginning of the attack, East Group chimpanzees farther eastwards were heard to drum. All the South Group members rushed to attack them, leaving the victim alone but he had by now much difficulty to move and just succeeded to sit. Two minutes later, Zora came back to sit near the stranger. Five minutes later, 3 of the 4 adult males from the South Group, including Sagu and Gogol, came back to the stranger and attacked him viciously for one minute. The South party started to move away, but twice Gogol came back and bit his arm and the noise of the breaking bones could be heard. Each time Sumatra followed him to chase him off the victim. After 39 minutes, the victim seemed dead. They left the inanimate body 46 minutes after the beginning of the attack.

The victim was dead, probably due to a wide 10 cm gash in his throat and upper chest. The testis and penis had been removed. It was impossible to say when the emasculationhappened. Later that day, observers saw that Sagu had three fresh cuts on his head, neck and one foot, and that Sumatra and Zora each had one fresh cut as well. The attack took place in the overlapping zone between the South and East Group. The victim could have been a young adult male of the East Group called Nérone who sometimes foraged on his own in the periphery of the East territory and who disappeared exactly at that time. Due to his numerous facial injuries and the rapid post-mortem changes, we could not confirm his identity.

Aggressive Non-lethal Encounters between Groups

Although the majority of encounters between groups involved only auditory contact, we followed 118 visual encounters (25 percent of all encounters) of which 47 included physical contacts (10 percent of all encounters). Here we describe two of them that occurred between habituated groups to illustrate some specific aspects of violent encounters.

Case 3: Multiple encounters between Middle Group and North Group (observers: Catherine Crockford for the MG and Honora Kapazhi for the NG)

On 5 May 2000, all three Middle Group males began a patrol of the North Group territory, starting at the same *Treculia* tree where they found Goma. They patrolled deep into the North Group territory, right into their core area, drumming once. They remained in the core area for two hours, listening continuously and intently. They drummed once again as they left the core area. No reaction was discernable from the North Group at any time. Six hours after starting the patrol they returned to the border area of the two territories, to the same *Treculia* tree as in the morning.

On May 7, Urs and Bob from the Middle Group returned to the same *Treculia* tree where they captured Goma. They approached the tree slowly and silently, and stopped to sniff some leaves. Both appeared unaware that Marius and Nino, the two adult males of the North Group, were silently sitting some 25 meters north watching them intently. After two minutes, and after looking around, Urs made an initial movement to retreat at which immediately Marius and Nino charged them. Urs and Bob fled southwards back into their territory. Marius and Nino chased the two males while giving loud barks for about two minutes. A minute after losing the Middle Group, Marius drummed. Five minutes later, Urs and Bob drummed after retreating several hundred meters to the south. Both groups of males continued drumming for some time. Next, Marius and Nino came back to the same area and rested.

Two hours and 50 minutes later, Léo, the alpha male of the Middle Group moved alone northwards, whimpering and pant hooting, seemingly looking for Urs and Bob. He arrived in the same area as the morning encounter and ate two *Sacoglottis* fruits. Suddenly he stood bipedally with piloerection, while looking around intently. After two minutes, the two males of the North Group, Marius and Nino, appeared from the undergrowth in a full charge toward Léo. Léo screamed loudly and fled south back into his territory. Marius and Nino chased him for 40 meters then stopped to bark and drum. Léo continued to flee southwards, screaming continuously for four minutes, and Marius and Nino continued drumming for one hour.

What happened to the male, Léo, demonstrates how risky foraging in the forest can be for a lone individual, particularly when moving toward the periphery of the community. This illustrates how the male could get caught in such an unequal and deadly situation.

Female Prisoners Taken by Neighboring Males

In Taï chimpanzees, the search for appropriate mating partners seems to play a key role in intergroup contacts. As mentioned in Boesch and Boesch-Achermann (2000), females can be made prisoners by males of a neighboring group, kept temporarily and unwillingly separated, and actively prevented from moving away. Here we describe such a situation with minimal human influence as it happened between the North and Middle Groups.

Case 4: 30 April 2000: North Group female taken prisoner for 22 hours by Middle Group males (observer: Catherine Crockford)

At 16:21, the three adult males of the Middle Group, Urs, Bob, and Léo, moved north into the North Group range and suddenly rushed forward and surprised two adult females of the North Group, Goma and Fossey, with their two infants and two juveniles. Goma, whose running abilities have been impaired for months by a handicap in both hips, bent over to cover her 4-year-old daughter, Gisèle, while the males displayed around her, hitting and jumping on her for one minute. Fossey and one juvenile disappeared immediately, while Fossey's 6-year-old daughter remained sitting and observing from a branch in a tree. The aggressive actions of the males toward Goma stopped rapidly. Then, Urs made his first friendly contact to Goma with an open-mouth kiss, followed by Bob two minutes later. All three males performed genital inspection on Goma who had no sexual swelling and was lactating. Four minutes after the initial encounter, Gisèle left her mother to greet Léo, the alpha male of the Middle Group. Gisèle tried repeatedly to greet the males, but Goma whimpering tried to have her come back to her. Urs tried without success to mate with Goma. After 15 minutes, Fossey's daughter disappeared as well, leaving Goma and Gisèle alone with the males. When Goma tried to climb a tree, Urs hit her many times but then openmouth kissed her and groomed her. Léo successfully mated with her after 45 minutes. The males fed a little bit on *Treculia* fruits, but Goma just looked at them. At 19:30, they all made their nests in nearby trees, the males making their nest near the one of Goma.

The next morning, the males tried to lead Goma south into their territory but it took Goma two hours to leave her nest and come to the ground. Urs displayed twice at her, and for the very first time Léo hit Gisèle. Afterwards many reassurances between Goma and Léo were observed, as males tried to lead Goma east into their territory. Léo mated twice with Goma, while Urs tried two more times without success. Three hours after leaving the nest, Goma tried to move back westwards, in the direction of the North Group territory. Léo mated with her. Urs and Léo groomed Goma. Gisèle and Goma received some fruit remains from Bob and Léo and ate for the first time since their capture. At 12:22, for the first time a drumming from the North Group was heard far in the west. The males tried to lead Goma to the east, whilst Goma tried to head in the direction of the drumming. As a result, little progress was made in any direction. Around 14:30, Goma started to move west for short distances, but the males came back to her twice. The third time, at 14:45, the males reacted too slowly and Goma escaped toward the west and hid in a dense tree fall, the males not trying hard to find her. Eighteen minutes later, Marius the alpha male of the North Group drummed close to the Middle Group males. The three Middle Group males retreated to the south, back in their territory, eventually drumming and pant hooting. (See case 3 for the subsequent interactions.)

As shown in Table 6.1, such kidnapping of females has been seen regularly (North Group, 9 times; Middle Group, 5; South Group, 4) and the duration they are kept prisoner is a direct function of the promptness of the support provided by their group males. In 11 of these 13 cases, sexual activities were observed between the female and her male aggressors. In the majority of the cases, noisy support from the victim group came within minutes, and kidnappers always first faced them, thus granting victims the time to escape. As observed previously (Boesch and Boesch-Achermann 2000), in only one instance were the infants of these females directly hurt by the members of the other community.

Females' Active Involvement in Aggressive Intergroup Interactions

Taï females have been recorded as being active participants of some of the intergroup encounters led by males (Boesch and Boesch-Achermann 2000). Our new observations confirm this, as seen in cases 1, 2, and 4 above. In addition, we have seen that females on their own could be quite aggressive towards strangers (Case 5) and might take risks in doing so (Cases 6 and 7).

Case 5: 3 August 2005: Females of South Group take a female prisoner from West Group (observer: Nicaise Oulaï)

At 8:56, a large party of 14 adults of the South Group heard drumming in the West; they screamed, and then moved silently in that direction. At 9:00, while the adult males of the group were ahead, chasing the West Group, five adult females of the South Group surprised a young female from the West Group on a tree. Some females immediately climbed the tree and pulled her to the ground, where Sumatra blocked her and all other females present attacked her. Young adolescent males Woodstock, Utan, and Taboo from the South Group tried toprotect her, but the adult females continued the attack. After two minutes, Woodstock hit Sumatra, who released the stranger to respond to this attack. The stranger then ran. South Group females pursued her, but she escaped.

In another instance, seven resident females of the South Group were aggressive against a female infant pair while three males of the South Group tried to stop them from attacking her. While the stranger female was injured, bleeding from cuts on her face and body, some females of the South Group were injured by South Group males during this confrontation. The support from some males of stranger female community interrupted this attack after eight minutes.

Case 6: 17 August 2002: A female of Middle Group chasing females from the West Group (observer: Louis-Bernard Bally)

At 9:21, Jessica was alone, with her two offspring eating some fruits in a tree of *Scotellia coriacea*, when she heard whimpers from a baby chimpanzee coming from the west. Jessica made a silent open grin face, took her 9-month-old daughter on her back and climbed down followed by her 4-year-old juvenile daughter. At 9:37, she arrived under a *Sacoglottis gabonensis* tree where chimpanzees had been eating very recently. She smelled the fresh food-wadges that were on the ground and after four minutes she started to eat. At 9:53, she climbed with her daughters in a tree, faced west, and stayed apparently listening for 2 hours and 13 minutes. At 13:18, she heard a little noise of a chimpanzee close by and both her daughters climbed onto her, the baby on the belly and the juvenile on her back. She moved very slowly toward the sound and, at 13:24, standing, she looked up to a *Uapaca* tree where two stranger females were eating some fruits, one with a little baby and the other with a juvenile female. At 13:25, Jessica barked loudly and displayed toward the tree. The stranger females in the tree immediately screamed and rushed down disappearing toward the west. Jessica barked and screamed for two minutes while drumming once. The stranger females remained silent. Jessica continued to bark five times during the following 20 minutes and advanced for 60 meters. At 13:53, Jessica retreated.

Jessica's behavior was remarkable for two reasons. First, she is part of the Middle Group that was already very small (one adult male and two adult females) and she could therefore not receive much support from her group. Second, being alone, it seems as if she was counting on the surprise effect of her appearance in such a low visibility environment.

Case 7: 24 January 1991: Goma, an adult female of the North Group, rescuing an adult male from a West Group's gang attack (observer: Christophe Boesch)

After arriving in the southern most ridge region of their territory, the chimpanzees of the North Group spread out to feed on *Landolphia* fruits. Macho and Goma were together. She climbed a tree with her 5-year-old daughter to eat some fruits, while Macho continued south to climb another tree to feed. At 12:50 loud calls came suddenly from where Macho was eating. Without hesitation, Goma with her daughter on her belly rushed down and ran toward the screams with aggressive barks. The attackers took some time to check who was attacking them, and Macho used that moment to immediately escape and ran to Goma and both individuals fled toward the observer. Two of the attackers followed them, but ran away after seeing the observer. At 12:52, three adult males arrived silently in support of Macho, and with him they immediately chased the neighbors away over a distance of 300 m. During this short attack, Macho received 18 cuts over all his body, including one that missed his right eye by one centimeter. The quick reaction of Goma apparently prevented him from receiving more serious injuries.

Voluntary Visits of Parous Females to Neighboring Groups

Although voluntary visits by young nulliparous females before transfer into new groups have been reported in all study chimpanzee populations, voluntary visits to neighboring males by multiparous adult females with or without infants have been rarely documented. The one exception was the secondary transfers of mothers following the dramatic decrease in the number of males within K-group in Mahale Mountains, Tanzania (Nishida et al. 1985; but see Thompson et al. 2006 for other potential cases in Budongo chimpanzees). Voluntary visits by multiparous females to neighboring groups were observed several times in our three study groups. We detail one situation that involved only individuals from habituated groups.

Case 8: 6 June 2002: Nadesh, a Middle Group multiparous female makes a repeated visit to the South Group (Observers: Nicaise Oulaï and Camille Bolé)

By June 2002, the Middle Group had lost two adult males, leaving only one adult male and no adolescent males in the group. Nadesh, an adult female estimated to be 40 years old, had just lost her second known infant to anthrax four months earlier. At 17:19, Nadesh, with a maximally swollen sexual swelling, joined a party of the South Group including four adult males and five adult females in a fig tree. At her arrival, she was greeted by some calls. A South female, Olivia, tried to attack her, but she was immediately chased away by Sagu, the alpha male of the South Group. Three adult males, including Sagu, and one adolescent male were observed to mate with Nadesh. Olivia attacked Nadesh once more, but Sagu and another male, Zyon, chased Olivia and another female away. Later, two males and two females groomed Nadesh. Nadesh spent the night with the South Group, making her nest in the same tree as some males.

The next day, Nadesh remained with the South Group males and was seen to interact quite freely with them. She copulated four times and was seen to be groomed by three adult males and three adult females. She had to sustain six attacks by three females but was vigorously protected by the males each time. She made her nest in the same tree as some of the males.

The next day, June 8, started just like the day before. She copulated twice with young males and was protected by the males on the three attacks by females. She left the group silently at 14:26 and entered her Middle Group range the same day. Eight days later, on June 16, she appeared again in the South Group and mated four times with the males but left early the next morning.

She returned in September 2002, and stayed 44 hours with the South Group males and mated with two of them. Nadesh gave birth to a new baby in July 2003, but unfortunately the baby died in December 2004 before samples for determining its paternity could be collected.

Thereafter, Nadesh reappeared for the first time in the South Group on 2 May 2005. She was observed for hours every day in the South Group until July 10. During the first 9 days of those repeated visits, she was seen to copulate 15 times with South Group males. However, the aggression of the resident females against her remained persistent, while the support of the South males was less systematic than before, so that she had to escape from the females repeatedly during this time. She came back for a one-day visit on 9 September 2005, and she was seen to mate three times with adult males. In October 2005, Nadesh was not seen in the Middle Group, and she might have been visiting another group. However, she remained a member of the Middle Group, which had now decreased to include only one adult male, Bob, and another adult female, Jessica. In October 2006, Nadesh was seen with a new baby that was born sometime in January 2006. If we count an eight-month pregnancy period, she would have conceived in May 2005, which coincides with her visit to the South Group.

Similar voluntary visits have also been observed with non-habituated multiparous females with infants, who visited members of each of the study groups (North, 1 visit; Middle, 2; South, 1). However, due to the presence of the human observers, these visits were much shorter and observations were far less detailed. Intriguingly, in three of those instances the females with infants were anestrus, suggesting that they might have visited previously. When a female with an infant visited the study groups, no threats or violence from resident group members were directed at the infants and the infants even sought direct contact with adult members of the new group (see also case 4).

InterPopulation Comparison of Intergroup Conflicts

Population differences in the occurrence of lethal violence in intergroup interactions in chimpanzees are revealed by a comparison of data on intergroup encounter and death rates for nine chimpanzee communities in five populations (Table 6.2). On average, for Taï, Mahale and Ngogo chimpanzees, encounters with neighboring groups take place between 1 to 1.5 times per month and visual contact occurs in one out of three to four contacts. Encounter rates are similar for Taï and Ngogo, despite different patrolling rates (Ngogo = 95 in 48 months [Watts et al. 2006], Taï = 38 in 45 months).

Most striking is the variation in the rate of intergroup killings (Table 6.2), with Ngogo chimpanzees having the highest rate at 2 deaths per year of observation, while at Taï none have been observed in two of the three groups despite decades of observations. This difference cannot be attributed to study duration, since some groups with shorter observation times have high death rates. Nor could it be attributed to the number of neighboring groups: if the low death rate at Bossou could be explained by the absence of neighboring groups, and the intermediate intergroup death rates observed in Gombe and Mahale communities may be due to them bordering the Tanganyika Lakes and having few neighbors, the lowest and highest rates are found in the three study communities at Taï and at Ngogo with neighbors in all directions. Finally, the number of males in the community does not seem to explain the differences in intergroup death rates (all populations: $r_s = 0.496$, N = 9, p = 0.176).

Table 6.2 Comparisons of intergroup encounter rates and intergroup death rates in different chimpanzee populations.

| Populations | Number of contacts | | Observation duration | Encounter rate | | # of death | Intergroup | Number |
	auditory	visual	Month (year)	auditory	visual	(Ad+Inf)	death rate	adult male
Taï NG	288	66	221 (22)	1.30	(0.30)	0+0	**0.00**	6.6
Taï MG	85	18	54 (6)	1.57	(0.33)	0+0	**0.00**	2.55
Taï SG	95	34	87 (9)	0.96	(0.39)	1+1	**0.27**	6.25
Budongo[1]			(10)			0+6[a]	**0.60**	16.0
Mahale M[2]	37	8	12[b] (20)	3.08	(0.66)	1+2	**0.15**	16.1
Mahale K			(17)			(7)[c]+1	**0.06** **(0.47)**	4.6
Gombe, Kasakela[3]			144 (12)			6+4	**0.83**	10.5
Kanyawara[5]			(14)			3+0	**0.21**	12.7
Ngogo[6]	68	20	48 (7)	1.41	(0.42)	4+7	**1.83**	24.0
Loango			20			1+1	**1.20**	

Encounter rate = # contact / # month of observation;

Intergroup death rate = (# death / (# month of observations/12))

[a] In Budongo chimpanzees, 7 bodies of unknown infants suspected to be killed as a result of intergroup encounters have been seen by observers, however one was suggested to belong to one female of the study community (Reynolds 2005).

[b] Encounter rate were provided only for the year 1974, thus the observation time for them is 12 months (Nishida 1979).

[c] In Mahale chimpanzees, the disappearance of 7 males of the K group was described in detail and attributed to violent interactions with the larger M group (Nishida et al. 1985). However, none of those interactions were witnessed nor were any of the bodies found. Keeping in line with our criteria, they would not qualify as intergroup violence victims and we consider them as such only in brackets. On another occasion, one female from the K group was seen to be attacked badly twice by the M group and her life spared twice thanks to the direct intervention of the researchers (Nishida and Hiraiwa-Hasegawa 1985).

[1] Reynolds 2005.

[2] Nishida et al. 1985 and Nishida and Hiraiwa-Hasegawa 1985 for the period 1965 to 1983, and Kutsukake and Matsusaka 2002 for the period 2000.

[3] Goodall 1986 (observational period: 71–82).

[4] Wilson et al. 2004 (observational period: 93–02).

[5] Wrangham et al. 2006.

[6] Watts et al. 2004, 2006, pers. com., Sylvia Amsler (pers. com.) shared the observation of four intergroup encounters that occurred during 2005 and 2006. Death rate accordingly includes two more years of observations.

The intergroup death rate will likely be influenced by the number of individuals present during encounters. This includes support by other group members once an encounter has started (Boesch and Boesch-Achermann 2000). Support can change the balance of power between opponents and influence encounter outcomes. Chimpanzee communities seem to vary in the extent to which

Table 6.3 Comparison of intergroup behavior in different chimpanzee populations (same references as for Table 6.2). Under female visit, we include only cases where adult parous female voluntary visited neighboring group members.

Chimpanzee population	# of visual contacts	Prisoner Sex	with severe attack	attack against infant	Sexual interactions	Support	Female visit
Taï NG	66	♀ 7(2)[a]	0	0	13	19	1
		♂ 1	0	–	–	1	
Taï MG	18	♀ 4	0	0	14	2	9
Taï SG	34	♀ 4	0	0	18	10	16
		Inf 1[b]	1	–	–	1	
		♂ 1[b]	1	–	–	0	
Taï (all)	**118**	**18**	**2**	**0**	**45**	**33**	**26**
Gombe[1]	97	♀ 19	16	3	3	0	0
		♂ 6[b]	6	–	–	0	
Gombe (Wilson)		♀ 2	2	3	0	0	0
		♂ 2[b]	–	–	–	0	
Mahale[2]		♀ 5(1)	5	3	6		6
Ngogo[3]	24	♀ 10(6[c])	5	10	0	3	0
		♂ 11[b]+1	11	–	–	0	
Kanyawara		♀ 1	–	–	–	1	0
		♂ 3[b]	3	–	–	–	

Notes:

[a] In two occasions, two females were made prisoners at the same time.

[b] Individuals were killed during the encounters.

[c] Low visibility or late arrival at the site prevented observer from seeing the beginning of the attacks. The resulting infanticide was assumed to result from females being seized by attackers before their infant was snatched away from them.

[1] Gombe: data included visual contact number for the period 1975–1992 (Williams et al. 2004) but detailed data on interactions from Goodall 1986. In 74 of the 97 encounters involving females, 41 of them were peaceful. Seventeen of those peaceful encounters included parous females with at least one infant, and in three instances mating with a swollen female was seen (Pusey pers. comm.). The remaining 33 encounters with females were classified as aggressive of which 16 were described to be severe (Williams et al. 2004).

[2] Mahale: Nishida et al. (1985) provide only data on the number of identified females of K Group that visited M Group and not information about the number of visits as we presented for Taï.

[3] Ngogo: Unpublished data to complement the published material on Ngogo chimpanzees were kindly provided by David Watts and Sylvia Amsler (pers. comm.). The descriptions of support so far are limited to hearing calls of neighboring group members.

supporting individuals join intergroup encounters (Table 6.3). Supports by additional community members at the scene after an individual has directly encountered neighbors has been observed in 28 percent of all visual contacts in Taï chimpanzees and is almost systematic in cases where one or two females were made prisoners

(83 percent, N = 15 of the 18 cases). In 13 cases, support arrived before an individual had been isolated by the attackers and thereby probably prevented the attackers from concentrating on one individual and inflicting severe injuries.

This seems to be in dramatic contrast to what has been reported from other chimpanzee populations (see Table 6.3), where no support was described in any of the 25 cases in which individuals were trapped by neighboring attackers in Gombe (Goodall 1986; Wilson et al. 2004). In the 24 cases of physical intergroup contacts reported in Ngogo chimpanzees, there were only three instances where supporting chimpanzees were noted to approach the site of the attacks. Although the supporters did not come into view and join those engaged in the physical contact with neighbors, observers had the impression that the attackers were nonetheless influenced by their approach (Watts et al. 2006; Watts et al. 2002; Amsler, personal communication). No mention of support could be found in the reports about Mahale encounters (Nishida et al. 1985). It remains difficult to interpret this data as support may have gone unreported in some instances. In addition, it is known that Taï chimpanzees are more gregarious than other chimpanzee populations, and it might be that support is not always available when needed in other populations. On the other hand, if support, like in Taï, would have directly influenced the outcome of the interactions, we would expect that support to be reported.

Two additional striking differences emerge from the comparative data collated in Table 6.3, and these involve the treatment of adult females during intergroup contact. In Taï, 17 females have been isolated from members of their own communities by males from neighboring communities, but not subjected to severe or life-threatening aggression. Aggression was mostly limited to slapping and biting of sexual swellings and its intensity was similar to that observed during within-community aggression. Infants, when present, were not subject to violence. In comparison, Gombe females were subject to severe aggression in 75 percent of encounters, and such violence was suspected to lead to several deaths (Goodall 1986). A review of the data including more recent observations suggested that aggression against stranger females occurred in 45 percent of encounters at Gombe and was most frequently directed at non-swollen females (Williams et al. 2004). This implies that 55 percent of encounters with stranger females were peaceful, but because this study included observations of young nulliparous females in the process of transfer (in contrast to Goodall 1986), this difference might reflect the fact that transferring nulliparous females are generally accepted by males, so we have not included them in Table 6.3. In Mahale, violent attacks against parous females were also reported (Table 6.3), despite the fact that under some specific demographic conditions peaceful transfers between communities of parous females have been observed (Nishida et al. 1985). Similarly, at Ngogo, adult females suffered severe attacks in at least five cases, and possibly more (Watts et al. 2002; 2006).

Finally, in Taï, sexual interactions between members of different communities have been observed in 39 percent of the inter-group encounters with 30 percent of the later instances resulting from voluntary visits of parous females (Table 6.3). As seen in case 3, the males' interest in sexual interactions was observed with anestrous mothers as well as with estrous females. If sexual interactions with parous females have been observed in Gombe chimpanzees (Goodall 1986; Williams et al. 2004), observers in Ngogo have not seen males mate with parous females from neighboring communities (Watts, personal communication). In addition, voluntary visits by adult parous females have not been reported in Gombe or at Ngogo (Table 6.3). In Mahale, voluntary transfer of parous females was described following the strong decline in the number of males in the K Group, when mothers started to pay visit to the neighboring groups, including M Group, before definitive transfer (Nishida et al. 1985, Table 6.3). A similar process of permanent transfer of parous females has been suggested recently in relation to a possible increase in female number among Budongo chimpanzees (Emery-Thompson et al. 2006).

Discussion

Warfare in humans can take many forms, but "the most lethal and common form of warfare was the raid, using surprise and mostly taking place at night. Raids were carried out by individuals or small groups and were intended to kill a specific enemy, or members of a specific family, usually when victims were asleep in camp" (Gat 1999). Adam Ferguson wrote in his *An Essay on the History of Civil Society* referring to the rude nations of America (1765, quoted in Gat 1999), "Their ordinary method of making war is by ambuscade; and they strive by overreaching an enemy, to commit the greatest slaughter or to make the greatest number of prisoners with the least hazard to themselves." Thus, the prevalence of raid in traditional warfare in human seems like a match to the intergroup interactions we observe in chimpanzees and this explains why some authors have proposed war to have some common origins with what we see in chimpanzees (Goodall 1986; Manson and Wrangham 1997; Boesch and Boesch-Achermann 2000).

These new observations on intergroup encounters in Taï chimpanzees confirm earlier suggestions that, in all known chimpanzee populations, those encounters are mostly aggressive (Boesch and Boesch-Achermann 2000). Our initial observations made with the North Group have been confirmed with two additional communities in Taï forest. These data, as well as recent data coming from chimpanzees in other populations (in Ngogo, Watts et al. 2002; 2006; in Budongo, Newton-Fisher 1999; Reynolds 2005; in Gombe, Wilson et al. 2004; and in Loango, Boesch et al. 2007), confirms the general occurrence of intergroup competition in chimpanzees. In addition, using data from three Taï chimpanzee groups, we have highlighted some aspects of intergroup conflicts that seem more specific to the Taï chimpanzees than to other populations, such as the high level of participation of females in intergroup encounters whether violent or friendly, the reduced level of violence displayed toward stranger infants by attacking males, and the possible more frequent occurrence of support to attacked individuals.

The frequency of lethal violence varies dramatically between chimpanzee populations. The Taï groups have undergone striking changes in size, particularly in the number of adult males. Demographic data reveals that only in the South Group was the general decline in community size associated with an increase in the number of adult males (Figure 6.1). Given that females prefer to transfer into communities with more than 6 adult males (Boesch and Boesch-Achermann 2000), recently observed lethal attacks in Taï could represent male efforts to signal their strength and to attract female immigrants. Gogol and Sagu, two young but high ranking males of the South Group, were very active in both lethal attacks and probably inflicted deadly injuries, which seems to illustrate this proposition. Variations in intergroup death rate between populations have been reported previously and seem not to be easily explained by the number of neighbors or the number of males in the community. We should not forget that emasculations of stranger male victims have regularly been observed, and that represents the paramount illustration that sexual conflicts are part of such violence.

Taï communities are also notable as "bisexually-bonded", because females are more gregarious than is typical for eastern chimpanzees

(Boesch and Boesch-Achermann 2000; Lehmann and Boesch 2004; 2005). Taï females take part in many of the intergroup encounters and initiate some of them. Visits and subsequent transfer of females from communities with decreasing number of males was nicely illustrated by the visits of Nadesh from the Middle Group to the larger South Group. Similar observations have been made with some females of the decreasing Kalande community in Gombe (Pusey et al. 2007), from the decreasing K-Group in Mahale (Nishida et al. 1985) and was inferred from Budongo recently (Emery Thompson et al. 2006). However, we suggest that female visits to neighboring groups happen recurrently, as well illustrated in the two cases of extragroup paternity in the South Group, at a time when seven adult and adolescent males were still present (Boesch et al. 2006). In addition, the data in Table 6.3 suggests that females in Taï chimpanzees participate in intergroup interactions more than reported in other populations, and stress the possibility that sex might play a more important role in influencing intergroup interactions.

The difference observed in the frequency of support is intriguing, because support can strongly modify the costs of intergroup encounters. Support in Taï chimpanzees has allowed many individuals to be rescued before they were injured, at little cost to supporters. We suggested previously that the low visibility within Taï forest favors such interventions compared to higher visibility environment like in Gombe (Boesch and Boesch-Achermann 2000). However, the mainly forested nature of the environment at Ngogo and Kanyawara would be equally favorable for this kind of support, and its rare occurrence would require an explanation. In Ngogo, observers have described three instances in which the presence of supporters made attackers wary and retreat more rapidly (Watts et al. 2004; Amsler, personal communication). Since detailed descriptions of many of those encounters are not provided, support might be underreported. However, a combination of higher gregariousness, due to leopard predation pressure in Taï, and lower visibility, reducing the accuracy of numerical assessment, could make support more frequent and more efficient in Taï chimpanzees compared to other populations. Support in intergroup conflicts makes imbalance of power between opponents uncertain. Therefore, support functions in a similar way as weaponry in humans by making imbalances of power less predictable and thereby altering the possible costs of intergroup conflicts (Kelly 2005; Knauft 1991). This also illustrates the importance of cooperation in chimpanzees, even in situations that are extremely risky and where the costs to supporters could be very high (Boesch, in preparation).

When should chimpanzees initiate an intergroup contact? Different options have been proposed, one suggesting that a drive to violence in males combined with imbalance of power would explain some of the intergroup interactions (Wrangham and Peterson 1996; Wrangham 1999), while another suggested a variability depending upon the demographic and ecological conditions of the communities under study (Boesch and Boesch-Achermann 2000; Mitani et al. 2002; Williams et al. 2002; 2004). The observation presented here shows that support regularly changes the balance of power and thus creates unpredictability. Second, small communities do not refrain from attacking larger communities (for example, when the Middle Group members attacked the much larger South Group or when the South Group members attacked the larger East group), even when in very small parties (Boesch et al. in press). Our general impression is that chimpanzees can take large risks when potential benefits are large or when failure to do so could inflict larger costs (see Grinnell et al. 1995 for examples in male lions). Males in communities with a relative small number of sexually active females might take more risks to attack groups with more females to try and improve their reproductive success, even if those groups have many more males (Boesch, in preparation).

In conclusion, in almost all populations of human and chimpanzees, "war-like" interactions with neighboring groups have been reported. This common propensity in both species for adult males to build large coalitions to attack neighboring group members is intriguing: such cooperative acts are systematically observed, but, in both species, they occur with very different levels of frequency and produce different death rates (Keeley 1996; Kelly 2000; Otterbein 2004). Discussion is still going on to identify the factors influencing this but many authors have mentioned sexual opportunities or competitions as well as foraging constraints as important for both species (Alexander 1989; Dennen 1995; Gat 1999; Otterbein 2004). Thus, multiple factors may account for the evolution of intergroup violence in both species, and more demographic data on neighboring communities would help to increase our understanding of the dynamics of intergroup conflict. The possible parallels in the origin of warfare in both species would support the suggestion of an old origin of this behavior (Manson and Wrangham 1996; Otterbein 2004) and make the presence of old signs of human violence understandable (Gat 2000).

Acknowledgments

We thank all the following persons for having contributed to the long-term data collection of the Taï chimpanzee project that were so important to allow the analysis presented in this chapter: Catherine Crockford, Roman Wittig, Ilka Herbinger, Emmanuelle Normand, Yasmin Moebius, Kohou Nohon Grégoire, Kpazahi Honora, Oulaï Daurid Nicaise, Bolé Camille, Bally Louis Bernard, Gouyan Bah Nestor, Kevin Charles Bally, Ignace Dezaï, Sylvain Guy, Gabriel Gnombouhou Kouya, Arsène Sioblo, Cristina Gomes, Rebecca Stumpf, Tobias Deschner. We thank all Ivorian authorities that allowed us to work in the Taï National Park and supported our work in many ways: Ministère de la Recherche Scientifique et Technique, Ministère des Eaux et Forêts et de l'Environnement. Thank to David Watts, Anne Pusey, Sylvia Amsler, Linda Vigilant, and two anonymous reviewers for constructive comments on an earlier version of this manuscript. For year-long, faithful financial support, we are very grateful to the Swiss Science Foundation and the Max Planck Society.

References

Alexander, R. 1989. Evolution of the human psyche. In *The Human Revolution*, edited by P. Mellar and C. Stringer, 455–513. Edinburgh: Edinburgh University Press.

Aureli, F., C. Schaffner, J. Verpooten, K. Slater, and G. Ramos-Fernandez. 2006. Raiding parties of male spider monkeys: Insights into human warfare? *American Journal of Physical Anthropology* 131(4):486–97.

Boesch, C. 1991. The effect of leopard predation on grouping patterns in forest chimpanzees. *Behaviour* 117(3–4):220–42.

Boesch, C., and H. Boesch-Achermann. 2000. *The chimpanzees of the Taï forest: Behavioural ecology and evolution*. Oxford: Oxford University Press.

Boesch, C., C. Crockford, I. Herbinger, R. Wittig, Y. Moebius, and E. Normand. 2008. Intergroup conflicts among chimpanzees in Taï National Park: Lethal violence and the female perspective. *American Journal of Primatology* 70(6):519–32.

Boesch, C., G. Kohou, H. Néné, and L. Vigilant. 2006. Male competition and paternity in wild chimpanzees of the Taï forest. *American Journal of Physical Anthropology* 130:103–15.

Boesch, C., J. Head, N. Tagg, M. Arandjelovic, L. Vigilant, and M. Robbins. 2007. Fatal chimpanzee attack in Loango National Park, Gabon: observational and genetic evidence. *International Journal of Primatology* 28:1025–34.

Boyd, W. 1990. *Brazzaville beach*. New York: Sinclair Stevenson Inc.

Clark, M. 2002. *In search of human nature*. London: Routledge.

Constable, J., M. Ashley, J. Goodall, and A. Pusey. 2001. Noninvasive paternity assignment in Gombe chimpanzees. *Molecular ecology* 10:1279–300.

Creel, S., and N. Creel. 2002. *The African wild dog: Behavior, ecology, and conservation*. Princeton: Princeton University Press.

van der Dennen, J. 1995. *The origin of war: The evolution of a male-coalitional reproductive strategy*. Groningen: Origin Press.

Emery Thompson, M., N. Newton-Fisher, and V. Reynolds. 2006. Probable community transfer of parous adult female chimpanzees in the Budongo Forest, Uganda. *International Journal of Primatology* 27(6):1601–17.

Fawcett, K., and G. Muhumuza. 2000. Death of a wild chimpanzee community member: Possible outcome of intense sexual competition. *American Journal of Primatology* 51:243–7.

Formenty, P., C. Boesch, M. Wyers, C. Steiner, F. Donati, F. Dind, F. Walker, B. 1999. Ebola outbreak among wild chimpanzees living in a rainforest of Côte d'Ivoire. Journal of Infectious Diseases 179 (Suppl. 1):120–6.

Gat A. 1999. The pattern of fighting in simple, small-scale, prestate societies. *Journal of Anthropological Research* 55(4):563–83.

Goodall, J. 1979. Life and death at Gombe. *National Geographic Magazine* 155:595–621.

Goodall, J. 1986. *The chimpanzees of Gombe: Patterns of behavior*. Cambridge, MA: The Belknap Press of Harvard University Press.

Goodall, J., A. Bandura, E. Bergmann, C. Busse, H. Matam, E. Mpongo, A. Pierce, D. Riss. 1979. Inter-community interactions in the chimpanzee populations of the Gombe National Park. In *The Great Apes*, edited by D. Hamburg and E. McCown, 13–53. Menlo Park, CA: Benjamin/ Cummings.

Grinnell, J., C. Packer, and A. Pusey. 1995. Cooperation in male lions: Kinship, reciprocity or mutualism? *Animal Behaviour* 49(1):95–105.

Gros-Louis, J., S. Perry, and J. Manson. 2003. Violent coalitionary attacks and intraspecific killing in wild white-faced capuchin monkeys (Cebus capucinus). *Primates* 44:341–6.

Harris, T. 2006. Between group contest competition for food in a highly folivorous population of black and white colobus monkeys (Colobus guereza). *Behavioral Ecology and Sociobiology* 61:317–29.

Hart, D., and R. Sussman. 2005. *Man the hunted: Primates, predators, and human evolution*. New York: Westview Press.

Herbinger, I., C. Boesch, H. Rothe. 2001. Territory characteristics among three neighbouring chimpanzee communities in the Taï National Park, Ivory Coast. *International Journal of Primatology* 32(2):143–67.

Hrdy S. 1977. *The langur of Abou: Female and male strategies of reproduction*. Cambridge, MA: Harvard University Press.

Kawanaka, K., and T. Nishida. 1974. Recent advances in the study of inter-unit-group relationships and social structure of wild chimpanzees of the Mahale Mountains. In *Proceedings of the 5th Congress of the International Primatological Society*, edited by S. Kondo, M. Kawai, A. Ehara, S. Kawamura, 173–85. Tokyo: Japan Science Press.

Keeley, L. 1996. *War before civilization*. New York: Oxford University Press.

Kelly, R. 2000. *Warless societies and the origin of war*. Ann Arbor, MI: University of Michigan Press.

Kelly, R. 2005. The evolution of lethal intergroup violence. *Proceeding of the Natural Academy of Science* 102(43):15294–98.

Knauft, B. 1991. Violence and sociality in human evolution. *Current Anthropology* 32(4):391–428.

Kutsukake, N., and T. Matsusaka. 2002. Incident of intense aggression by chimpanzees against an infant from another group in Mahale Mountains National Park, Tanzania. *American Journal of Primatology* 58:175–80.

Leendertz, F., H. Ellerbock, C. Boesch, E. Couacy-Hymann, and K. Mätz-Rensing, R. Hakenback, C. Bergmann, P. Abaza, S. Junglen, Y. Moebius, L. Vigilant, P. Formenty, G. Pauli. 2004. Anthrax kills wild chimpanzees in a tropical rainforest. *Nature* 430:451–2.

Leendertz, F., G. Pauli, K. Maetz-Rensing, W. Boardman, C. Nunn, H. Ellerbrok, S. Jensen, S. Junglen, and C. Boesch. 2006. Pathogens as drivers of population declines: the importance of systematic monitoring in great apes and other threatened mammals. *Biological Conservation* 131(2):325–37.

Lehmann, J., and C. Boesch. 2004. To fission or to fusion: effects of community size on wild chimpanzees (Pan troglodytes verus) social organisation. *Behavioral Ecology and Sociobiology* 56:207–16.

Lehmann, J., and C. Boesch. 2005. Bisexually-bonded ranging in chimpanzees (Pan troglodytes verus). *Behavioral Ecology and Sociobiology* 57(6):525–35.

Manson, J., and R. Wrangham. 1991. Intergroup aggression in chimpanzees and humans. *Current Anthropology* 32(4):369–90.

Mech, D., and L. Boitani. 2003. Wolf social ecology. In *Wolves: Behavior, Ecology, and Conservation*, edited by D. Mech and L. Boitani, 131–60. Chicago: University of Chicago Press.

Mitani, J., and D. Watts. 2005. Correlates of territorial boundary patrol behaviour in wild chimpanzees. *Animal Behaviour* 70:1079–86.

Mitani, J., D. Watts, and M. Muller. 2002. Recent development in the study of wild chimpanzee behaviour. *Evolutionary Anthropology* 11(1):9–25.

Muller, M. 2002. Agonistic relations among Kanyawara chimpanzees. In *Behavioural Diversity in Chimpanzees and Bonobos*, edited by C. Boesch, G. Hohman, and L. Marchant, 112–23. Cambridge: Cambridge University Press.

Newton-Fisher, N. 1999. Infant killers of Budongo. *Folia Primatologica* 70:167–9.

Nishida, T. 1968. The social group of wild chimpanzees in the Mahali Mountains. *Primates* 9:167–224.

Nishida, T. 1979. The social structure of chimpanzees of the Mahale Mountains. In *The Great Apes*, edited by D. Hamburg and E. McCown, 73–122. Menlo Park, CA: Benjamin/Cummings.

Nishida, T. 1989. Social interactions between resident and immigrant female chimpanzees. In *Understanding Chimpanzees*, edited by P. Heltne and L. Marquardt, 68–89. Cambridge, MA: Harvard University Press.

Nishida, T. 1996. The death of Ntologi, the unparalleled leader of M group. *Pan Africa News* 3(1).

Nishida, T., and M. Hiraiwa-Hasegawa. 1985. Responses to a stranger mother-son pair in the wild chimpanzee: A case report. *Primates* 26(1):1–13.

Nishida, T., and K. Kawanaka. 1985. Within-group cannibalism by adult male chimpanzees. *Primates* 26(3):274–84.

Nishida, T., M. Hiraiwa-Hasegawa, T. Hasegawa, and Y. Takahata. 1985. Group extinction and female transfer in wild chimpanzees in the Mahale National Park, Tanzania. *Zeitschrift fur Tierpsychologie* 67:284–301.

Otterbein, K. 2004. *How War Began*. College Station: Texas A&M University Press.

Packer, C., L. Herbst, A. Pusey, J. Bygott, J. Hanby, S. Cairns, M. Borgerhoff-Mulder. 1988. Reproductive success in lions. In *Reproductive Success*, edited by T. Clutton-Brock, 363–83 Chicago: University of Chicago Press.

Packer, C., D. Gilbert, A. Pusey, and S. O'Brien. 1991. A molecular genetic analysis of kinship and cooperation in African lions. *Nature* 351:562–5.

Power, M. 1991. *The Egalitarians: Human and Chimpanzee*. Cambridge: Cambridge University Press.

Reynolds, V. 1965. *Budongo: A Forest and its Chimpanzees*. London: Methuen and Co.

Reynolds, V. 2005. *The Chimpanzees of the Budongo Forest: Ecology, behaviour and conservation*. Oxford: Oxford University Press.

Robbins, M. 1995. A demographic analysis of male history and social structure of mountain gorillas. *Behaviour* 132(1–2):21–47.

Sherrow, H., and S. Amsler. 2007. New intercommunity infanticides by the chimpanzees of Ngogo, Kibale National Park, Uganda. *International Journal of Primatology* 28(1):9–22.

Starin, E. 1994. Philopatry and affiliation among red colobus. *Behaviour* 130:253–70.

Stumpf, R., and C. Boesch. 2005. Does promiscuous mating preclude female choice? Female sexual strategies in chimpanzees (Pan troglodytes verus) of the Taï National Park, Côte d'Ivoire. *Behavioral Ecology and Sociobiology* 57:511–24.

Stumpf, R., and C. Boesch. 2006. The efficiency of female choice in chimpanzees of the Taï forest, Côte d'Ivoire. *Behavioral Ecology and Sociobiology* 60:749–65.

Sugiyama, Y., S. Kawamoto, O. Takenaka, K. Kumazaki, N. Miwa. 1993. Paternity discrimination and inter-group relationship of chimpanzees at Bossou. *Primates* 34(4):545–52.

Suzuki, A. 1971. Carnivority and cannibalism observed among forest-living chimpanzees. *Journal of the Anthropological Society of Nippon* 79:30–48.

Townsend, S., K. Slocombe, M. Emery Thompson, and K. Zuberbühler. 2007. Female-led infanticide in wild chimpanzees. *Current Biology* 17(10):355–6.

Tsukahara, T. 1993. Lions eat chimpanzees: The first evidence of predation by lions on wild chimpanzees. *American Journal of Primatology* 29:1–11.

Vigilant, L., M. Hofreiter, H. Siedel, and C. Boesch. 2001. Paternity and relatedness in wild chimpanzee communities. *PNAS* 98:12890–5.

Watts, D. 1996. Comparative socio-ecology of gorillas. In *Great Apes Society*, W. McGrew, L. Marchant, and T. Nishida, editors, 16–28. Cambridge: Cambridge University Press.

Watts, D., and J. Mitani. 2000. Infanticide and cannibalism by male chimpanzees at Ngogo, Kibale National Park, Uganda. *Primates* 41(4):357–65.

Watts, D., J. Mitani, and H. Sherrow. 2002. New cases of inter-community infanticide by male chimpanzees at Ngogo, Kibale National Park, Uganda. *Primates* 43(4):263–70.

Watts, D., M. Muller, S. Amsler, G. Mbabazi, and J. Mitani. 2006. Lethal intergroup aggression by chimpanzees in the Kibale National Park, Uganda. *American Journal of Primatology* 68:161–80.

Williams, J., G. Oehlert, J. Carlis, and A. Pusey. 2004. Why do male chimpanzees defend a group range? *Animal Behaviour* 68:523–32.

Wilson, M., and R. Wrangham. 2003. Intergroup relations in chimpanzees. *Annual Review of Anthropology* 32:363–92.

Wilson, M., W. Wallauer, and A. Pusey. 2004. New cases of intergroup violence among chimpanzees in Gombe National Park, Tanzania. *International Journal of Primatology* 25(3):523–48.

Wrangham, R. 1999. Evolution of coalitionary killing. *Yearbook of Physical Anthropology*, 42:1–30.

Wrangham, R., and D. Peterson. 1996. *Demonic Males: Apes and the Origins of Human Violence*. Boston: Houghton Mufflin Co.

Wrangham R., Wilson M., Muller M. 2006. Comparative rates of violence in chimpanzees and humans. Primates 47: 14–26.

7

The Causes of War in Natural and Historical Evolution

Azar Gat

This article suggests that societies throughout history have manifested a remarkably similar set of reasons for fighting. Cultural diversity in human societies is stressed for excellent reasons, but all too often to the point of losing sight of our easily observed core of species specificity (Tooby and Cosmides 1992). Arguing that the human motivational system as a whole should be approached from the evolutionary perspective, we begin with an examination of what can be meaningfully referred to as the "human state of nature," the 99.5 percent of the genus *Homo*'s evolutionary history in which humans lived as hunter–gatherers. In this "state of nature" people's behavior patterns are generally to be considered as having been evolutionarily adaptive. The interaction of biological propensities and cultural development in shaping the causes of war in historical state societies is examined in the second part of the article.

Although I shall now survey the reasons for warfare among hunter–gatherers one by one, it is not my intention to provide yet another "list" of elements, such as provided in Thomas Hobbes's *Leviathan* (Ch. 6), or by modern psychologists (e.g., Maslow 1970; Burton 1990). In the absence of an evolutionary perspective, these lists typically have something arbitrary and trivial about them. They lack a unifying regulatory rationale that suggests why the various needs and desires came into being, or how they relate to one another. Instead, I seek to show how the various reasons come together in an integrated motivational complex. This complex has been shaped by the logic of evolution and natural selection for geological times. It is the *totality* of human motivation – in relation to the causes of violence and war – that this article seeks to lay out and explain.

The Human State of Nature

Subsistence Resources

In contrast to long-held Rousseauite beliefs that reached their zenith in the 1960s, widespread deadly violence within species – including humans – has been found to be the norm in nature (Keeley 1996; LeBlanc 2003; Gat 2006). Competition over resources is a prime cause of aggression and deadly violence. The reason for this is that food, water, and, to a lesser degree, shelter against the elements are tremendous selection forces. As Darwin, following Malthus, explained, living organisms, including humans, tend to propagate rapidly. Their numbers are constrained and checked only by the limited resources of their particular ecological habitats and by all sort of competitors. Contrary to the Rousseauite imagination, humans, and animals, did not live in a state of primordial plenty. Even in lush environments plenty is a misleading notion, for it is relative, first, to the number of mouths that have to be fed. The more resource-rich a region is, the more people it attracts from outside, and the greater the internal population growth that takes place. As Malthus pointed out, a new equilibrium between resource volume and population size would eventually be reached, recreating the same tenuous ratio of subsistence that was the fate of pre-industrial societies throughout history. Hence the inherent state of competition and conflict found among Stone Age people.

Competition over resources was largely about nourishment, the basic and most critical somatic activity of all living creatures, which often causes dramatic fluctuations in their numbers. Resource competition – and conflict – is not, however, a given quantity but a highly modulated variable, depending on the varying nature of the resources available and of human population patterns in diverse ecological habitats. The basic question, then, is what the main scarcities, stresses, and hence objects of human competition are in any particular circumstances.

In extreme cases such as the mid–Canadian arctic, where resources were highly diffused and human population density was very low, resource competition and conflict barely existed. In arid and semi-arid environments, like those of Central Australia, where human population density was also very low, water holes were often the main cause of resource competition and conflict. They were critical in times of drought, when whole groups of Aborigines are recorded to have perished. For this reason, however, there was a tendency to control them, also violently, even when stress was less pressing (Meggitt 1965b, 42). In well-watered environments, where there was no water shortage and hence no water competition, food often became the chief cause of resource competition and conflict, especially at times of stress, but also in expectation of and preparation for stress (Ember and Ember 1992, 242–62; also Hamilton 1975, 146). As Lourandos (1997, 33) writes with respect to Aboriginal Australia: "In southwestern Victoria, competition between groups involved a wide range of natural resources, including territory, and is recorded by many early European observers throughout Victoria." Lourandos's next sentence shows that his "competition" also includes "combat."

The nature of the food in question varied with the environment. Still, it was predominantly meat of all sorts that was hotly contested among hunter-gatherers. This fact, which is simply a consequence of nutritional value, is discernible throughout nature. Herbivores rarely fight over food, for the nutritious value of grass is too low for effective monopolization. Fruit, roots, seeds, and some plants that are considerably more nutritious than grass are often the object of competition and fighting, both among animals and humans. Meat, however, represents the most concentrated nutritional value in nature and is the object of the most intense resource competition.

Let us understand more closely the evolutionary calculus that can make the highly dangerous activity of fighting over resources worthwhile. In our affluent societies, it might be difficult to comprehend how precarious people's subsistence in premodern societies was (and still is). The specter of hunger and starvation was ever-present. Effecting both mortality and reproduction, they constantly trimmed down population numbers. Thus struggle over resources was very often evolutionarily cost-effective. The benefits of fighting also had to be matched against possible alternatives (other than starvation). One of them was to move elsewhere. This, of course, often happened, especially if one's enemy was much stronger, but this strategy had clear limitations. By and large, there were no "empty spaces" for people to move to. In the first place, space is not even, and the best, most productive habitats were normally already taken. Furthermore, a move meant leaving a habitat with whose resources and dangers the group's members were intimately familiar. Such a change could involve heavy penalties. Moreover, giving in to pressure from outside might establish a pattern of victimization. Encouraged by its success, the alien group might repeat and even increase its pressure. Standing for one's own might mean lessening the occurrence of conflict in the future. No less, and perhaps more, than actual fighting, conflict is about deterrence.

Reproduction

The struggle for reproduction is about access to sexual partners of reproductive potential. There is a fundamental asymmetry between males and females in this respect, which runs throughout nature. At any point in time, a female can be fertilized only once. Consequently, evolutionarily speaking, she must take care to make the best of it. It is quality rather then quantity that she seeks. She must select the male who looks the best equipped for survival and reproduction, so that he will impart his genes, and his qualities, to the offspring. In those species, like the human, where the male also contributes to the raising of the offspring, his skills as a provider and his loyalty are other crucial considerations. In contrast to the female, there is theoretically almost no limit to the number of offspring a male can produce. He can fertilize an indefinite number of females, thus multiplying his own genes in the next generations. The main obstacle to male sexual success is competition from other males.

Around this rationale, sexual strategies in nature are highly diverse and most nuanced, ranging from extreme polygamy to monogamy (Symons 1979; Daly and Wilson 1983; Ridley 1994; Buss and Malamuth 1996). However, although monogamy reduces male competition, it by no means eliminates it. If the male is restricted to one partner, it becomes highly important for him as well to choose the partner with the best reproductive qualities he can get: young, healthy, and optimally built for baring offspring; that is, in sexual parlance, the most attractive female. The need to take care of very slowly maturing offspring, which required sustained investment by both parents, turned humans in the monogamous direction. However, competition over the best female partners remains. Furthermore, humans, and men in particular, are not strictly monogamous. In most known human societies polygamy was legitimate, though only a select few well-to-do men were able to support, and thus have, the extra wives and children. Also, in addition to official or unofficial wives, men tend to search for extra-marital sexual liaisons.

How does all this affect human violent conflict and fighting? The evidence across the range of hunter-gatherer peoples tells the same story. Within the tribal groupings, women-related quarrels, violence, so-called blood feuds, and homicide were rife, often constituting the principal category of violence. Between groups, the picture was not very different, and was equally uniform. Warfare regularly involved the stealing of women, who were then subjected to multiple rape, or taken for marriage, or both.

So hunter-gatherer fighting commonly involved the stealing and raping of women, but was this the cause or a side effect of hunter-gatherer fighting? This is a pointless question that has repeatedly led scholars to a dead end. It artificially takes out and isolates one element from the wholeness of the human motivational complex that may lead to warfare, losing sight of the overall rationale that underpins these elements. Both somatic and reproductive elements are present in humans; moreover, both these elements are intimately interconnected, for people must feed, find shelter, and protect themselves in order to reproduce successfully. Conflict over resources was at least partly conflict over the ability to acquire and support women and children, and to demonstrate that ability in advance, in order to rank worthy of the extra wives. Resources, reproduction, and, as we shall see, status, are interconnected and interchangeable. Motives are mixed, interacting, and widely refracted, yet this seemingly immense complexity and inexhaustible diversity can be traced back to a central core, shaped by the evolutionary rationale.

Polygyny was a significant factor in many hunter-gatherer societies. Again Australia constitutes our best laboratory. Its size, nearly complete isolation, and ecological diversity make it far superior to other, more recently studied and more publicized cases that are mostly confined to arid environments. Polygyny was legitimate among all the Aborigines tribes of Australia and highly desired by the men. However, comparative studies among the tribes show that men with only one wife comprised the largest category among married men, often the majority. Men with two wives comprised the second largest category. The percentage of men with three or more wives fell sharply, to around 10 to 15 percent of all married men, with the figures declining with every extra wife (Meggitt

1965a; Long 1970). To how many wives could the most successful men aspire? There was a significant environmental variation
here. In the arid Central Desert, four, five, or six wives were the
top. Five or six was also the top figure mentioned by Buckley for
the Aborigines living in the region of Fort Philip (Melbourne), in
the south-east, in the early nineteenth century. However, in the
more rich and productive parts of Arnhem Land and nearby islands
in the north, a few men could have as many as 10 to 12 wives,
and in some places, in the most extreme cases, even double that
number. There was a direct correlation between resource density,
resource accumulation and monopolization, social ranking, and
polygyny (Morgan 1980, 58; Hart and Pilling 1964, 17–18, 50;
Meggitt 1965b, 78, 80–1; Berndt and Berndt 1964, 172; Keen 1982;
Lournados 1988, 151–2).

Data from other hunter-gatherer societies reveal a similar picture.
Resource scarcity reduced social differentiation, including in marriage, but did not eliminate it. The leaders of the Aka Pygmies were
found to be more than twice as polygynous as ordinary people and to
father more children (Betzig, Denton, and Rodseth 1991, 410). Among
the !Kung of the arid Kalahari Desert, polygyny was limited, but
5 percent of married men still had two wives (Daly and Wilson 1983,
285). Women-related feuds were the main cause of homicide among
them. In the extremely harsh conditions of the mid-Canadian arctic, where resources were scarce and diffused, fighting over resources
barely existed. Because of the resource scarcity, marriages among the
native Eskimo were also predominantly monogamous. One study
registered only 3 polygynies out of 61 marriages. Still, wife-stealing
was a widespread, probably the main, cause of homicide and "blood
feuds" among the Eskimo (Betzig, Denton, and Rodseth 1991). "A
stranger in the camp, particularly if he was travelling with his wife,
could become easy prey to the local people. He might be killed by
any camp fellow in need of a woman" (Daly and Wilson 1983, 222,
citing Balikci 1970, 182). Among the Eskimo of the more densely
populated Alaskan Coast, abduction of women was a principal cause
of warfare. Polygyny, too, was more common among them, although
restricted to the few (Irwin 1990, 201–2; Nelson 1983 [1899], 292,
327–9; Oswalt 1967, 178, 180, 182, 185, 187, 204; Burch and Correll
1972, 33; Dickemann 1979, 363; Symons 1979, 152). Strong *Ingalik*
("big men") often had a second wife, and "there was a fellow who
had five wives at one time and seven at another. This man was a great
fighter and had obtained his women by raiding" (Betzig 1991, 410).

Many wives naturally meant a large number of children for a man, sometimes scores, who often comprised a large part of the next generation in the tribe (Keen 1982; Daly and Wilson 1983, 88–9, 332–3; Symons 1979, 143; Chagnon 1979, 380). Again, women are such a prominent motive for competition and conflict because reproductive opportunities are a very strong selective force indeed. This does not mean that people always want to maximize the number of their children. Although there is some human desire for children *per se* and a great attachment to them once they exist, it is mainly the desire for sex – Malthus's "passion" – which functions in nature as the powerful biological proximate mechanism for maximizing reproduction. As humans, and other living creatures, normally engage in sex throughout their fertile lives, they have a vast reproductive potential, which, before the introduction of effective contraception, mainly depended for its realization on resource availability.

Polygyny (and female infanticide) created women scarcity and increased men's competition for – and conflict over – them (Divale and Harris 1976). Among Aboriginal Australian tribes, about 30 percent of the Murngin adult males are estimated to have died violently, and similar findings have been recorded for the Tiwi. The Plains Indians showed a deficit of 50 percent for the adult males in the Blackfoot tribe in 1805 and 33 percent deficit in 1858, while during the reservation period the sex ratio rapidly approached 50–50. Among the Eskimo of the central Canadian arctic, the rate of violent deaths was estimated at one per thousand persons per year, 10 times the 1990 US rate which is the highest in the developed world. Among the !Kung of the Kalahari Desert, known as the "harmless people," the rate of killing was 0.29 person per thousand per year, and had been 0.42 before the coming of state authority, 3–4 times higher than the 1990 US rate (Gat 2006, 129–32).

The data for pre-state agriculturalists is basically the same. Among the Yanomamo of the Orinoco about 15 percent of the adults died as a result of inter- and intra-group violence: 24 percent of the males and 7 percent of the females. The Waorani (Auca) of the Ecuadorian Amazon hold the registered world record: more than 60 percent of adult deaths were caused by feuding and warfare. In Highland New Guinea violent mortality estimates are very similar: among the Dani, 28.5 percent of the men and 2.4 percent of the women; among the Enga, 34.8 percent of the adult males; among the Goilala, whose total population was barely over 150, there were 29 (predominantly men) killed during a period of 35 years; among the Lowland Gebusi, 35.2 percent of the adult males and 29.3 percent of the adult females (ibid.).

Dominance: Rank, Power, Status, Prestige

The interconnected competition over resources and reproduction is the *root* cause of conflict and fighting in humans as in all other animal species. Other causes and expressions of fighting in nature, and the motivational and emotional mechanisms associated with them, are derivative of, and subordinate to, these primary causes, and *originally* evolved this way in humans as well. It is to these "second level" causes and motivational mechanisms, directly linked to the first, that we now turn.

Among social animals, possessing higher rank in the group promises one a greater share in the communal resources, such as hunting spoils, and better access to females. For this reason, rank in the group is hotly contested. It is the strong, fierce, and – among our sophisticated cousins, the chimpanzees – also the "politically" astute, that win status by the actual and implied use of force. Rivalry for rank and domination in nature is, then, a proximate means in the competition over resources and reproduction. For this reason people jealously guard their honor. In traditional societies in particular, people were predisposed to go to great lengths in defense of their honor. The slightest offence could provoke violence. Where no strong centralized authority existed, one's honor was a social commodity of vital significance.

To avoid a misunderstanding: the argument is not that these behavior patterns are a matter of conscious decision and complex calculation conducted by flies, mice, lions, or even humans. It is simply that those who failed to behave adaptively became decreasingly represented in the next generations, and their maladaptive genes, responsible for their maladaptive behavior, were consequently selected against. The most complex structural engineering and behavior patterns have thus evolved in even the simplest organisms, including those lacking any consciousness (Dawkins 1989, 96, 291–2).

As with competition over women, competition over rank and esteem could lead to violent conflict indirectly as well as directly. For instance, even in the simplest societies people desire ornamental, ostentatious, and prestige goods. Although these goods are sometimes lumped together with subsistence goods, their social function and significance are entirely different. Body and clothes ornamentation are designed to enhance physically desirable features that function everywhere in nature as cues for health, vigor, youth, and fertility (Darwin 1871, 467–8; Low 1979; Diamond 1992, Ch. 9). It is precisely on these products of the "illusions industry" – cosmetics, fashion, and jewelry – that people everywhere spend so much money. Furthermore, where some ornaments are scarce and therefore precious, the very fact that one is able to afford them indicates wealth and success. Hence the source of what economist Thorstein Veblen, referring to early twentieth century American society, called "conspicuous consumption." Similarly, in Stone Age societies, luxury goods, as well as the ostentatious consumption of ordinary ones, became in themselves objects of desire as symbols of social status. For this reason, people may fight for them.

Indeed, plenty and scarcity are relative not only to the number of mouths to be fed but also to the potentially ever-expanding and insatiable range of human needs and desires. Human competition increases with abundance – as well as with deficiency – taking more complex forms and expressions, widening social gaps, and enhancing stratification. While the consumption capacity of simple, subsistence, products is inherently limited, that of more refined, lucrative ones is practically open-ended. One can simply move up the market.

Revenge: Retaliation to Eliminate and Deter

Revenge is one of the major causes of fighting cited in anthropological accounts of pre-state societies. Violence was activated to avenge injuries to honor, property, women, and kin. If life was taken, revenge reached its peak, often leading to a vicious circle of death and counter-death.

How is this most prevalent, risky, and often bloody behavior pattern to be explained? From the evolutionary perspective, revenge is retaliation that is intended either to destroy an enemy or to foster deterrence against him, as well as against other potential rivals. This applies to non-physical and non-violent, as well as to physical and violent action. If one does not pay back on an injury, one may signal weakness and expose oneself to further injuries. A process of victimization might be created. This rationale applies wherever there is no higher authority that can be relied upon for protection, that is, in so-called anarchic systems. In modern societies it thus applies to the wide spheres of social relations in which the state or other authoritative bodies do not intervene. In pre-state societies, however, it applied far more widely to the basic protection of life and property.

Thus the instinctive desire to strike back is a basic emotional response which evolved precisely because those who struck back were generally more successful in protecting their own. This is remarkably supported by the famous computerized game that found tit-for-tat the most effective strategy a player can adopt (Hamilton and Axelrod 1984). But tit-for-tat poses a problem. One's offender cannot always be eliminated. Furthermore, the offender has kin who will avenge him, and it is even more difficult to eliminate them as well. In many cases tit-for-tat becomes a negative loop of retaliation and counter-retaliation from which it is very hard to exit. One original offence may produce a pattern of prolonged hostility. Retaliation might produce escalation rather than annihilation or deterrence. In such cases, fighting seems to feed on, and perpetuate, itself, bearing a wholly disproportional relation to its "original" cause. People become locked into conflict against their wishes and best interests. It is this factor that has always given warfare an irrational appearance that seems to defy a purely utilitarian explanation.

How can this puzzle be explained? In the first place, it must again be stressed that both the original offense and the act of retaliation arise from a fundamental state of inter-human competition that carries the potential of conflict, and is consequently fraught with suspicion and insecurity. Without this basic state of somatic and reproductive competition and potential conflict, retaliation as a behavior pattern would not have evolved. However, while explaining the root cause of retaliation, this does not in itself account for retaliation's escalation into what often seems to be a self-defeating cycle. A prisoner's dilemma situation is responsible for the emergence of such cycles. In the absence of an authority that can enforce mutually beneficial cooperation on people, or at least minimize their damages, the cycle of retaliation is often their only rational option – though, exposing them to very heavy costs, is not their best option.

The prisoner's dilemma is of great relevance when explaining the war complex as a whole and not only that of revenge and retribution. Still, it ought to be emphasized that not all violent conflicts or acts of revenge fall under the special terms of the prisoner's dilemma. In the context of a fundamental resource scarcity, if one is able to eliminate, decisively weaken, or subdue the enemy, and consequently reap most of the benefits, then this strategy is better for one's interests than a compromise.

Power and the Security Dilemma

Revenge or retaliation is an active reaction to an injury, emanating from a competitive and, hence, potentially conflictual basic state of relations. However, as Hobbes saw (*Leviathan*, Ch. 13), the basic condition of competition and potential conflict, which gives rise to endemic suspicion and insecurity, invites not only reactive but also preemptive response, which further magnifies mutual suspicion and insecurity. It must be stressed that the source of the potential conflict here is again of a "second level." It does not necessarily arise directly from an actual conflict over the somatic and reproductive resources themselves, but from the fear, suspicion, and insecurity that the potential of those "first level" causes for conflict creates. Potential conflict can thus breed conflict. When the "other" must be regarded as a potential enemy, his very existence poses a threat, for he might suddenly attack one day. For this reason, one must take precautions and increase one's strength as much as possible. The other side faces a similar security problem and takes similar precautions. Things do not stop with precautionary and defensive measures, because such measures often inherently possess some offensive potential. Thus measures that one takes to increase one's security in an insecure world often decreases the other's security and vice versa.

What are the consequences of this security dilemma (Herz 1950; Jervis 1978)? In the first place, it tends to escalate arms races. Arms races between competitors take place throughout nature. Through natural selection, they produce faster cheetahs and gazelles; deer with longer horns to fight one another; more devious parasites and viruses and more immune "hosts." Many of these arms races involve very heavy costs to the organisms, which would not have been necessary if it were not for the competition. This, for example, is the reason why trees have trunks. Trees incur the enormous cost involved in growing trunks only because of their life-and-death struggle to outgrow other trees in order to get sunlight. As with humans, competition is most intense in environments of plenty, where more competitors can play and more resources be accumulated. This is why trees grow highest in the dense forests of the water-rich tropical and temperate climates.

Arms races often have paradoxical results. The continuous and escalating effort to surpass one's rival may prove successful, in which case the rival is destroyed or severely weakened. However, in many cases, every step on one side is matched by a counter-step on the other. Consequently, even though each side invests increasing resources in the conflict, neither gains an advantage. This is called, after one of Alice's puzzles in Lewis Carroll's *Through the Looking-Glass*, the "Red Queen effect": both sides run faster and faster only to find themselves remaining in place. Arms races may become a prisoner's dilemma.

The special feature of arm races created by the security dilemma is that their basic motivation on both sides is defensive. Since suspicion is difficult to overcome, there is another way to reduce the insecurity. The sides may chose to actively pre-empt, that is, take not only defensive precautions but attack in order to eliminate or severely weaken the other side. Indeed, this option in itself makes the other side even more insecure, making the security dilemma more acute. Warfare can thus become a self-fulfilling prophecy. Since full security is difficult to achieve, history demonstrates that constant warfare can be waged, conquest carried afar, and power accumulated – all truly motivated by security concerns, "for defense." Of course, in reality motives are often mixed, with the security motive coexisting with a quest for gain.

World-View and the Supernatural

But what about the world of culture that after all is our most distinctive mark as humans? Do not people kill and get killed for ideas and ideals? From the Stone Age on, the spiritual life of human communities was imbued with supernatural beliefs, sacred cults and rituals, and the practice of magic.

The evolutionary status of religion is beyond our scope here. Like warfare, religion is a complex phenomenon which is probably the result of several different interacting factors. For example, from Emile Durkheim (1965) on, functionalist theorists have argued that religion's main role was in fostering social cohesion, *inter alia* in war.[1] This means that in those groups in which common ritual and cult ceremonies were more intensive, social cooperation became more habitual and more strongly legitimized, which probably translated into an advantage in warfare.

But how did hunter-gatherers' supernatural beliefs and practices affect the reasons for conflict and fighting? I argue that on the whole they added to, sometimes accentuating, the reasons we have already discussed. The all-familiar glory of the gods, let alone missionary quests, never appear as reasons for hunter-gatherers' warfare. These will appear later in human cultural evolution. The most regular supernatural reason cited by anthropologists for fighting among hunter-gatherers is fear and accusations of sorcery. It should be noted, however, that these did not appear randomly, but were directed against people whom the victim of the alleged sorcery felt had reasons to want to harm him. This, of course, does not necessarily mean that they really did. What it does mean is that competition, potential conflict, animosity, and suspicion were conducive to fears and accusations of sorcery. To a greater degree than with the security dilemma, the paranoia here reflects the running amok of real, or potentially real, fears and insecurity, thus further exacerbating and escalating the war complex.

Fighting in the Evolutionary State of Nature

Conflict and fighting in the human state of nature, as in the state of nature in general, was fundamentally caused by competition. While violence is evoked, and suppressed, by powerful emotional stimuli, it is not a primary, "irresistible" drive; it is a highly tuned, both innate and optional, evolution-shaped tactic, turned on and off in response to changes in the calculus of survival and reproduction. It can be activated by competition over scarce resources, as scarcity and competition are the norm in nature because of organisms' tendency to propagate rapidly when resources are abundant. Deadly violence is also regularly activated in competition over women, directly as well as indirectly, when men compete over resources in order to be able to afford more women and children.

From these primary somatic and reproductive aims, other, proximate and derivative, "second level" aims arise. The social arbiters within the group can use their position to reap somatic and reproductive advantages. Hence the competition for – and conflict over – esteem, prestige, power, and leadership, as proximate goods. An offense or injury will often prompt retaliation, lest it persists and turns into a pattern of victimization. Tit-for-tat may end in victory or a compromise, but it may also escalate, developing into a self-perpetuating cycle of strikes and counter strikes, with the antagonists locked in conflict in a sort of prisoner's dilemma situation.

Similarly, in a state of potential conflict, security precautions are called for, which may take on a defensive but also offensive or pre-emptive character. The security dilemma variant of the prisoner's dilemma breads arms races that may produce an advantage to one side but often merely produces a "Red Queen" effect, by which both sides escalate their resource investment only to find themselves in the same position vis-á-vis one another. Organisms can cooperate, compete, or fight to maximize survival and reproduction. Sometimes, fighting is the most promising choice for at least one of the sides. At other times, however, fighting, while being their rational choice, is not their best one.

Finally, a few comments on the evolutionary perspective that underpins this study. As our grand scientific theory for understanding nature, evolutionary theory does not compete in explaining motivation with scholarly constructs such as psychoanalytic theories or the realist approach in the study of international relations; rather, evolutionary theory may encompass some of their main insights within a comprehensive interpretative framework. For instance, Freud, Jung, and Adler were divided over the elementary drive which each posited as the underlying regulating principle for understanding human behavior. These were respectively: sex; creativeness and the quest for meaning; and the craving for superiority. All these drives in fact come together and interact within the framework of evolutionary theory, which also explains their otherwise mysterious origin. Similarly, realist theory in the study of international relations is an analytical construct, whose fundamental assumptions and insights capture some important, albeit partial, truths about reality, explained by evolutionary theory (cf. Thayer 2000, 126, 137–8, 140; 2004, 11–12, 93).

Some readers may wonder why evolutionary theory should be presented here as different from and superior to other scholarly approaches. It is because evolutionary theory is nature's *immanent* principle rather than an artificial analytical construct. It is the only non-transcendent mechanism for explaining life's complex design. This mechanism is blind natural selection in which at every stage those who are endowed with the most suitable qualities for surviving and reproducing survive. There is no reason for their survival other than that they proved successful in the struggle for survival. "Success" is not defined by any transcendant measurement but by the immanent logic of the evolutionary process.

This brings us to another widespread cause of resistance to sociobiology: the belief that it upholds biological determinism in a subject which is distinctively determined by human culture. For once humans developed agriculture some ten thousand years ago, which led to the growth of the first states about five thousand years ago, they set in motion a continuous chain of developments that have taken them far away from their evolutionary natural way of life. Original, evolution-shaped, innate human wants, desires, and proximate behavioral and emotional mechanisms now express themselves in radically altered, artificial conditions. In the process, they were greatly modified, assuming novel and diverse appearances. All the same, cultural evolution did not operate on a clean slate, nor was it capable of producing simply anything. Its multifarious and diverse forms have been built on a clearly recognizable deep core of innate human propensities. Cultural takeoff took place much too recently to affect human biology in any significant way.[2] Biologically, we are virtually the same people as our Stone Age forefathers and are endowed with the same predispositions. With cultural evolution all bets are not off – they are merely hedged. We now turn to examine these gene–culture interactions to see how they shaped the motives for human fighting throughout history.

Historical State Societies

As we have seen, the motivations that lead to fighting are fundamentally derived from the human motivational system in general. Fighting, to change Clausewitz, is a continuation of human aims and the behavior designed to achieve them by violent means, and, now, on a progressively larger scale and with increasing organization, mainly associated with the state. How did cultivation, accumulated resources, stratification, coercive structuring, and a growing scale affect the motivational system that led to fighting?

Resources

Territories for cultivation (and for pasture) replaced hunting and foraging territories as an object for competition. However, where both of the above involved competition over the right of access to nature, the real novelty brought about by cultivation was the exploitation of human labor. With cultivation it became possible to live off of other people's work. Accumulated foodstuffs and livestock could be appropriated by looting. Other somatic-utility objects, such as fabrics, tools, and metal, were also desirable targets. In addition to their utility value, objects possessed decorative, status, and prestige value. Precious objects that acquired the role of money, most notably precious metals, became the most highly prized booty. Control over both natural sources of raw materials and trade intensified as a source of competition. Furthermore, not only products but also the producers themselves could be captured and carried back home as slaves, to labor under direct control. Finally, looting could be further upgraded into tribute extraction, a more systematic and more efficient appropriation of labor and resources through political subjugation, which did not involve great destruction, waste, and disruption of productive activity.

The balance of costs and gains is the most intricate and intriguing issue here. Cultivation greatly increased the material costs of fighting. Hunter-gatherers' fighting harmed mainly the antagonists and their productive activity, but (with minor exceptions) barely the resources themselves. Cultivation, however, added to the above the ability to inflict direct damages on the resources and on other somatic and labor-intensive hardware. Antagonists regularly ravaged crops, livestock, production implements and settlements in order to weaken and/or increase the cost of war incurred by the opponent. Furthermore, growing political units and technological advancement meant that fighting no longer took place close to home, during lulls in productive activity, and with simple arms and improvised logistics. Metal weapons, fortifications, horses, ships, pay for long-term soldiers, and provisions consumed huge resources. Exact data is sparse, but it is clear that military expenditure regularly constituted by far the largest item of states' expenditure, in most cases the great majority of it. States' tax revenues may have reached as much as 10 percent of the national product and rose to even higher levels during military emergencies.[3] In premodern subsistence economies, where malnutrition was the rule and starvation an ever-looming prospect, such a burden literally took bread out of people's mouths.

Resources ravaged by and invested in war thus constituted a new, massive addition to the cost-side of fighting. Whereas among hunter-gatherers the struggle for resources approximated a zero-sum-game, wherein resource quantity remained generally unaffected, fighting now invariably *decreased* the sum total of resources, at least so long as the fighting went on. Only the relative *distribution* of these decreased resources and, moreover, the re-channeling of their *future yield* might result in net gains for one at the expense of the other.

Who was that "one"? Neither humanity nor even individual societies counted as real agents or units of calculation in the competition. Unequal distribution was the rule not only between but also within rival sides. Chiefs and their war hosts might accumulate wealth through raiding, while the rest of the tribal people suffered the consequences, in the form of enemy reprisals, counter raiding, and ravaging. Indeed, the state itself was largely the outgrowth of such processes: power gave wealth, which, in a self-reinforcing spiral, accentuated intra-social power relations in a way that obliged people down a progressively more hierarchic social pyramid to follow their superiors while receiving a lesser and lesser share of the benefits.

Thus cultivation, resource accumulation, and the state for the first time made possible a predatory, "parasitical" existence on the fruits of other people's labor. Whereas productivity-related competition generally increases productive efficiency, predatory-parasitical competition increases predatory-parasitic efficiency while decreasing productive efficiency. All the same, by being efficient in the predatory competition, one was able to secure the benefits of production.

There were also spin-off and long-term net productive gains resulting from the power race. How much of a substantial independent spin-off effect military innovation in metallurgy, engineering, horse breeding, naval architecture, and supply had on society is difficult to establish. But the most significant spin-off effects seem to have come from the state itself. It was through violence that one power established authority over a territory or society, thereby securing increased internal peace and imposing coordinated collective efforts, some of which, at least, were in the common good, decreasing "free-riding." Large states introduced economies of scale, and, as long as they did not become monopolistically big and overburdened by overheads, they generated and accelerated innovation (cf. Mann 1988, 64–5). War was a "two-level game" in which both external and internal power relations and external and internal benefit extraction were linked.

Sex and Harems

The same logic applies to that other principal source of human competition – the sexual – considered from the perspective of male fighting. Students of war scarcely think of sexuality as a motive for fighting. The underlying links that connect the various elements of the human motivational system have largely been lost sight of.[4]

Silence is one reason for this blind spot. While some aspects of sexuality are among the most celebrated in human discourse, others are among the least advertised and most concealed by all the sides involved. Nonetheless, the evidence is overwhelming and has recently retuned to the headlines, shocking Western public with mass documentation from the wars in Bosnia, Rwanda and the Sudan. Throughout history, widespread rape by soldiers went hand in hand with looting as an inseparable part of military operations. Indeed, like looting, the prospect of sexual adventure was one of the main attractions of warlike operations, which motivated people to join in. Young and beautiful captured women were a valued prize, in the choice of which – as with all other booty – the leaders enjoyed a right of priority. While in heroic sagas of semi-barbaric societies, such as the *Iliad*, the sexual value of that prize was barely veiled, the practice was no less in force – openly or more discretely – in the armed forces of more civilized societies.[5]

The other major reason – apart from the silence of both victors and victims – for the oversight of sexuality as one of the potential benefits of fighting was the exponential rise in large-scale civilized societies of accumulated wealth, which functioned as a universal currency that could be exchanged for most of the other good things in life. Even more than before, fighting advanced reproductive success not only directly, as women were raped and kidnapped, but also indirectly, as the resources and status won by fighting advanced one in the intra-social competition for the acquisition and upkeep of women domestically. By and large, power, wealth, and sexual opportunity comprised overlapping and interlinked hierarchic pyramids.

Where polygyny was permitted, the rich and powerful acquired a greater number of wives and enjoyed a marked advantage in choosing young, beautiful and otherwise worthy ones. In addition to wives, many societies sanctioned official concubines, and there were, of course, unofficial concubines or mistresses. Yet another avenue of sexual opportunity was females in the household, some of whom were slave girls captured in war and raiding. Finally, there was the sex trade *per se*, where again the most consummate and graceful exponents of the trade could be highly expensive.

The manner in which power, wealth, and sexual opportunity were linked is most strikingly demonstrated at the apex the hierarchic pyramids, most notably in the figure of the so-called Oriental despot, who had his counterpart in the empires of pre-Columbian America. Rulers possessed large harems. According to the Greek authors (Cook 1985, ii. 226–7), Alexander the Great captured 329 of King Darius III's concubines after the Battle of Issus (333 BC). Only slightly later, Kautilya's *Arthashastra* (i.20 and i.27) provides a detailed description of the construction and procedures of the harem, as well as an account of the bureaucratic apparatus that supervised over the march of prostitutes who were invited to the court.

Bureaucratic records, where they survived, constitute the most solid source, from which verified numbers can be derived. The most bureaucratic and most magnificent of empires was China. According to the state's records (Bielenstein 1980, 73–4), the imperial harem of the Early Han (second and first centuries BC) comprised some 2000–3000 women, whereas that of the Later Han (first and second centuries AD) reached 5000–6000. Imperial China represented the ultimate in terms of harem size. The records of the Ottoman Privy Purse indicate that at its zenith, during the first half of the seventeenth century, the sultan's harem comprised some 400 women, with another 400 kept on a "retired list" (Peirce 1993, 122–4).

Gardens of Pleasure and Cherubs with a Flaming Sword at Their Gates

All this should not to be regarded as a piece of exotic piquancy, something peripheral to the real business of government. Quite the contrary, as with the other elements in the human motivational system, it was for the supreme commanding position over the garden of pleasures that people reached for or fought in defense of, killed and got killed. As Ibn Khaldun (1958, Ch. 3.1) wrote: "royal authority is a noble and enjoyable position. It comprises all the good things of the world, the pleasures of the body, and the joys of the soul. Therefore, there is, as a rule, great competition for it. It rarely is handed over (voluntarily), but may be taken away. Thus discord ensues. It leads to war and fighting." The same reality was vividly captured by the ancient Greek tale of wisdom regarding the sword of Damocles. The ruler, according to this tale, was seated at a table packed full with all the world's delights and objects of desire, while a sword hanged on a horse-hair above his head, liable to fall down and kill him at any moment. Ruling was a high-stake – high-risk, high-gain – affair, with force as its mainstay.

A rigorous study of royal violent mortality rates has yet to be undertaken. All the same, some data may illustrate the point. According to the Biblical record, only 9 out the 19 kings of the northern kingdom of Israel died naturally. Of the others, 7 were killed by rebels, 1 committed suicide to escape the same fate, 1 fell in battle, and 1 was exiled by the Assyrians. Four or five out of Achaemenid Persia's 13 kings were assassinated and one was apparently killed in war (Cook 1985, 227, 331). During the last century of the reign of the Hellenistic Seleucids, practically all of the 19 reigning monarchs became victims (after having been perpetrators) of usurpation and violent death. During the five hundred years of the Roman Empire, roughly 70 percent of its rulers died violently, not to mention the countless contenders who were killed without ever making it to the imperial crown (Southern and Dixon 1996, x–xii, for the data on the late Empire). During the lifespan of the Eastern Roman Empire or

Byzantium (395–1453 AD), 64 out of its 107 emperors, more than 60 percent, were deposed and/or killed (Finer 1997, 702). Six out of eight kings of Northumbria in the seventh century AD died in war (Abels 1988, 12). It is estimated that during the later Viking period more than a third of the Norwegian kings died in battle, and another third were banished (Griffith 1995, 26).

All these are merely examples taken from countless similar tales of insecurity, violent struggle, and bloodbaths at the apex of political power. Violent usurpations spelled doom not only for the ruler or contender, but also for their families and followers, and, if the struggle turned into a full-fledged civil war, for masses of soldiers and civilians. All the same, there was no shortage of candidates to take up this high-risk, high-gain game.

Was it "worth it" and in what sense? Did people who engaged in the high-gain, high-cost, intra- and inter-social, two-level game of power politics improve their ultimate reproductive success? The answer to this question seems very difficult to compute. On the one hand, rulers enjoyed much greater reproductive opportunities, most strikingly represented in the autocratic harem. On the other hand, contenders to the throne, and even incumbent rulers, played a highly risky game for both themselves and their families. Some light on the question is shed by a remarkable study recently conducted on the Y (male) chromosome in Central and Eastern Asia, which demonstrates how great the rulers' reproductive advantage could be (Zerjal, Xue, Bertorelle et al. 2003). It reveals that some 8 percent of the population in the region (0.5 percent of the world's population) carry the same Y chromosome, which can only mean that they are the descendants of a single man. Furthermore, the biochemical patterns indicate that this man lived in Mongolia about a thousand years ago. It was not difficult to identify the only likely candidate, Chinggis Khan, an identification confirmed by an examination of the Y gene of his known surviving descendents. This, of course, does not mean that Chinggis Khan alone sired so many children from a huge number of women, an obvious impossibility even if he had ceased his military conquests altogether. The tremendous spread of his Y chromosome is due to the fact that his sons succeeded him at the head of ruling houses throughout Central and East Asia for centuries, all enjoying staggering sexual opportunities.

To be sure, Chinggis Khan was among the greatest warlords ever, and his dynasty probably the most successful. Countless unsuccessful bidders for power, whose lines ceased because of their failures, have to be figured into the other side of the equation. All the same, the apex of the social pyramid held such a powerful attraction for people because it was there that evolution-shaped human desires could be set loose and indulged on a gigantic scale. On a more modest scale, the same considerations held true farther down the social hierarchy.

The Quest for Power and Glory

Status, leadership, and power were sought out in the evolutionary state of nature because of the advantages that they granted in access to somatic and reproductive resources. With resource accumulation and hierarchic organization, the scope and significance of coercive social power rocketed. Furthermore, since both resources and power could now be accumulated and expanded on a hitherto unimaginable scale, while being closely intertwined and interchangeable, power, like money, grew into a universal currency by which most objects of desire could be secured. Power became the medium through which all else was channeled, and the quest for power thus represented all else. For this reason, the quest for power seemingly acquired a life of its own and was also pursued for its own sake. To be sure, power was desired not only for positive reasons; the security dilemma in itself drove people and political communities to expand their power as a defensive measure, for in a competitive race one would rather swallow than be swallowed.

Like status and power, and closely linked to them, the quest for honor and prestige was originally "designed" to facilitate access to somatic and reproductive resources. As such, it too is stimulated by powerful emotional gratifications, which give it a seemingly independent life of its own. Again, the potential for the fulfillment of this quest increased exponentially in large-scale societies. The stellas on which autocrats celebrated their achievements in super-human images are interpreted by scholars as instruments of royal propaganda; but, equally, they express the quest for the ultimate fulfillment of the craving for boundless glory and absolute domination, which could now be extended to the "four corners of the world" and "everything under the sun," as the mightiest of imperial rulers boasted.

All the above also applied to individuals in general and to political communities at large. Community members bathed in their collective glory and were willing to pay for its advancement and protection. This again was derived from the conversion value of honor and glory in terms of power, deterrence, and inter-state bargaining. Individuals and political communities jealously guarded their honor and responded forcefully even to slight infringements, not because of the trifle matters involved, but because of the much more serious ones that might follow if they demonstrated weakness. To paraphrase Winston Churchill: choosing shame rather than war might very likely beget shame and then war.

Kinship, Culture, Ideas, Ideals

Are people only interested in these crude materialistic objectives, which even after humankind's dramatic cultural takeoff can ultimately be shown to derive from evolution-shaped sources? They undoubtedly do, but, as I claim above, as a continuation rather than a negation of the above. A highly intricate interface links the natural with the cultural.

Let us begin with the factor of identity. People exhibit a marked, evolution-shaped innate predisposition to favor closer kin over more remote ones, or "strangers" – that is, to favor those with whom they share more genes. Roughly this means that people in any kin circle struggle among themselves for the interests of their yet closer kin, while at the same time tending to cooperate against more distant circles. In this incessant multi-level game, internal cooperation tends to stiffen when the community is faced with an external threat, while inner rivalries variably diminish, though never disappear. It should, of course, be added that non-kin cooperation and alliances for mutual gain are commonplace, becoming only more so with the growth of large-scale organized society.

While the above limitations on kin cooperation must always be kept in mind, the range of kin affinities and kin bonds expanded dramatically in large-scale state societies. Wherever they took place, agricultural expansions in particular created ethnic groups which often encompassed hundreds of thousands, but were divided into separate, competing, and often hostile tribes, tribal confederations, and, later, petty-states. It is not sufficiently recognized that above all it is within such ethnic spaces that larger states tended to emerge and expand, for people of a similar ethnicity could be more easily united and kept united, relying on shared ethnocentric traits and bonds. Indeed, it was primarily on their loyal native ethnic core that states and empires relied when they expanded beyond that core to rule over other ethnicities. Thus, contrary to a widely held view, ethnicity mattered a great deal in determining political boundaries and affinities from the very start, rather than only achieving that effect with modernity.[6]

To be sure, it is overwhelmingly cultural traits rather than genetic gradations that separate ethnicities from one another. The point is entirely different. Since in small hunter-gatherer groups kinship and culture overlapped, not only phenotypic resemblance (similarity in physical appearance) but also shared cultural traits functioned as cues for kinship, as well as proving vital for effective cooperation. Thus, whether or not national communities are genetically related (and most of them are), they feel and function as *if* they were, on account of their shared cultural traits. Independence from foreign domination has been perceived as crucial to a people's prosperity as a community of kinship and culture, often evoking most desperate expressions of communal devotion in its defense. To be blind to the sources and workings of these intricate mental mechanisms of collective identity formation inevitably means to misconceive some of the most powerful bonds that shape human history.

The power of ideas is even more far-reaching. People everywhere kill and get killed over ideas, irrespective of kinship and across nations. How is this lofty sphere – the often most abstract of metaphysical ideas, indeed, all too often seemingly absurd notions – connected to the practicalities of life? The key for understanding this query is our species' strong propensity for interpreting its surroundings as deep and as far as the mind can probe, so as to decipher their secrets and form a mental map that would best help to cope with their hazards and opportunities. *Homo sapiens sapiens* possesses an innate, omni-present, evolution-shaped predisposition for ordering its world, which *inter alia* extends to form the foundation of mythology, metaphysics, and science. We are compulsive meaning-seekers. It is this propensity that is responsible for our species' remarkable career.

Thus the array of ideas regarding the fundamental structure and working of the cosmos, and the means and practices required for securing its benevolent functioning have been largely perceived as *practical* questions of the utmost significance, evoking as powerful emotions and motivation for action – including violence – as any other major practical question might (cf. Boyer 2001, 135–42). They hold the key to individual, communal, and cosmic salvation in this and/or other worlds, worthy of the greatest dedication and even of dying for.

Although religious, and later secular, salvation-and-justice ideologies regularly emerged and sometimes remained grounded within a particular people, they often carried a universal message that transcended national boundaries. Furthermore, the relationship of the new universal religious and secular ideologies with war was complex. The obligation of a "just war" was already evident in many of the older religions. With the new universal ideologies, this obligation was reinforced, as was the ban on belligerency among the faithful. At the same time, some of the salvation ideologies incorporated a strong missionary zeal that could be translated into holy belligerency against non-believers. Furthermore, militant salvation ideologies generated a terrific galvanizing effect on the holy warrior host.[7]

Christianity, starting as a religion of love, compassion, and non-violence, later developed a brutal militant streak towards non-believers and heretics, which awkwardly coexisted with its opposite in both doctrine and practice. With regards to the relations among the faithful its position was more consistently pacifist. Islam incorporated the holy war against the non-believers as an integral part of its doctrine from its inception, while preaching unity and non-belligerency within its own house. The blatant fact that within both Christianity and Islam fighting went on incessantly despite religious condemnation merely indicates that, while being a very potent force, religious ideology was practically powerless to eradicate the motivations and realities that generated war. Much the same applies to Eastern Eurasia, where spiritual ideologies such as Buddhism and Confucianism were more tolerant and even more conflict-averse.[8]

Conclusion

Attempts to find the root cause of war in the nature of either the individual, the state, or the international system are fundamentally misplaced. In all these "levels" there are necessary but not sufficient causes for war, and the whole cannot be broken into pieces.[9] People's needs and desires – which may be pursued violently – as well as the resulting quest for power and the state of mutual apprehension which fuel the security dilemma are all molded in human nature (some of them existing only as options, potentials, and skills in a behavioral "tool kit"); they are so molded because of strong evolutionary pressures that have shaped humans in their struggle for survival over geological times, when all the above literally constituted matters of life and death. The violent option of human competition has been largely curbed within states, yet is occasionally taken up on a large-scale between states because of the anarchic nature of the inter-state system. However, returning to step one, international anarchy in and of itself is not an explanation for war were it not for the potential for violence in a fundamental state of competition over scarce resources that is embedded in reality and, consequently, in human nature.

Wars have been fought for the attainment of the same objects of human desire that underlie the human motivational system in general – *only by violent means*, through the use of force. Politics – internal and external – of which war is, famously, a continuation, is the activity intended to achieve at the intra- and inter-state "levels" the very same evolution-shaped human aims we have already seen. Some writers have felt that "politics" does not fully encompass the causes of war. John Keegan (1994) rightly criticized Clausewitz for equating warfare with the state. In opposition to Clausewitz he also argued that the reasons for war are "cultural," rather than merely "political," in the sense that they express a far broader causal array, reflecting a society's whole way of life, identity, religion, and ideology. Even Thayer (2004, 178–9), who correctly argues that evolutionary theory explains ultimate human aims, nonetheless goes on to say, inconsistently, that Clausewitz needs extension because war is caused not only by political reasons but also by the evolutionarily-rooted search for resources, as if the two were separate, with politics being somehow different and apart, falling outside of the evolutionary logic.

What is defined as "politics" is of course a matter of semantics, and like all definitions is largely arbitrary. Yet, as has been claimed here, if not attributed to divine design, organisms' immensely complex mechanisms and the behavioral propensities that emanate from them – including those of human beings – *ultimately* could only have been "engineered" through evolution. The challenge is to lay out how evolution-shaped human desires relate to one another in motivating war.

The desire and struggle for scarce resources – wealth of all sorts – have always been regarded as a prime aim of "politics" and an obvious motive for war. They seem to require little further elaboration. By contrast, reproduction does not appear to figure as a direct motive for war in large-scale societies. However, as we saw, appearance is often deceptive, for somatic and reproductive motives are the two inseparable sides of the same coin. In modern societies, too, sexual adventure remained central to *individual* motivation for going to war, even if it usually failed to be registered at the level of "state politics." This may be demonstrated by the effects of the sexual revolution since the 1960s, which, by lessening the attraction of foreign adventure for recruits and far increasing the attraction of staying at home, may have contributed to advanced societies' growing aversion to war. Honor, status, glory and dominance – both individual and collective – enhanced access to somatic and reproductive success and were thus hotly pursued and defended, even by force. The security dilemma sprang from this state of actual and potential competition, in turn pouring more oil into its fire. Power has been the universal currency through which all of the above could be obtained and/or defended, and has been sought after as such, in an often escalating spiral.

Kinship – expanding from family and tribe to peoples – has always exerted overwhelming influence in determining one's loyalty and willingness to sacrifice in the defense and promotion of a common good. Shared culture is a major attribute of ethnic communities, in the defense of which people can be invested as heavily as in the community's political independence and overall prosperity. Finally, religious and secular ideologies have been capable of stirring enormous zeal and violence; for grand questions of cosmic and socio-political order have been perceived as possessing paramount *practical* significance for securing and promoting life on earth and/or in the afterlife. In the human problem-solving menus, ideologies function as the most general blueprints. Rather than comprising a "laundry list" of causes for war, all of the above partake in the interconnected human motivational system, *originally* shaped by the calculus of survival and reproduction.

This calculus continues to guide human behavior, mostly through its legacy of innate proximate mechanisms – human desires – even where the original link between these proximate mechanisms and the original somatic and reproductive aims may have been loosened or even severed under altered conditions, especially during modernity: more wealth is desired even though above a certain level it has ceased to translate into greater reproduction; with effective contraception much the same applies to sexual success; power, status, honor and fame – connected to the above – are still hotly pursued even though their reproductive significance has become ambivalent.

To the extent that the industrial-technological revolution, most notably its liberal path, has sharply reduced the prevalence of war, the reason for this change is that the violent option for fulfilling human desires has become much less promising than the peaceful option of competitive cooperation. Furthermore, the more affluent and satiated the society and the more lavishly are people's most pressing needs met, the lesser their incentives to take risks that might involve the loss of life and limb. This does not mean a millenarian era of selfless altruism. People continue to compete vigorously over scarce objects of desire, partly because much of the competition among them concerns relative rather than absolute allocation of gains. On this realists are on firmer ground than radical liberals. However, liberals have been right in stressing that human reality is not static and, indeed, has been changing dramatically over the past generations, with the growth of affluent-liberal society going hand in hand with deepening global economic interdependence and mutual prosperity. As conditions have changed – indeed, only for those for whom they have changed, most notably within the world's affluent and democratic "zone of peace" – the violent option, the "hammer," in the human behavioral tool kit seems to have declined in utility for attaining desired aims.

Notes

1. Durkheim was followed in the functionalist tradition by Bronislav Malinovski and A. R. Radcliffe-Brown. More recently see Heiden 2003. For an evolutionary perspective see: Ridley 1996, 189–93; Wilson 2002.
2. Except for some well know aspects such as genes for lactose absorption, disease resistance, and a few other cases of strong selection: Lumsden and Wilson 1981; Cavalli-Sforza and Feldman 1981; Boyd and Richerson 1985; 2005; Durham 1991.
3. Rome is the best documented case: Frank 1959, i. 146, 228, and *passim.*; v. 4–7, and *passim.*; Hopkins 1980; more broadly see Goldsmith 1987, 18, 31–2 (Athens), 48 (Rome), 107, 121 (Moghal India), 142 (Tokugawa Japan).
4. Even Thayer generally shies away from sexuality in his evolutionary account of war. There have been, of course, attempts to connect sexuality with politics, most famously, in Freud's footsteps, those by Wilhelm Reich and Michel Foucault.
5. Thornhill and Palmer 2000 is an evolution-informed study. See also Buss and Malamuth 1996; Goldstein 2001, 362–9; van Creveld 2001, 33.
6. Cavalli-Sforza, Menozzi, and Piazza 1994. This is not the place to go into the vast literature on nationalism.
7. For a similar argument see: Stark 1996, Ch. 8; Wilson 2002. Both works overlook the military aspect.

8. Schwartz' thesis regarding the bellicosity of monotheism (1997) is historically naive and overstates a good case, overlooking the fact that pagans too fought for common, partly religious identity, sacred territory, and the glory of the gods, as well as relying on heavenly support. Dawkins' (2006) and Hitchens' (2007) charges that religion is responsible for all ills, including war, is entirely one-sided. Martin (1997), while idiosyncratic and apologetic, rightly claims that religion was merely one interacting element within a complex array of factors. Stark (2001), Ch. 3, is the closest to the approach presented here.
9. See Sugnami 1996, an excellent work of analytical philosophy that dissects Waltz 1979 and 1959.

References

Abels, Richard. 1988. Lordship and Military Obligation in Anglo-Saxon England, Berkeley: U. of California.

Balikci, A. 1970. *The Netsilik Eskimo*. Garden City, NY: Natural History.

Berndt, R. M., and C. H. Berndt. 1964. *The world of the first Australians*. London: Angus and Robertson.

Betzig, L., R. K. Denton, and L. Rodseth. 1991. Comments on Bruce Knauft, violence and sociality in human evolution. *Current Anthropology* 32:391–428.

Bielenstein, Hans. 1980. *The bureaucracy of the Han times*. Cambridge: Cambridge University Press.

Boyd, Robert, and Peter J. Richerson. 1985. *Culture and the evolutionary process*. Chicago: University of Chicago Press.

Boyd, Robert, and Peter J. Richerson. 2005. *Not by genes alone: how culture transformed human evolution*. Chicago: University of Chicago.

Boyer, Pascal. 2001. *Religion explained: The evolutionary origins of religious thought*. New York: Basic Books.

Burch, Ernest, and Thomas Correll. 1972. Alliance and conflict: interregional relations in North Alaska. In *Alliance in Eskimo Society,* edited by L. Guemple, 17–39. Seattle: University of Washington.

Burton, John (ed.). 1990. *Conflict: Human needs theory*. London: Macmillan.

Buss, D., and N. Malamuth (Eds.). 1996. *Sex, power, conflict: evolutionary and feminist perspectives*. New York: Oxford University Press.

Cavalli-Sforza, L. L., and M. W. Feldman. 1981. *Cultural transmission and evolution*. Princeton: Princeton University Press.

Cavalli-Sforza, L. L., Paolo Menozzi and Alberto Piazza. 1994. *The history and geography of human genes*. Princeton: Princeton University Press.

Chagnon, Napoleon. 1979. Is reproductive success equal in egalitarian societies? In *Evolutionary Biology and Human Social Behavior,* edited by N. Chagnon and W. Irons. North Scituate, MA: Duxbury Press.

Cook, J. 1985. The rise of the Achaemenids and establishment of their empire. In Vol. II of *The Cambridge History of Iran*, edited by I. Gershevitch. Cambridge University Press.

Daly, Martin, and Margo Wilson. 1983. *Sex, evolution, and behavior*. Boston: Willard Grant.

Darwin, Charles. n.d. [1871]. *The origin of the species and the descent of man*. New York: The Modern Library.

Dawkins, Richard. 1989. *The selfish gene*. Oxford: Oxford University Press.

Dawkins, Richard. 2006. *The God delusion*. Boston: Houghton Mifflin.

Diamond, Jared. 1992. *The rise and fall of the third chimpanzee*. London: Vintage.

Dickemann, Mildred. 1979. Female infanticide, reproductive strategies, and social stratification: A preliminary model. In *Evolutionary Biology and Human Social Behavior*, edited by N. Chagnon and W. Irons. North Scituate, MA: Duxbury Press.

Divale, William, and Marvin Harris. 1976. Population, warfare and the male supremacist complex. *American Anthropologist* 78:521–38.

Durham, W. H. 1991. *Coevolution: Genes, culture, and human diversity*. Stanford: Stanford University Press.

Durkheim, Emile. 1965. *The elementary forms of religious life*. New York: Free Press.

Ember, M., and C. R. Ember. 1992. Resource unpredictability, mistrust, and war: A cross-cultural study. *Journal of Conflict Resolution* 36:242–62.

Finer, S. E. 1997. *The history of government from the earliest times*. Oxford: Oxford University Press.

Frank, Tenney. 1959. *An economic survey of Ancient Rome*. Paterson, N.J.: Pageant Books.

Gat, Azar. 2006. *War in human civilization*. Oxford: Oxford University Press.

Goldsmith, Raymond. 1987. *Premodern financial systems: A historical comparative study*. Cambridge: Cambridge University Press.

Goldstein, Joshua. 2001. *War and gender: How the gender shapes the war system and vice versa*. New York: Cambridge University Press.

Griffith, Paddy. 1995. *The viking art of war*. London: Greenhill, 1995.

Hamilton, W. D. 1975. Innate social aptitude of man: An approach from evolutionary genetics. In *Biosocial Anthropology*, edited by R. Fox. New York: John Wiley and Sons.

Hamilton, W. D., and Robert Axelrod. 1984. *The evolution of cooperation*. New York: Basic Books.

Hart, C. W. M., and Arnold Pilling. 1964. *The Tiwi of North Australia*. New York: Holt, Reinhart and Winston.

Heiden, Brian. 2003. *A prehistory of religion: shamanism, sorcerers and saints*. Washington DC: Smithsonian.

Herz, John. 1950. Idealist internationalism and the security dilemma. *World Politics* 2:157–80.

Hitchens, Christopher. 2007. *God is not great*. New York: Hachette.

Hopkins, Keith. 1980. Taxes and trade in the Roman Empire (200 B.C.–A.D. 400), *Journal of Roman Studies* 70:101–25.

Ibn Khaldun. 1958. *The Muqaddimah: An introduction to history*. New York: Pantheon.

Irwin, Colin. 1990. The inuit and the evolution of limited group conflict. In *Sociobiology and Conflict*, edited by J. van der Dennen and V. Falger, 189–226. London: Chapman.

Jervis, Robert. 1978. Cooperation under the security dilemma. *World Politics* 30:167–214.

Keegan, John. 1994. *A history of warfare*. New York: Knopf.

Keeley, Lawrence. 1996. *War before civilization*. New York: Oxford University Press.

Keen, Ian. 1982. How some murngin men marry ten wives. *Man* 17:620–42.

LeBlanc, Steven, with Katherine Register. 2003. *Constant battles: The myth of the peaceful noble savage*. New York: St Martin's.

Long, Jeremy. 1970. Polygyny, acculturation and contact: aspects of aboriginal marriage in Central Australia. In *Australian Aboriginal Anthropology*, edited by R. M. Berndt. Nedland: University of Western Australia.

Lournados, Harry. 1988. Palaeopolitics: Resource intensification in aboriginal Australia and Papua New Guinea. In Vol. I of *Hunter and Gatherers*, edited by T. Ingold, D. Riches, and J. Woodburn. New York and Oxford: Berg.

Lournados, Harry. 1997. *Continent of hunter-gatherers: New perspectives in Australian prehistory*, Cambridge: Cambridge University Press.

Low, Dobbi. 1979. Sexual selection and human ornamentation. In *Evolutionary Biology and Human Social Behavior*, edited by N. Chagnon and W. Irons, 462–87. North Scituate, MA: Duxbury Press.

Lumsden, C. J., and E. O. Wilson. 1981. *Genes, mind and culture*. Cambridge, MA: Harvard University Press.

Mann, Michael. 1988. States, ancient and modern. In his *State, War and Capitalism*. Oxford: Blackwell.

Martin, Daniel. 1997. *Does Christianity cause war?* Oxford: Oxford University Press.

Maslow, Abraham. 1970. *Motivation and personality*. New York: Harper.

Meggitt, M. J. 1965a. *Desert people*. Chicago: University of Chicago.

Meggitt, M. J. 1965b. Marriage among the Walbiri of Central Australia: A statistical examination. In *Aboriginal Man in Australia*, edited by R. M. Berndt and C. H. Berndt, 146–59. Sidney: Angus and Robertson.

Morgan, John. 1980 [1852]. *The life and adventures of William Buckley: Thirty-two years a wanderer among the aborigines of the unexplored country round Port Philip*. Canberra: Australian National University Press.

Nelson, E. W. 1983 [1899]. *The Eskimo about Bering Strait*. Washington DC: Smithsonian.

Oswalt, Wendel. 1967. *Alaskan Eskimos*, San Francisco: Chandler.

Peirce, Leslie. 1993. *The Imperial harem: Women and sovereignty in the Ottoman Empire*. New York: Oxford University Press.

Ridley, Matt. 1994. *The Red Queen: Sex and the Evolution of Human Nature*. New York: Macmillan.

Ridley, Matt. 1996. *The origins of virtue: Human instincts and the evolution of cooperation*. New York: Viking.

Schwartz, Regina. 1997. *The curse of Cain: The violent legacy of monotheism*. Chicago: University of Chicago Press.

Southern, Pat, and Karen Dixon. 1996. *The late Roman army*. London: Batsford.

Stark, Rodney. 1996. *The rise of Christianity*. Princeton: Princeton University Press.

Stark, Rodney. 2001. *One God: Historical consequences of monotheism*. Princeton: Princeton University Press.

Sugnami, Hidemi. 1996. *On the causes of war*. Oxford: Oxford University Press.

Symons, Ronald. 1979. *The evolution of human sexuality*. New York: Oxford University Press.

Thayer, Bradley. 2000. Bringing in Darwin: Evolutionary theory, realism, and international politics. *International Security* 25.2:124–53.

Thayer, Bradley. 2004. *Darwin and international relations: On the evolutionary origins of war and ethnic conflict*. Lexington: University of Kentucky.

Thornhill, Randy, and Craig Palmer. 2000. *A natural history of rape: Biological bases of sexual coercion*. Cambridge, MA: MIT.

Tooby, John, and Leda Cosmides. 1992. The psychological foundations of culture. In *The Adapted mind: Evolutionary psychology and the generation of culture*, edited by L. Cosmides, J. Tooby, J. Barkow, 19–136. New York: Oxford University Press.

Van Creveld, Martin. 2001. *Men, women and war*. London: Cassell.

Waltz, Kenneth. 1959. *Man, the state, and war*. New York: Columbia University Press.

Waltz, Kenneth. 1979. *Theory of international politics*. Reading, MA: Addison.

Wilson. David S. 2002. *Darwin's Cathedral: Evolution, religion, and the nature of society*. Chicago: University of Chicago Press.

Zerjal, Tatiana, Yali Xue, Giorgio Bertorelle, et al. 2003. The genetic legacy of the Mongols. *The American Journal of Human Genetics* 72:717–21.

8

Groups in Mind: The Coalitional Roots of War and Morality

John Tooby and Leda Cosmides

War, Coalitions, and the Human Condition

War is older than the human species. It is found in every region of the world, among all the branches of humankind. It is found throughout human history, deeply and densely woven into its causal tapestry. It is found in all eras, and in earlier periods no less than later. There is no evidence of it having originated in one place, and spread by contact to others. War is reflected in the most fundamental features of human social life. When indigenous histories are composed, their authors invariably view wars – unlike almost all other kinds of events – as preeminently worth recording. The foundational works of human literature – the *Iliad,* the *Bhagavad-Gita,* the *Tanakh,* the *Quran,* the *Tale of the Heike* – whether oral or written, sacred or secular – reflect societies in which war was a pervasive feature.

War is found throughout prehistory (LeBlanc and Register 2003; LeBlanc 1999; Keeley 1996). Wherever in the archaeological record there is sufficient evidence to make a judgment, the traces of war are to be found. It is found across all forms of social organization – in bands, chiefdoms, and states. It was a regular part of hunter-gatherer life wherever population densities were not vanishingly low, and often even in harsh and marginal habitats. The existence of intergroup

191

conflict in chimpanzees suggests that our ancestors have been practicing war for at least 6 million years, and that it was a selective presence acting on the chimpanzee-hominid common ancestors and their
descendants (Manson and Wrangham 1991; Wilson and Wrangham
2003; Boehm 1992). The evidence indicates that aggressive conflict
among our foraging ancestors was substantial enough to have constituted a major selection pressure, especially on males (Keeley 1996;
Manson and Wrangham 1991). Careful ethnographic studies of living peoples support this view (Chagnon 1983; Heider 1970). Indeed,
in some ethnographically investigated small-scale societies where
actual rates can be measured, a third of the adult males are reported
to die violently (Keeley 1996), with rates going as high as 59 percent,
reported for the Achuar (Bennett Ross 1984). Coalitions – especially
male coalitions – and intergroup rivalries are a cross-culturally universal feature of human societies ranging from hunter-gatherer societies
to complex, post-industrial societies. Expressions of coalitionalism
include states, politics, war, racism, ethnic and religious conflict, civil
war, castes, gang rivalries, male social clubs, competitive team sports,
video games, and war re-enactment (Alexander 1987; Keegan 1994;
Sidanius and Pratto 2001; Tiger 1969; Tooby and Cosmides 1988;
Tooby, Cosmides, and Price 2006).

Our core claim is that theoretical considerations and a growing body of empirical evidence support the view that the human
mind was equipped by evolution with a rich, multicomponent
coalitional psychology. This psychology consists of a set of species-typical neurocomputational programs designed by natural
selection to regulate within-coalition cooperation and between-
coalition conflict in what, under ancestral conditions, was a fitness promoting way (Tooby and Cosmides 1988; Kurzban, Tooby,
and Cosmides 2001; Price, Cosmides, and Tooby 2002; Tooby,
Cosmides, and Price 2006). Ancestrally, coalitions and alliances
ranged from dyads to (rarely) hundreds of individuals. Across
human evolution, the fitness consequences of intergroup aggression (war), intimidation, and force-based power relations inside
communities (politics), were large, especially when summed over
coalitional interactions of all sizes.

These selection pressures built our coalitional psychology, which
expresses itself in war, politics, group psychology, and morality. The
evolutionary dynamics of war, coalitional behavior, and moral interactions are worth studying because the past world of conflict and cooperation is reflected in the present architecture of the human mind.

The Logic of Conflict

It is impossible to understand the social dynamics of collective aggression and alliance without first understanding, at least broadly, the psychological adaptations that evolved in response to the adaptive problems posed by individuals interacting with each other. It is on these foundations that subsequent adaptations for collective interactions were built.

Entropy and aggression: Aggression is the targeted infliction of disorder on one organism by another. There are two classes of benefits animals derive from aggression, and that therefore drive the evolution of control circuitry and weaponry for the targeted infliction of disorder.

The benefit of removing obstacles to fitness promotion: The first benefit occurs when the continued survival or activity of the other organism (the target) is harmful to the actor. If the target's continued survival suppresses the actor's fitness, then the actor increases its fitness by causing the death or incapacitation of the target. A typical example occurs in langurs. Langur infants whose nursing inhibits maternal ovulation are killed by the unrelated new resident male (Hrdy 1980).

Genetic relatedness and cooperative networks inside the same band and (to a lesser extent) the same tribe place restraints on the violent elimination of others whose fitness is negatively correlated with the actor. But members of other groups, outside the boundary of kinship and cooperative networks often fall into the category of fitness suppressors – for example, by virtue of occupying habitat that could benefit the aggressors, or because they threaten displacements of their own sooner or later if left unchecked. Intergroup raiding among chimpanzees (Wilson and Wrangham 2003; Boesch this volume) fits into this category. One can view neighboring groups of males locked into long-term demographic competition over productive habitat, and possibly also over the females that would be supported by it. Much raiding among small-scale human societies appears to fit into the same pattern (e.g., Chagnon 1983; Manson and Wrangham 1991; Boehm 1992). Unlike chimpanzees, however, humans also engage in more dramatic and organized wholesale slaughters and population displacements (Zimmerman 1981). History and prehistory are full of conflict-driven population displacements, and historical analysis of small face-to-face groups typically shows the same patterns (Chagnon 1983).

Aggression as bargaining power: The second class of benefit organisms accrue from aggression is bargaining power, which can be used to modify the behavior of others favorably. Obvious examples include using threats or the actuality of aggression to induce others to cede contested resources that otherwise would be monopolized by rivals; punishing others for taking actions which are fitness reducing; and deterring others from attack or exploitation. Wars among foragers commonly also have these characteristics, and power-based bargaining forms the heart of political interactions within groups.

Hate and anger as evolved computational programs: We suggest that in humans these two benefits of aggression, the elimination of fitness suppressors and bargaining, are regulated by two different motivational programs, which we will call "hate" and "anger." Hate is (1) generated by cues that the existence and presence of individuals or groups stably imposes costs substantially greater than the benefits they generate, and (2) is upregulated or downregulated by cues of relative power (formidability), and by cues signaling the degree to which one's social network is aligned in this valuation. (It is also worth investigating whether, as seems likely, there is a special emotion mode "rage" designed for combat, which orchestrates combat adaptations along with murderous motivational processes.)

We and our colleagues have proposed that anger is an evolved emotion program that evolved in the service of bargaining (Sell, Tooby, and Cosmides, 2009; Tooby, Cosmides et al. 2008). There are two bargaining tools which social organisms have available to them: (1) the threat or actuality of inflicting costs, and (2) the threat or actuality of withholding benefits. According to the recalibrational theory of anger, anger is an evolved regulatory program designed to orchestrate the deployment of these tools in order to cost-effectively bargain for better treatment and to resolve conflicts of interest in favor of the angry individual.

Welfare trade-off ratios, formidability indices, and conferral indices: We hypothesize that there are three families of computed regulatory variables that interact in the anger system to regulate decisions. The first is the *welfare trade-off ratio*, or WTR_{ij}. For a given individual i, the WTR regulates the weight that the actor i places on the welfare of a specific individual j compared to the weight the actor places on the self (i), when making decisions that have impacts on the welfare of i and j (Tooby et al. 2008; Delton et al. forthcoming; Sell et al. 2009).

The bargaining specialization outlined by the recalibrational model of anger computes the WTR it expects from specific other to self. Its function is to elicit the maximum WTR from each specific other that it can enforce cost-effectively, given its bargaining position. This bargaining position is set by the individual's relative ability to inflict costs and to confer benefits – external variables that the cognitive architecture must internally register to regulate the individual's negotiative behavior in a fitness promoting way. Hence, the anger system uses two different families of internal variables to regulate behavior: formidability indexes, designed to track the ability of self and others to inflict costs; and conferral indexes, designed to track the ability of self and others to confer benefits. The anger system registers the formidability of self and other, and the ability to confer benefits of self and other, to set the conditions of acceptable treatment by the other.

The design and operation of the anger program: On this theory, when the anger program detects that the other party is not placing "sufficient" weight on the welfare of the actor (i.e., its WTRji is too low), anger is triggered. Indeed, experimental evidence supports the view that it is a low WTR, and not just harm per se, that triggers anger (Sell, Cosmides, and Tooby, 2009). When activated, the anger program then deploys its negotiating tactics, by the threat or actuality of inflicting costs (aggression); or where cooperation exists, by the threat or actuality of withdrawing or downregulating expected benefits. Acts or signals of anger communicate that, unless the target sufficiently increases the weight it places on the angry individual's welfare, the actor will inflict costs on, or withdraw benefits from, the target. When these anticipated or experienced fitness costs are greater for the target than the cost of placing more weight on the actor's welfare, then the target's motivational system should increase its WTR toward the actor. It will only be advantageous for the target of the anger to recalibrate its WTR_{ji} upward when the inflicted costs or withdrawn benefits would be greater than the costs of placing more weight on the welfare on the angry individual. This threshold therefore defines the conditions where anger will be effective in recalibrating the target. Because organisms are selected to pursue strategies when they are effective, this therefore also defines the conditions in which anger should be triggered in the actor. That is, the WTR that the actor considers itself "entitled to" (i.e., the level of treatment that will not provoke its anger) is a function of the actor's relative ability to inflict costs (formidability) compared to the target, or (in cooperative relationships) a function of the actor's relative ability to confer or withhold benefits. The anger system motivates the actor to undertake actions to recalibrate the target of its anger by showing the target that it will be worse off by continuing to behave in ways that place too little weight on the actor's interests. Other things being equal, high formidability individuals are able to create incentives for low formidability individuals to assign a greater weight on their welfare.

Formidability and male combat identity: Formidability or fighting ability is the capacity to inflict costs on others (Sell, Cosmides, and Tooby 2008). Formidability is therefore a major determinant of bargaining position. Accordingly, natural selection favors the evolution of design features that enhance the ability to inflict costs – both circuitry for the effective deployment of violence, and physical structures like fangs or muscles that support successful aggression. In the human case, evidence supports the predictions from the recalibrational theory of anger that stronger men feel more entitled, anger more easily, prevail more in conflicts of interest, and more strongly approve of war as a means of settling disputes (Sell, Tooby and Cosmides, 2009).

In order to make advantageous decisions about when to persevere or defer in conflicts, humans should have evolved specializations to make accurate assessments of individual differences in formidability, and there is now strong evidence of this (Sell, Cosmides, and Tooby 2009). Moreover, humans are among the more sexually dimorphic primates particularly in upper body strength – the strength component most relevant to combat – where males are 75 percent stronger (Lassek and Gaulin 2009). Because of this, a female will almost never find herself the strongest individual in mixed sex groups, and so dispute resolution through violence or its threat tends to be a near monopoly of adult males. Across surveyed cultures and time periods, women deploy physically aggressive strategies far less often than men do (Archer 2004; Campbell 1999; Daly and Wilson 1988).

The differential use of aggression by males and females has been a long-enduring feature of human sociality. Its enduring presence among our ancestors selected for a sexually dimorphic psychology (Daly and Wilson 1988; Tooby and Cosmides 1988) in which a central constituent of masculine identity is formidability and its deployment – individual fighting ability (which may be used in dispute resolution internal to the group) and warriorship (the characteristics responsible for successful participation in intergroup aggression). The male combat identity hypothesis is the claim that in addition to whatever cultural support there is for (or against) a masculine identity involving formidability, there is a core of evolved adaptations and sexually dimorphic calibrations in anatomy and physiology, systems of representation, and regulatory variables in motivation and emotion that orient males to cultivate an identity that navigates the challenges and opportunities of individual and collective aggression.

Males are designed by selection to be physically stronger; to threaten or deploy aggression more readily; to have sensorimotor and motivational adaptations to combat; to participate more readily and effectively in formidability-based coalitions, and to identify with them more strongly; to respond more to the potentiality of coalitional aggression by other groups; to have a more elaborated aggression-based coalitional psychology; to be aesthetically attracted to weapons and their skilled use; to be more interested in information and observations relevant to aggression; to have an appetite to improve one's formidability and maximize one's reputation for high formidability; to exhibit greater courage in potentially lethal physical encounters; to scrutinize and police others' perceptions of their formidability, status, courage, pain thresholds, competence in emergencies, and alliances; to represent others in terms of their formidability; and to be attentive to the skills and natural aptitudes in others relevant to formidability. Male status will be more based on formidability than female status. Men have more to win and to lose in intergroup conflicts. Hence, in conditions of intergroup rivalry, men should have higher evolved welfare trade-off weightings calibrated to trade-off individual welfare for group success. Broadly speaking, males should be more competitive with respect to coalitional rivalries. We expect these dimensions of male anatomical and neurocomputational architecture to be coupled together, so that they can be upregulated or downregulated by epigenetic cues (e.g., maternal condition, testosterone, methylation), as well as by neurocomputational regulation that turns dimensions of masculine combat identity up or down based on developmental environment, social context, and personal characteristics (e.g., strength). It seems likely that male combat identity should heavily overlap with a hypothesized sexually dimorphic hunting identity, an activity in which similar skills are also deployed. Both males and females should have a "theory of group mind" parallel to "theory of mind" specializations, but in males this interpretive orientation should be more easily activated and should process information relevant to alliance-based formidability more readily.

Selection for Alliances and Coalitions

Benefits flow to individuals with higher formidabilities, and one important way an individual can increase its formidability is by coordinating his or her potential for aggression with one or more others: that is, by constituting alliances and coalitions. In conflicts, the individual not only has its own formidability, but also a coalition-derived formidability that under normal conditions will be large. In general, it is plausible to suppose that when formidabilities are not too unequal, two individuals can defeat one individual, three can defeat two, and so on. Resources and reproductive advantage flow to those who form alliances over those who do not, revolutionizing the social world. Once alliances enter the social world, and individuals are no longer social atoms, individual formidability no longer necessarily generates outcomes, and linear dominance hierarchies are no longer necessarily the overriding social dimension. The game dynamics and cognitive challenges of social interactions become far more complex. The efficiency (or inefficiency) with which individual formidability could be combined into coalitional formidability would have had a major impact on ancestral human social ecologies.

The benefits of augmenting one's own formidability with coalition-derived formidability is seemingly such a general selection pressure that it poses the puzzle of why virtually all animal species are not driven to high levels of coalitional behavior. In reality, relatively few are. Why? We think that there are a series of adaptive information processing problems that must be solved if this pathway to formidability-enhancement and mutual goal realization is to be exploited (Tooby and Cosmides 1988).

When closely analyzed, the adaptive information processing problems posed by coalition formation and its associated game dynamics are numerous and difficult to solve, restricting the evolutionary emergence of robust coalitions (Tooby and Cosmides 1988; Tooby, Cosmides, and Price 2006). The actual distribution of alliances and coalitions among animal species suggests a series of answers to this puzzle (Tooby and Cosmides 1988; Tooby, Cosmides, and Price 2006). In particular:

1. Close kinship collapses or reduces many of the game-dynamical obstacles to coalition formation because inclusive fitness effects can often outweigh costs to individual direct fitness (as among social insects or, to a lesser extent, among female matrilines in primates);
2. Cognitive sophistication in large-brained social species (e.g., mammals, especially primates) preadapts certain species for evolving cognitive specializations capable of overcoming the game-dynamic obstacles to

extending coalitions beyond close kinship; robust coalitions that extend beyond close kin are particularly notable features of the social life of the more cognitively sophisticated species (e.g., chimpanzees, dolphins, humans), supporting the view that the computational complexity of coalitional behavior is a key piece of the puzzle of why so many species lack robust coalitions;

3. Coalitions are easier to evolve where there are conditions that promote fitness lotteries (such as mobbing or hunter-gatherer combat); that is, where coalition members are behind a veil of ignorance as to who will pay the costs and who will reap the benefits of a coalitional event (see Tooby and Cosmides 1988, for discussion);

4. Fast-acting weaponry or tools that operate at a distance can probabilistically decouple inflicting costs from incurring costs (e.g., in carnivores such as hyenas and lions; or in humans equipped with weapons). This is one key factor precipitating coalitional fitness lotteries. Fast-acting weaponry can shorten the interval between the time the participant detects it will incur a major injury and the time it can withdraw (the harm imminence-withdrawal interval); when this interval is routinely too short to withdraw, the cost of being in a coalition is distributed as a probability cloud that collapses unforeseeably on random participants; in such cases, the aggressing individual's fitness prospects are predicted by the average payoff minus the average cost accruing to the group – an easier threshold to cross. In contrast, in close combat (such as unarmed chimpanzees engage in), striking blows invites receiving blows, and so more aggressive individuals incur higher costs. We expect that the introduction of projectile weapons by themselves should have intensified warfare, simply because of their game theoretic effects (i.e., randomizing who pays costs, and socializing the costs of combat. Changes in technology relevant to these variables should also have an impact on social structure. Stoning, thrusting spears, throwing spears, atlatls, bows, expensive bronze weapons, inexpensive iron weapons, flintlocks – these should all have changed warfare and the associated social structure. Weaponry that reduces the advantages of individual strength and/or allows multiple individuals to cost-effectively combine their formidabilities could contribute to more egalitarian social forms. Changes in social structure over human history can be broadly linked to these technological changes. More broadly, human hunter-gatherers tend to be egalitarian to some degree. This is an outcome that can be attributed to our cognitive capacities for coalition formation – a capacity that allows the many to limit exploitation that would otherwise be perpetrated by dominating individuals (see, for example, Boehm 1992).

Indeed, the harm-imminence – withdrawal-interval is a critical variable regulating the game dynamics of alliances, as is the link between injury, post-combat formidability, and post-combat bargaining position. The problem begins with the fact that when fighting, incurring a cost for the coalition lowers the formidability the individual can deploy to bargain for its share of the winnings. Consider elephant seals, or other species whose combat involves relatively slow attrition. Inflicting a cost in such species is closely associated with incurring damage, and at a relatively slow rate. When damage is incurred, the formidability of the animal is lowered. If the attacker is part of a dyadic alliance, the attacker's future ability to enforce its share of the winnings against its ally depends on its subsequent formidability. If attacking will decrease the attacker's formidability to a point where it cannot enforce its share of the winnings, then the individual should refrain from attacking in the first place, or withdraw when the rate of damage predicts the imminence of formidability decline. Such attacks would constitute one-shot games. In short, when the harm imminence-withdrawal interval is large, then the alliance dynamics unravel cooperation. In contrast, when the harm imminence-withdrawal interval is too short, then there is not time enough for the attacker to respond by withdrawing from the fight. The individual should withdraw at the point when the attacker ceases to share risks equally with its partner, and begins to receive unequal damage to its formidability. So, at the point of attack, each attacker faces a veil of ignorance that averages payoffs across the coalition members. As long as the net payoff is positive, the coalition should not unravel. It is also easy to see how inclusive fitness effects among related individuals could cushion and stabilize these dynamics.

Forming and Maintaining Alliances

Alliances pose a series of adaptive problems that selected for cognitive and motivational specializations for their solution: For example, individuals must be able to form and maintain alliances, recruit allies, evaluate and select allies, motivate allies to support them, influence alliances to take those actions which are beneficial to the individual, and map the alliance structure of their social world. Cognitively, individuals in a world with coalitions must be equipped with programs that detect alliances (evidence supports the view that humans have such an alliance detector; Kurzban, Tooby, and Cosmides 2000); these neurocomputational programs must be able to assign formidability estimates to alliances as well as to individuals (using a formidability-integrating function of some kind);

they must be able to integrate their estimate of an individual's formidability with their estimate of the individual's coalition-derived formidability (Ermer 2008).

Assigning formidabilities to coalitions underlies a range of human social realities: group rank, the redirection of resources from less formidable to more formidable groups, displacement from territories, and the entire panhuman suite of wars, intergroup rivalries and conflicts, group-based privileges, and power differentials. This superstructure requires a psychology of group formidability, including alliance formidability detection.

Formidability can also be altered behaviorally: It is typically too costly for humans to carry their weapons with them on all occasions, and so formidability asymmetries are magnified during ambushes and surprise attacks. Where conflicts are likely or endemic (e.g., chimpanzee or ancestral hunter-gatherer zero sum territory competition) such a payoff structure favors "first strikes," raiding, and the offensive initiation of conflicts. In short, the human entry into the cognitive niche (which carries with it the human ability to act in coalitions over long distances and extended time periods in a coordinated way) intensifies the payoffs to initiating collective aggression (Tooby and DeVore 1987; Wilson and Wrangham 2003).

The two biggest obstacles to the evolution of alliances and coalitions are the problem of free-riding (Tooby and Cosmides 1988; Price, Cosmides, and Tooby 2002), and the problem of coordination (Tooby, Cosmides, and Price 2006). A coalition can be defined as a group of individuals that coordinate their actions to achieve common goals and share the resultant benefits. From this definition, it is apparent that coalitions depend on (1) adaptations for solving problems of coordination, and (2) adaptations for solving problems arising from benefit allocation not being conditioned on contributory behavior (i.e., free-riding). If individuals do not coordinate their behavior toward some common goal or benefit, then there is no coalition. If free-riders outcompete cooperators, then coalitions cannot stably evolve.

Anti-free rider adaptations: How is the problem of free-riding solved? From a cognitive perspective, a coalition is an *n*-party exchange, in which each participant is entitled to receive benefits from the action of co-participants conditional on the participant's supplying contributions to the exchange (Tooby, Cosmides, and Price 2006). Free riders are individuals who take disproportionate benefits from coalitional projects compared to other participants without paying proportionate costs. Evidence supports the view that humans have a cognitive specialization for detecting free riders (Delton, Cosmides, and Tooby, forthcoming).

Secondly, we and our colleagues have found evidence that humans evolved a motivational program that generates punitive sentiment toward free-riders in coalitions (Price, Cosmides, and Tooby 2002; Tooby, Cosmides, and Price 2006). Contributors to collective actions are motivated to have a negative WTR toward free riders. Another line of defense is a basic anti-exploitation orientation, including a motivational circuit to downregulate contribution as a function of how much free-riding is going on (Tooby, Cosmides, and Price 2006).

Adaptations for coordination: Coordination poses even greater difficulties for the formation and operation of alliances and coalitions (for discussion, see Tooby, Cosmides, and Price 2006): An individual is a unitary information processor, and can be expected to support itself. Even a dyadic alliance is not a unitary information processor, and coalitions only exist and function when their members coordinate their actions to some productive extent. Individuals have different interests, locations, loyalties, values, social relationships, formidabilities, and information. Moreover, humans are presented with an uncountably large number of alternative cooperative projects (n-party exchanges), each with a different matrix of payoffs for the participants. Indeed, coalitions are by their nature coordination games in which payoffs are a function of the number of participants who contribute to the same project productively, and their contingent interrelationships.

To coordinate on a single project, potential coalition members must mutually collapse the space of possibilities down in their minds to the same one (or a few that can be carried out simultaneously). We think that adaptations for coalitional coordination include programs implementing a theory of group mind; programs implementing a theory of interests; programs implementing a theory of human nature; programs for leadership and followership; the outrage system; theory of mind; coregistration programs for solving common knowledge problems; language; and an underlying species-typical system of situation representation which frames issues in similar ways for different individuals.

Common knowledge: One kind of difficulty of coordination can be clarified by the concept of common knowledge, which the philosopher David Lewis introduced to describe knowledge of the following kind (Lewis 1969; see also Nozick 1963; Aumann 1976; Chwe 2003). For a group of agents, common knowledge exists of proposition x when all the agents in the group know x; they all know that they all know x, they all know that they all know that they know x, a recursion that continues ad infinitum. Cognitively speaking, this is an implausible set of representations, not least because it requires infinite storage and infinite time. Obviously, it needs to be recast in computationally realizable, adaptationist terms. But why is this important? An *n*-party exchange is an example of intercontingent behavior (Tooby, Cosmides, and Price 2006): What I do is contingent on what you will do, while what you do is simultaneously contingent on what I will do. That makes my behavior contingent on my knowing your knowledge of my behavior, which is itself contingent on your knowing my knowledge of your representation of my behavior (and so on) – mirrors reflecting each other endlessly. Mutually coordinated behavior among two or more actors cannot be achieved without some analog to the set-theoretic relationships analyzed by logicians as common knowledge. If cooperation and coalitions require common knowledge, and common knowledge requires infinite cognitive resources, how can coalitions or cooperation exist?

The first thing to recognize is that the standard common knowledge formulation rests on a flawed folk concept of "knowledge," a flawed assumption of economic rather than ecological rationality, and the flawed blank slate view of the mind. In contrast, a large number of neurocomputational adaptations involve specialized systems of valuation, and depend on internal regulatory variables that do not correspond to beliefs or communicable representations ("knowledge"), but rather to value-related settings in motivational, emotional, and other decision-making structures (Tooby, Cosmides, Sell, et al. 2008; Tooby and Cosmides 2008; for a detailed example, see Lieberman, Tooby, and Cosmides 2007). As discussed, these include such computational elements as WTRs, formidability indexes, kinship indexes, sexual value indexes, and so on. For successful behavioral coordination to occur, agents must (1) converge on a common representation of a situation, (2) converge on similar (or compatible) regulatory variable weights relevant to the situation, (3) recognize the convergence, and (4) converge implicitly or explicitly on a cooperative response. The requirement that the architectures "recognize the convergence" does not mean they represent common knowledge in the formal sense. It only means that the architecture has one or more regulatory variables that are increased when there are cues of convergence, and that when a threshold is passed (set by a selective history of payoffs that exceed uncertainty-caused costs), implements the cooperative behavior. There need be no explicit and deliberative representation of others' knowledge states at all. Such a design acts as if it satisfied the common knowledge criterion for game play, without actually having or representing common knowledge.

Sharing the same evolved architecture provides a partial foundation for resolving the game theoretic problem of common knowledge with finite cognitive resources. For many basic aspects of jointly experienced situations, humans, by virtue of being members of the same species, already share a common architecture containing a rich and detailed set of adaptations for interpreting and responding to the world largely in the same way. The space of logical possibilities is radically pared down to manageable proportions by possession of the same situation-interpretive machinery. If humans have adaptations for different families of evolutionarily recurrent games and strategies of play, then they can count on others having the same adaptations – what might be called architectural coordination. (Because the coordination required between psychological architectures diverges from the normal meaning of knowledge, we prefer to call this necessary parallelism *mental coordination* rather than *common knowledge*.)

The more similar the information states of the two architectures, the more likely they will be to arrive at the same situation representation. Hence, the more similar the experiences of two architectures, the more coordinated they will be. We will call the process in which two or more individuals experience parallel inputs that bring about mental coordination *coregistration*. Spending time together, joint attention, being together at critical events – all obviously increase the frequency of coregistration and hence mental coordination. That is why these factors, along with the ease of mind-reading, spontaneous rapport, being *simpatico*, etc. are important facilitators of friendships and other alliances, as well as of leadership-followership relations. Indeed, the payoffs to coordination also plausibly selected for complementary adaptations that produce leadership-followership roles (Tooby, Cosmides, and Price 2006; Tooby and Cosmides, 1979). Coregistered events can also play the role of coordinating coalitions ("outrages" – coregistration of outgroup members harming ingroup members; Tooby, Cosmides, and Price 2006).

Emotions and the psychophysics of mental coordination: For cooperative action to be taken, evolved procedures must exist for inducing or recognizing sufficient coordination in situation representation (e.g., others represent a joint threat) and regulatory variables (e.g., our formidability indices are too low to resist them). It is worth noting that specific emotions are evolved systems of internal coordination activated in response to evolutionarily recurrent situations such as danger, contamination, conflict, or pleasure (Tooby and Cosmides 2008). Their activation signals that the individual has assigned the particular situation encountered to one of a finite set of interpretations recognizable to the entire species. Emotions also organize motivational variables in predictable ways. Because of this, they are ideally suited, when signaled through facial and postural expressions of emotion, to show the individual's situation representation, and associated regulatory variable recalibrations. That is, coregistration of emotional broadcasts provides one solution to mental coordination, and its role in coordination may offer a selectionist explanation for the puzzle of why expressions of emotion are nearly automatic and quasi-involuntary.

More generally, there seems to be a psychophysics of mutual coordination and coregistration, involving (for example) joint attention and mutual gaze, especially timed when salient new information could be expected to activate emotional or evaluative responses in one's companions. The benefits of coregistration and mental coordination can explain (at least in part) an appetite for co-experiencing (watching events is more pleasurable with friends and allies), the motivation to share news with others, for emotional contagion, for gravitation in groups toward common evaluations, for aversion to dissonance in groups, for conformity, for mutual arousal to action as with mobs (payoffs shift when others are coordinated with you), and so on. The weightings occurring when information is coregistered should be more intense, because mentally coordinated weightings can be acted on with fewer costs. Issues of coordination provide a reason why coalitions should form around denser social networks whose connectivity provides faster coordination among its individual constituents. Fractal fissures in coalitional structure around which factions form should similarly track network structure.

Group interests: The problem of coordination includes but is not limited to common knowledge problems. Even if all parties had perfect mutual knowledge (which they do not), each would still be confronted with the unlimited set of alternative n-party exchanges, and the fact different payoffs and different characteristics among potential participants will typically lead each to favor different projects and coalitional boundaries. Negotiating common projects, maintaining allies, and choosing courses of action in the context of coalitions all require the ability to predict and understand others' values, because one individual's actions affect others' interests or welfare.

Groups as agents: Another critical coalitional adaptation was the widening of the concept of agent in evolved procedures so that representations that formerly could have referred solely to human individuals become able to refer also to coalitions, alliances, communities, and other collectives (Tooby, Cosmides, and Price 2006). That is, groups can be mentally represented to be agents (a useful delusion), and so to be things to which we can attribute mental states as if they had a single mind. This delusion is a useful one, because groups sometimes do arrive at mental coordination making them similar to an agent. Common intentional states, joint action, mental coordination – and cues that increase the probability of these – should increase the perception of groups as entities – what social psychologists call *entitativity* (Ip, Chiu, and Wan 2006).

The ability to represent groups as agents allows us to construe groups as having intentions, attitudes, emotions, knowledge, and so on. Groups can have status, formidability, rank, stigma, and dominance relations, not to mention alliances, friendships and enmities. The group-as-agent construal allows individuals to represent themselves in exchange relationships with groups. Being able to represent a group as an agent allows us to apply the intuitive theory of interests specialization to groups – that is, it allows humans to think of groups as having interests, and therefore to approve or disapprove of an individual's actions. This last step is one of several keys to understanding morality. Not only can groups "have" emotions, but equally, they become interpretable as objects of our emotions and motivational programs, such as anger, gratitude, guilt, shame, welfare-trade-off representations, formidability, kin-oriented representations, and so on. That is, the whole apparatus that evolved to deal with individuals was modified so that it could be extended to groups.

Alliances, coalitions, and amplification coalitions. We define a *coalition* as a group of individuals that coordinate their actions to achieve a common goal. A coalition constitutes an *n*-party exchange, with the compliance of its participants dependent on the compliance of the others. The common goal could be anything, and therefore the coalition could be transient. However, coordination once achieved is intrinsically valuable, because it can be turned to many ends, and realize gains of many types. So coalitions among people who repeatedly interact tend to gravitate toward becoming amplification coalitions (Tooby, Cosmides, and Price 2006). That is, an *amplification coalition* is defined as an *n*-party exchange system whose function is the amplification of the ability of each of its members to realize her interests in daily events by cost-effectively combining welfare trade-offs and joint efforts with the other members. The underlying principle is Dumas' one for all, and all for one. We use *alliance* to mean a a dyadic or small-scale amplification coalition (primarily formed out of dyadic links), whose major function is prevailing in conflicts of interest against other individuals or coalitions.

The characteristics of a given kind of social relationship (e.g., mateship, friendship, or kinship) may involve the operation of multiple adaptations reflecting distinct selection pressures. Social relationships that are coalitions are not reduced to being only coalitions. For example, we hypothesize that friendship circuits have a strong alliance/amplification dimension, sensitive to the registration of mutual support when either party is challenged by third parties. (The closeness of a friendship can be operationalized by the intensity with which one person is favored over another when there is a conflict of interest between them.) But as engagement relationships they also have strong elements of fitness interdependence, which reinforces their stability as alliances (Tooby and Cosmides 1996). And there is also the expectation that each friend's welfare will be more greatly realized in daily events by exchange, by cost-effectively combining welfare trade-offs (such as risk-pooling), and by cooperative labor.

Moreover, public signals of support (or their absence) lead individuals and sets of individuals to revise what they attempt to possess, consume, or do. In consequence, our species-typical psychology evolved to represent coalitions as having rank, status, or formidability-justified entitlement. Because everything can be taken from a powerless individual or group, humans (especially men) have evolved specializations that motivate forming or affiliating with groups, that motivate affiliating with a coalition over no coalition, and that motivate affiliating with higher status coalitions (that will accept them) over lower status coalitions. That is, we have specializations for coalitional identity formation, and these operate even when the coalitional activities they result in have no obvious function (see, for example, Tiger 1969 on the case of fraternal organizations in developed societies; and Rofe 1984, on anxiety and the need for affiliation). Ancestral wars were intercommunity conflicts, but this system of dispute and alliance extended all the way down to the

dyadic level. Our coalitional adaptations should guide us to participate in coalitions at all fractal and nested levels, so that at whatever
scale a dispute occurs, one has allies to press one's case (see Sahlins
1961; Boehm 1992 on segmentary social organization).

The dynamics of unification and fractionation: Unless there are large
benefits that can only be obtained by large-scale coalitions, the
interests of smaller scale factions will undermine the cohesion or
preclude the existence of larger, encompassing coalitional levels.
Conversely, to form a large-scale coalition, individuals and lower
level cells must surrender their agendas to the labor contributions
required by the larger scale project. Negotiating phase changes to
different scales of coalitional cooperation in a fitness promoting way
has been a chronic adaptive problem for humans, and we appear
to have circuits specialized for this function. Both strategic *faction-
alization* (fragmentation of a larger coalition) and strategic unification and inclusion appear to happen in response to cues of (1) the
payoffs existing at different scales, and (2) cues of mental coordination, such as coregistration of collective events. The underlying
theme for increasing unification is the evocation of cues of fitness
interdependence (Tooby and Cosmides 1996). Coalitional identity
and affiliation can shift upwards, with existing coalitional identities
being shed like clothes. Computationally, this involves recalibrating
WTRs upwards toward those who were previously outgroup members, as well as toward higher-level coalitions. Of course, the most
reliable facilitator for higher-level coalitions is external conflict with
a large competing coalition – something repeatedly found in the
historical record. The prospect of large gains or huge losses through
displacement, expropriation, subordination, or extermination is one
of the few reliable signals that the formation of large-scale coalitions
would be worthwhile.

Alliance mapping and coalitional evaluation: Social life is riddled with
implicit and explicit coalitions across a range of fractal scales, and
choosing courses of action requires anticipating which responses and
latent coalitions might materialize in response to various actions. To
accomplish this, we think there are a number of evolved inferential
elements for alliance mapping (e.g., between two people, patterns of
assistance and prosociality, such as sharing, close kinship, maintained
proximity and approach, coresidence, positive affect, mirrored affect,
empathy, etc. imply alliance and stable high WTRs; in contrast,
zero-sum conflict, anger, disgust, contempt, avoidance, resource
confiscation, unmirrored affect, counterempathy, unwillingness to

share, nonassistance and goal-blocking, exploitation and aggression obviously imply enmity and negative WTRs). These are combined with other evolved inferential circuits, such as generalization of social relationships to allies: e.g., positive action by one person towards a target recruits positive recalibration in the target's allies; and especially negative action towards a target recruits anger and punitive sentiment in the target's allies toward the malefactor. Such inferential and motivational elements (with proper scope limitations) can be combined recursively to deduce a social map and associated mental contents (e.g., the friend of my enemy is my enemy; the enemy of my enemy is my ally; the enemy of my friend is my enemy, etc.).

These inferential elements provide input to the alliance detector, which we have begun to map (Kurzban et al. 2001). Its ideal output should be an alliance map (perhaps resembling a social network map) that not only represents individuals in terms of the ongoing coalitions they belong to, but also: (1) the differential strength or clustering of their actual and potential alliances to others in the social system, for each likely issue; (2) factors that predict alliance value and disposition: e.g., their trustworthiness, duration of their participation in the coalition, history or summary of their level of contribution (their welfare trade-off propensity to the group account compared to self), observed WTRs, individual characteristics (like kinship) that predict interests, individual and alliance formidability, etc. The discriminative alliance system should use such characteristics to assess others' value as coalitional members or enemies, and to regulate motivations for recruitment, rejection, price setting for inclusion (e.g., subordination or required level of contribution). Coalition membership should be associated with indices that track how valuable the individual's membership is – with membership being a fuzzy set relationship. They should also track an estimated WTR propensity from the individual to the coalition. Acts of sacrifice for a coalition or individual are highly informative, as are acts of contribution and allegiance cues. Such acts should trigger categorization as coalition members, as well as changes in the index tracking how strong membership is – how "good" a member a person is.

Status. As discussed, formidability – the ability to inflict costs – is only one kind of bargaining tool. The second family of bargaining tools is the ability to withhold or confer benefits. Formidability is tracked by formidability indices, and the ability to confer or withhold benefits is tracked by implicitly registered conferral indices. Among humans, evidence indicates that both appear to be registered, both appear to determine who prevails in conflicts of interest, and both regulate the deployment of anger as an implicit bargaining system (Sell, Tooby, and Cosmides 2009). During human evolution the ability to cooperate and to produce alienable benefits greatly expanded, so the force-based logic of animal conflict has been greatly elaborated to include a co-equal cooperative dimension. Representations of formidability and the ability to confer or withhold benefits are the two direct components of individual status (Tooby and Cosmides 1996). Secondary components of formidability and benefit control include support in each of these negotiative modalities provided by others as individuals or coalitions. A third factor is the relative support one's supporters have, the support their supporters have in turn, and so on, as devalued by the probabilistic decay of support along network links – something akin to Google's page rank algorithm. A fourth factor is the ability to mentally coordinate others in the community (leadership). A fifth factor is common knowledge or mental coordination (or discoordination) of how these representations and weightings are ecologically distributed in the relevant population of social actors. That is, do I register that everyone else registers this person as high status? A sixth factor is moral status, to be discussed later. While we hypothesize that each of these (formidability, conferral, support, leadership, coregistration of these variables, etc.) has its own proprietary representations or regulatory variables, they all need to be integrated into a single summary variable, status. A primary function of assigning a status index to an agent is to be able to assign weight to the bargaining power (and related properties) of the agent – whether that agent is an individual or coalition. That is, the function of a status index is to predict the fitness consequences that arise by engaging in conflict, cooperation, affiliation, proximity, welfare modifications, and other interactions with the agent. The status index is the summary function that evolved to track status. This index is based on an evolved status estimating system that takes the subcomponents (formidability indices, conferral indices, etc.) and integrates them into a decision-making data-structure. In general, the higher the status of the agent, the greater the WTR one expresses toward the agent.

The alliance detection system needs to assign status to individuals, clusters (potential coalitions), and mentally coordinated (actualized) coalitions, in order to usefully navigate the social world. The mental coordination of representations and status evaluations is crucial, because the reigning social reality is governed by how the population represents status. So, humans have motivational programs whose objects are status representations in the minds of others, and their distribution and coordination in the local population. Status is zero sum, at least among non-allies, generating a status rival matrix in the population. People like status increases for themselves and their friends and allies, and status reductions in their status rivals. They respond to the prospect of alternative courses of action in part by their status consequences. They engage in status operations, designed to increase status of themselves or their allies, or reduce status in others.

Coregistration cues – that is, the mutuality of social observation –should be an important regulator of decisions. A fight that no one else observes may only change the formidability indexes in the two participants, so the winner pays a given cost to accrue greater status in the mind of a single individual. If the entire community coregistered the fight, then the same cost would purchase a recalibration of his status in the minds of everyone – and a mental coordination of his enhanced status. So the motivational intensities of the status recalibrational emotions – shame and pride – will be proportionately greater to the extent that they lead to mental coordination (common knowledge) of the changed status among a larger set of individuals. Cues of coregistration are an important regulator of status operations (see, for example, Ermer, Cosmides, and Tooby 2008). High coregistration is a lubricant of recalibration, while low coregistration produces friction in social recalibration.

Musical chairs – competitive behavior under scarcity: In addition to a territory displacement game, a power-based bargaining game, and a demographic attrition game, we think that humans ancestrally played what might be called the musical chairs game: there is one less chair than there are players, when the music stops players rush to find a chair, and the one left standing is eliminated. The abundance of habitats varied greatly and unpredictably over time. The alliance maps of local populations involve clusterings, and areas where network links are sparser. Persons who might be tolerated or welcomed as part of the community during abundance might shift to imposing fitness costs by merely existing during times of scarcity. If the social network were equally dense everywhere, then any attempted exclusion would be difficult and involve costly conflict, recruiting equal numbers of allies on both sides. To the extent that there is mental coordination on network fissures (signaled, perhaps, by small daily acts of humiliation), then a spontaneous coalition of the well networked with high potential formidability could actualize itself to exclude marginal segments of the population. Hunger, for example, should provoke shifts in tolerance, acceptance, and themes of inclusion – not to mention, drops in oxytocin. The emergence of social dominance in complex societies that Sidanius and Pratto (2001) document may be rooted not only in adaptations for coalitional and intercommunity competition and status interactions, but also ancestral musical chairs interactions in more egalitarian societies.

Coregistration and the game of chicken: Imagine that two forager communities are locked, for example, in an ancestral, chimpanzee-like demographic war of attrition (i.e., where larger groups eventually replace groups that are slowly whittled away by raids). A male resident of the community benefits when members of the other community are killed. It weakens them as a threat, moves the territorial line so that more food is available to the male and his children, and so on (see Wilson and Wrangham 2003, on chimpanzees). Why wouldn't a sane male designed by selection to promote his fitness share in the benefits of others' actions, but shirk himself? (That is, why would not selection shape male psychology to avoid participation in offensive war?). His participation would only marginally increase these benefits, but he gets the full benefit of the costs he avoids (Olson 1965). The common participation of adult males in such situations has led some to argue that group selection is the driving force in human warfare (Bowles 2006). The risk contract of war (Tooby and Cosmides 1988) is one model of selection pressures involved in war, and models of punitive sentiment as an anti-free-riding adaptation may help to answer this question (Price, Cosmides, and Tooby 2002). However, there are other selection pressures which we think also operated. We think these act in a complementary fashion to reinforce selection for an evolutionarily stable coalitional psychology that accrues benefits from war.

Ethnographically, lethal conflict inside groups is treated very differently than homicide in intergroup conflict – within group homicide is typically punished, while attacks on enemies are typically socially valued. Death or maiming of a community member triggers factional within group conflict, the activation of allies, and potentially serious consequences. Still, conflicts of interest do occur inside communities, and may even erupt into violence. Further, humans can deploy lethal violence quickly, through the use of weapons – which are brandished and sometimes used in intracommunity conflicts (Chagnon 1983; Lee and DeVore 1976). Moreover, anger as a bargaining emotion (as well as male combat identity) causes face offs. Such encounters can be considered a game of chicken: One or both may be injured or killed unless one defers to the other. Yet, individuals are sanctioned for killing or maiming ingroup members – an event which would otherwise cause fitness-enhancing coregistration of the formidability of the winner.

Given these facts, one strategy that might stabilize contributions to offensive war arises from the fact that killing or defeating outgroup enemies – in contrast to ingroup members – is not sanctioned, but is seen as laudable. If a group of males conduct a raid or a battle, coregistration of their mutual exploits allows the mutual assessment of their relative formidabilities within the community and between the rivals – including characteristics like courage that are hard to assess in restrained ritual combat. These then set precedents about who should defer when conflicts with the potential for escalation occur among them. The individual who is mentally coordinated as being more formidable will not defer in games of chicken, because the expectation has been set that the other will defer. This is one pathway through which coalitional contributions are good for the individual – at least for the more formidable. Research, for example, supports the prediction that stronger males are more pro-war (Sell, Tooby, and Cosmides, 2009). They have an opportunity to display (and at lower risk than weaker and less skilled individuals), from which they will derive status benefits. To stay home is not only undercontribution (free-riding), and a failure to exploit an opportunity for status enhancement ("glory," "honor"), but could potentially be interpreted as weakness and cowardice by other males in the community. Many cultural practices that seem instrumentally bizarre (such as counting coup or trophy-taking; Turney-High 1949) make sense as displays designed to coregister one's formidability with ingroup members. This dynamic is why, in so many cultures, warriorship is constitutive of masculine identity. "Glory" and "honor" – intuitive concepts that correspond to the coregistration of formidability – have been major motivations for participating in war across the historical and ethnographic record.

Morality, Valuation, and the Ability to Act in Concert

We have argued that humans have a far more elaborated evolved psychology for forming, participating in, and dealing with coalitions than other species do. Although morality seems superficially unrelated to coalitions, we hypothesize that the evolution of adaptations for coalitions was a key trigger for the evolution of adaptations for morality (Tooby and Cosmides, 1979). That is, the evolution and elaboration of morality was midwifed by the capacity for the rapid recruitment of individuals into a coalition around a common interest that could be punitively enforced. More fully, we think that our moral psychology evolved (in part) as a natural extension of the adaptations underlying our coalitional psychology, as well as adaptations for social assortment and exclusion, in interaction with a number of other elements. As we will detail, these other elements include (1) pre-existing adaptations that evolved to solve other adaptive problems (e.g., language; negotiation); (2) a novel set of games (i.e., structured social interactions with payoffs) that were unleashed by the evolutionary expansion of coalitional and communicative adaptations; (3) novel features and adaptive problems inherent in the resulting social ecologies; and (4) adaptations that specifically emerged for successfully navigating the family of "moral" games that were endemic to this new coalitionally infused social world. We think that sketching out how these disparate elements interacted during our evolution can illuminate what the kind of thing morality is; how our species evolved a specialized moral psychology; and why, although our moral psychology is partly an outgrowth of our coalitional psychology, it is nonetheless distinct.

Negotiation and situation evaluation – the primary elements: Several kinds of pre-existing, premoral adaptations naturally interacted to produce first- order moral games. First, humans like many other animal species have adaptations for situation evaluation – values – that allow them to plan and choose more over less fitness- enhancing courses of action (Tooby, Cosmides, and Barrett 2005). Second, there exist suites of adaptations in humans that are designed to negotiate with others over the conduct of both self and others, based on valuations, alternatives, power, formidability, and status. As discussed, anger (for example) is one evolved program that implicitly organizes human bargaining, orchestrating the infliction or costs or the withdrawal of benefits in the service of prevailing (e.g., Sell, Tooby, and Cosmides, 2009). Negotiation occurs when we make our behavior conditional on others' conduct (through threatening to harm them, or to reduce or withhold benefit delivery); and vice versa. So, third, we are designed to attempt to influence others to act in conformity with our values. Fourth, others are simultaneously designed to incentivize us to act in conformity with their values.

Hence, first- order "moral games" are constituted by these complementary tugs of war, in which each agent negotiates to license the best obtainable course of action for the self, and each agent negotiates to obtain the most self-beneficial modification of the behavior of the other. Although these selection pressures operate to some extent on other species, the explosion in human instrumental behavior, and the human ability to communicate propositions with great precision vastly expanded the scope of social negotiation (far beyond messages such as "go away," or "mine" that are characteristics of other species). Whether one chooses to categorize these games of mutual influence as involving morality *per se*, it will subsequently become clear how they are foundational for phenomena that are widely categorized as moral.

The fact that first-order games of influence – even in a dyad – are treated by the mind as moral can be shown by considering the typical relationship of a parent and a young child, where the power asymmetry is large. The parent unproblematically uses the terms "right" and "wrong" to differentiate the parent's preferred courses of action for the child from those she dislikes (e.g., put away your toys when you are done; don't throw balls in the living room). Conduct in this case is moralized for the child, but not for the adult, since the child is too powerless to threaten the adult. Negotiating power is one ingredient that contributes to the formation of the moral domain. Exchange (or reciprocity), with its associated concept of "cheater" is an example of a dyadic first- order game in which the two participants have more equal power, and exercise it to modify each other's behavior advantageously.

The risk of others' coordinated action produces some components of the moral sense: The fifth element involved in the evolution of a distinctively moral psychology is an adaptive problem introduced by coalitions into the social ecology: From the perspective of any individual, there is a potentially dangerous power asymmetry. There are many others, and only one self, and others may join to form a powerful coalition (momentary or permanent) against any individual. This danger is relaxed to the extent an individual is powerful (such as a tyrant), and exacerbated to the extent an individual is powerless. If you take an action others strongly disvalue, they may combine to punish (harm) you, to your severe detriment. If you propose that others behave in ways that they strongly disvalue, they may combine to act against you. Because others' punishments or rewards are conditional on an individual's conduct, for any course of conduct being considered, the individual needs to add to the direct payoffs (e.g., the benefits of obtaining money from the till) the contingencies of reward and punishment that will be triggered in others (e.g., retaliation for theft). In short, the existence of others, together with their ability to respond, selected for adaptations that were designed to implicitly represent the values of others, and that weight others' values cost-effectively in the individual's own decision-making process. The values of even a single other may need to be taken into account (as in dyadic exchange), but the ability of others to rapidly form coalitions greatly multiplied their power and therefore the intensity of selection for adaptations that spontaneously weighted others' values.

Adaptations that register others' values and weight them (according to predictors of the consequences) constitute one key component of what Darwin called the "moral sense or conscience" (Darwin 1871; see also Hume 1751; Hutcheson 1728; Alexander 1979) and what Freud called the superego (Freud 1923). Indeed, this system should be designed to modify the mind's native valuations by adopting others' values implicitly as one's own (to a calibrated extent). The degree of this internalization of others' values should depend on the registration of how often one is monitored, how uncertain the identification of conditions of privacy are (i.e., what the information ecology is like), how great the penalties for detected deviance are, and how great the potential power imbalance is.

The opportunity to recalibrate others' choices produced additional, complementary components in the moral sense: Ancestrally, each individual faced the risk that one or more individuals would punish her for acting in defiance of their wishes. This selected for adaptations often characterized as "conscience" or the moral sense. The sixth element is simply the reciprocal of this: Each individual has the complementary potential to join with others to enforce their values on one or more others. We expect the human mind evolved adaptations for exploiting this social opportunity – that is, adaptations for (1) leveraging one's bargaining position by recruiting others into a coalition (however transient) around common values; and (2) enforcing its values by downregulating benefits or inflicting costs on those who deviate from these values. The fact that the anger program evolved to negotiate conflicts by inflicting costs or downregulating benefits explains why anger is evoked in the negotiations characteristic of moral games. The adaptations underlying the moral sense are designed not only for cost-effectively internalizing others values, but also for causing others to internalize the individual's values. One subsystem invites conformity to others' values, while the other unleashes morally censorious judgments, punitive sentiments or outrage designed to intimidate others into adopting one's values as their own.

Second order moral games: First- order moral games of individual mutual influence are transformed into second order moral games by the addition of coalitions. In second order games, coalitions are formed around enforcing the values that the coalition members commonly hold.

The moral domain is not a content-domain, and potentially encompasses an unlimited number of moral projects: The seventh element is a feature of the informational ecology faced by our post-coalitional ancestors. That is, agents playing second order moral games confronted a vast superset of alternative, potentially coalition-enforced values – far more than could possibly be actualized, especially given that many values and sets of values are mutually incompatible. For a morality to be actualized, this space of possibilities must be collapsed down to one. Indeed, one can get a sense of how large the set of potential moralities is by considering the immense cross-cultural range of real, documented moral projects and issues. The content that individual and local moralities are endowed with encompasses not only cross-culturally recurrent themes (e.g., don't murder an ingroup member) but extraordinarily heterogeneous and often contradictory contents (from Aztec ritual cannibalism and the National Socialist project to the psychedelic movement, Puritanism, sexual liberation, not revealing magicians' secrets, shocking the bourgeoisie, the Jainist prohibition on killing insects, and the restoration of the Caliphate). One answer to the question of why moral stances show such endless diversity is that our evaluative adaptations are designed to accept open input: All possible situations or outcomes must be able to be evaluated, in order for choice to operate with respect to encountered situations. If moral responses are derived in part from evaluative responses, and evaluation is open, it follows that morality is not a special content domain (like allocation or justice), but a posture with respect to any content that can be evaluated. Moreover, the surface contents of moralities often function merely as coalitional coordinative signals rather than as doctrines selected for their intrinsic attractiveness (e.g., the doctrine of predestination). Often moral contents are selected in order to signal the emergence of a new coalition, or to morally legitimize attacks on rivals based on pretexts arising from the surface properties of the rivals' moralities. Indeed, people often support moral projects not because they hold any intrinsic attraction but because of their downstream effects on rivals – for example, reducing the their status or weakening their social power.

Payoff distributions, coalitional maneuvering, and situation evaluation: The eighth element is the adaptive problem agents face because different moralities make different social group members winners and losers. That is, alternative values potentially distribute different payoffs among the participants (e.g., tolerance of infidelity favors attractive men at the expense of unattractive husbands and investment-deprived wives). The fact that different moralities privilege different individuals, combined with the fact that there are an unlimited number of possible alternative moralities, creates moral games concerning which moralities should reign in the social community. That is, there will be conflict between individuals and coalitions over which values out of the potential superset should spread in the social group. Second order games of morality involve individuals and emergent coalitions endlessly jockeying to advantageously actualize their values as the standard for punishment and reward, and to displace or preclude competing value projects that do not pay off as well for them. This approach explains why morality in a community is dynamic, and changes over time; why it is historically and culturally contingent; why it is contested and debated; why in the same time and place, whenever different sets of individuals are gathered – say, coalitions at different fractal scales – subtly or grossly different moralities are evoked within each group (e.g., men in their fraternities versus when they are with their mates). Which morality will be actualized depends on the specific set of coregistering individuals. Given the heterogeneous and fractal structure of groups in a population, moralities will be evoked with respect to the anticipated circle of players who will become aware of the deployment of a jointly defended value.

These games are further complexified by the fact that there are different roles in moral games, and the characteristics of different individuals will yield higher payoffs if they adopt some roles more than others. Roles include potential targets of moral attacks, who need to defend themselves; potential initiators of moral attacks; those who monitor; those who inflict punishment; those who withhold cooperation or deliver rewards; those who ostracize; and, of course, those who support and those who oppose the moral project. The distribution of individuals positioned to embody strategies advantageously, as well as the efficiencies of their combining forces, makes a difference to the dynamics of play. For example, high formidability individuals are better positioned to be enforcers and punishers, while leaders will be better situated to bring about mental coordination on the necessity for enforcement and punishment. Low power individuals will be more inclined to transfer information about the moral deviance of their fitness suppressors. Different adaptations should be associated with each role, although, of course, all of the different adaptations should be present in all normal individuals.; After all, individuals may often play more than one role simultaneously, and sooner or later might end up playing each role).

Moral communication to potential allies and targets: The ninth element shaping our moral adaptations involves the requirements that moral games place on moral communication. For an agent to successfully recruit others in support of her preferred value project, the value must be communicated first to potential recruits (the proponents of the value) − and (if there is enough support) then to those whose behavior is to be modified. That is, if it is to have the desired effect on modifying behavior, then it must also be communicated to its targets (e.g., potential robbers; partisans of equality for a dominated group, potentially unfaithful wives). Morality is "public" within a certain circle of players, however small. The issue of joint awareness within a circle of players is one factor that makes the moral game different from just any individual or small-scale bargaining or wielding of social influence. Approval and disapproval are exploratory probes that allow potential proponents to assess how widespread support will be for the proposed value. They also warn violators that they are being categorized as transgressing. Moral communication also often involves deception. Leaders, for example, may play a moral game in which they acquire moral power by conflating themselves and their discretionary actions with widely supported value projects (e.g., wrapping themselves in the flag). To attack them is to be seen as opposed to the moral project they are emblematic of.

The ladder effect and the pull toward depersonalization: The tenth element is what might be called the ladder effect in second order moral games − that is, what is the effect of larger and larger audiences on the content of successful moral projects. If individuals' interests often conflict, then the expression of a value in its personal form − this allocation injures me − will have only limited and small-scale appeal as a value around which to recruit the support of others. Only personal allies will support the cause of the injured individual, and so individualized disputes will have moral resonance only in small groups. To gain wider support, the value an individual launches can be recast in broader terms so that it simultaneously works in the interest of enough others to become the winning coalition-propelled value of its kind. As the moral representation moves from individual to individual and coalition to coalition, it will "evolve" – be progressively modified – by the set of players who engage it. Equally important, it will evolve (morph) because of how those who engage the value anticipate it will be received by a broader set of players.

To climb the ladder of increasingly wide support, a moral project cannot be seen as the instrument of simple parochial self-interest. This means that moral issues, as they encompass more players, increasingly take the form of rules, with "I support individual i" in an initial dispute evolving toward a rule, "for all x's in condition c must do/must not do action a." As the value spreads more widely within a circle, and is perceived as applying to more individuals, the different players will take sides depending on how they represent the proposal as potentially affecting them and their family and local allies. The contagious moral result therefore often sums up to outcomes not wholly divorced from average population utility (as distorted by social power, such as male privilege or the divine right of kings). However, this does not mean the evolved function of morality is maximizing group utility.

Morality, common knowledge, and mental coordination: The eleventh element is the effect on moral games of mental coordination about (or common knowledge of) different candidate values. The payoffs to behavioral conformity to or deviation from a given value depends on (1) the distribution of supporters, neutrals, and opponents, and (2) the aggregate effects of how each person represents what positions everyone else will publicly take and behaviorally support. There is much less risk to defying a rule that only some people support. In contrast, a winning rule is one that is coregistered as being supported by everyone (or by a winning combination of power holders, at least). To the extent individuals can spread the representation to others that everyone is mentally coordinated on the proposition that some value is moral (supported), then this flips the incentives on dissent. Dissenters risk widespread withdrawal of support or community wide punishment, motivating them to conform. In the highest level of the moral game, what individuals and groups are perpetually jockeying to do is to actualize mental coordination about which values will reign within the moral community. The ideal outcome is to forge a value project that is beneficial to its proponents, which then wins enough support that everyone publicly endorses it, and that finally is coregistered by everyone as universally endorsed. For an individual, that is winning the jackpot in second order moral games.

The motivational bias toward moral realism: The twelfth element is moral *antirelativism* – the preference to spread and enforce the belief that morality is objective and has an intrinsic reality. This follows from the role that mental coordination plays in empowering moral values. The winning outcome in social negotiation is to get everyone to adopt your position as their own, so that they conform to it, effectively enforce it, and carry the costs of enforcement. Mental coordination is defeated to the extent that it is publicly recognized that there are differences of position. This is usually recast not as moral relativism, but as individual mistakes in perceiving what the moral position "really" or "truly" is. It is almost definitional of morality that people intuitively represent morality to be intrinsically good, and support its being seen as real and objective. We argue that this is an evolved circuit.

There are a set of games that humans have played so intensively over the course of our evolution (such as dyadic exchange and collective action) that we have reasoning and motivational adaptations that were specialized by natural selection for these particular games (Cosmides and Tooby 2005; Price, Cosmides, and Tooby 2002). These games have what might be thought of as their own proprietary moral concepts (e.g., cheater, free-rider) and moral sentiments (e.g., punitive sentiment toward free-riders). When situations fall into the domains of these evolved games, our moral stance tends to be organized by these dominating evolved interpretations and motivational agendas. Yet, the scope of possible moral contents is so large, we cannot have evolved responses to all of them, and so many of our moral responses must come from other sources. Obviously, explicit representations of self-interest play a large role in our attraction to, or resistance to candidate moralities, and help to fill this gap. There are many moral phenomena, however, which do not fit either pattern. For example, it is in each male's fitness interest for reproductively competing males to adopt a homosexual orientation. Yet across many cultures, homosexuality is intuitively viewed as immoral. One might similarly ask why people in so many societies are morally concerned with third party incest that has no impact on them. These and other cases can be explained by considering that selection would have favored a tendency to endow a modest moral realism to one's personal evaluative reactions to others' behaviors, when reframed as if it were a first- person experience. On this view, what happens when the mind's evaluative systems implicitly assess a represented situation positively (e.g., if I were to experience that, I would like it)? When this reaction is not overruled by more powerful and specific features of our moral psychology, by conformity, or by self-interested strategic thinking (e.g., if this person gets away with theft, then that will injure me), then this first-person situation assessment migrates toward being positively moralized (or less negatively moralized). If the mind evaluates the situation as negative (if I were to experience it myself), then our moral psychology migrates toward viewing it as immoral. Thus, heterosexuals imagining themselves engaging in homosexual acts tend to have a disgust reaction, underpinning a negative moralization. Indeed, our data shows that subjects' moral objections to sibling incest by third parties track their preferences for their own personal sexual behavior toward siblings – as activated by the evolved anti-incest system (Lieberman, Tooby, and Cosmides 2003). While there is no logical relationship between the two, this moral circuit would be favored by selection because individuals would usually have benefited by having their preferences moralized. On balance, such an adaptation would make the local moral consensus more favorable to realizing the individual's preferences, even though sometimes such outputs are functionless or fitness reducing (e.g., opposition to homosexual behavior).

N-party exchange, hypocrisy, and private versus public behavior: The thirteenth element is that moral proposals in second order games are treated by our moral adaptations as a variant of n-party exchange or collective action. Just like for any other collective action, support from others for a moral proposal is purchased by the proponent's conformity with it – their contribution is their following the moral rule, and (to a lesser extent) their enforcing the moral rule. Evidence for this can be seen by the fact that our moral psychology includes an anti-hypocrisy circuit. This feature deflates both support for a proposal and the willingness to adhere to it when its proponents are discovered to be not following it themselves (Tooby, Cosmides, and Price 2006). There is no logical reason why others' adherence or abandonment makes a moral precept more or less worth following. It makes perfect sense, however, if morality is an n-party exchange, and our adherence to a costly moral rule is equivalent to the sucker's payoff when others have abandoned the rule. Because the negative reaction to hypocrisy closely parallels the negative reaction to free-riding, individuals prefer not to be seen as hypocrites. Obviously, there are benefits to evading the negative consequences of detected hypocrisy, as well as other advantages of evading others' responses to other kinds of moral defection undertaken to obtain gains. This dynamic leads to evolved programs for distinguishing one's own private behavior from public behavior, registering when acts are private, and modifying behavior in private to be more self-interested. As a consequence, moral games (among equally powerful players) favor individuals to be privately non-Kantian (do not act as you would if everyone were to do it) but publicly Kantian (publicly acting in conformity with those values that you are motivated to spread).

The fact that second order moral games are intuitively treated as n-party exchanges is one of the things that distinguishes morality from negotiation, politics, trade, aggression, or other ordinary paths to influencing others' behavior. This implicit framing explains why acting out of self-interest is intuitively contrasted with moral behavior (i.e., to fulfilling one's part in the implicit exchange). Moreover, it explains why, if other people feel no stake in a dispute, it is not seen a moral issue. In contrast, if people feel actions in a dispute would set a precedent for future actions by others, then the issue intuitively becomes moralized. Precedents implicitly define the terms of the n-party exchange that members coregister as being obligated to follow. These neurocognitive circuits provide the intuitive seeds for the common law practices of using precedent, and (when trying to escape precedent) distinguishing cases.

Partisanship and impartiality: Together, the combination of the ladder effect, morality as n-party exchange, the recognition of hypocrisy as cheating, the requirements of mental coordination for morality, and the moral realism bias explain the complex game dynamics revolving around representations of moral impartiality. The collective action of moral support for a value project is sustained or unraveled to the extent there are cheaters or free riders – people who benefited or would benefit from the moral rule applying to others, but depart from it when it costs them. People recognize the advantages individuals derive from benefits flowing to their kin, friends, and allies. This means that those who are not intrinsically drawn to being impartial moral actors when it injures them (i.e., everyone) are tempted to be cheaters. Partiality is (sometimes) restrained by the recognition that acting on this temptation leads to anti-free-riding punitive sentiments or the costs to the cheating individual of others' ceasing to adhere to the moral rule. Moreover, the proportion of a group's members that are the targeted beneficiaries of an act of partiality will be smaller the larger the group, while

the number of individuals with punitive sentiments will be proportionately larger. If the group size (moral community) becomes large
enough, impartiality can become a publicly endorsed (if secretly
unpracticed) ideal. In contrast, the perception that a value is being
flexibly deployed to serve someone else's self-interest undermines
recruitment of support to that value.

As moral projects climb the ladder to broader audiences (being
recast and potentially applied to increasingly broad sets of individuals), any given individual will be bombarded with increasing numbers of candidate moral rules. Although these moral rules were not
initially formulated with him or her in mind, the fortunes of life
may make them applicable. Each individual can help to propel, or
help to extinguish a rule or value, and should modulate their support
based on their evaluative response. The evaluative response in each
individual should be guided by which role (beneficiary or target)
the individual anticipates as most likely to apply to him or her (and
to those whose welfare matters to that individual). To the extent the
individual is uncertain which role she might end up in, she should
balance the two. This should lead to some tendency for rules to
mutate toward greater "fairness" when large numbers of players are
involved who are uncertain about their future role in the rule. If for
most individuals, what one gives up if the rule is adopted (the probability that the rule applies to you as target, plus its cost if it does) is
less than the benefit derived from having the rule to apply to everyone
else, then the community will tend to move toward making the rule
general and mentally coordinated. In principle, an individual could
benefit by retaining the option to rob or commit murder without
community opposition, but benefits even more giving up that option
in order to have all others in the community prevented from doing
so (Hobbes 1651). In this case, the individual will publicly support
the rule, even if privately she may not always follow it. Thus, moral
rules forbidding murder (of ingroup members), robbery (of ingroup
members), and the like, will often become mentally coordinated,
reigning moral rules within human communities, without having
been favored by group selection, uncompensated self-restraint, or
individual dedication to group welfare.

Moral cascades and moral warfare: Cognitive adaptations for moralizing disputes, attacking others' transgressions, and for launching contagious coalitional value projects are products of a selective history
of offensive moral warfare. The ultimate prize in the moral game
is one that causes a moral cascade that leads an advantageous value

project or attack to increase in frequency until it becomes accepted by the community as the reigning or equilibrium understanding: that is, by crafting and launching a representational bundle whose contagious runaway adoption by others amplifies the individual's preferences into a mentally coordinated valuation that recruits others and reaches high frequency in the local population. It recruits allies, and disadvantages opponents or rivals, for example by mobilizing punishment against rivals. While complete victories in moral warfare are rare, it is common for individuals and groups to better their position by playing second order moral games, both offensively and defensively. We expect motivational and cognitive adaptations in our moral psychology evolved to play these games well. To create a well-crafted project, the individual must, for example, have a good intuitive map of the local moral and social ecology. To be successful, the set of launched representations must be packaged to appeal to others (and to publicly disarm opposition). It must be apparently de-personalized, so that the issue does not begin or end just with the launcher's self-interest. To be successful in larger populations, it needs to attract supporters who have no particular interest in the launcher, the launcher's situation, or in the dispute, except as it sets a precedent that might be useful to them. Ideally, the project should be crafted so that others can see that is in their interests as well, and can foresee how it will apply. To reward the launcher, it must be self-interested, yet not appear self-interested. The constraints on a moral project are twofold: Finding a convergence of interest between launcher and potential allies; and finding a convergence of interest among a large and powerful enough set of potential allies that they successfully advance the project to the necessary level of social support. Moral offensives often focus on behavior of the target. Allies are more easily recruited if there are cues that make it easier to arrive at mental coordination on the wrongness of the behavior of the target (as well as the "facts"). For example, sins of omission are considered much less wrong than sins of commission, even though a utilitarian logician would defensibly equate them. Computationally, however, everyone is always omitting to take an infinite number of actions. With few exceptions, attaining a meeting of the minds that one omission out of this amorphous set is uniquely immoral is far harder to cognitively arrange than is the joint identification of a mutually objectionable act of commission. In contrast to sins of omission, sins of commission are finite, and knowably specific to the person or persons who commit them. Moral outrage, if it evolved to be useful in coordinating joint action should show intensities that correspond to how easily a type of action can be used to mobilize joint assault. Hence, because of the lower payoffs, people should be far less outraged by omissions than commissions. Reciprocally, from the perpetrator's point of view, acts of omission are more masked from moral retaliation – so humans should feel far less guilty about them. Equally, outrage elicited from an individual should be stronger when the underlying value is known to be shared by others. For example, someone who shows very low WTRs toward others poses an exploitive threat to others, and intentional behavior is more revelatory of underlying WTR dispositions than are actions with unintended consequences. This predicts that unintended negative consequences will trigger less outrage than intended consequences. This prediction is also supported by evidence (see, for example, Sedlak 1979; Hauser 2006).

The game of fault and blame: One particularly important moral game is the attribution of responsibility. We have special terms for social causality: fault, blame, credit, and so on. These terms have two components, one explanatory and one evaluative: First, the explanatory attribution is the claim that the causal source of the event originates in the person or group identified as responsible, and causation is not traced to other agents beyond them. Second, the evaluative implication is that the agent's n-party social exchange account and status is decreased or increased as a result (if you were at fault, you owe something; and you are worth less as a social partner, either because of bad character – bad intentions – or incompetence). Third, analyses of blame and credit are strongly affected by the benefits or costs that the actor and those affected experience as a consequence of the act that "caused" the outcome. These are the elements that allow the actor's WTR toward others to be computed, a third evaluative implication (see below). Others are morally blameworthy if they exhibit unusually low WTRs toward others.

Because human agents are complexly computational, there are usually an uncountably large number of possible paths and interactions involving many persons that could have prevented a negative outcome, or could have led to a better positive outcome. There is usually a large range of possible choices of individuals or groups who, if they had acted differently, would have changed the outcome. Any of these people could be said to have caused the outcome – allowing choice about which thread in the tapestry of causation to isolate as culpable. Positive and especially negative events provoke complex representational contests over just who is to blame (or to credit).

Disasters (such as the Black Plague, the 9–11 attacks, the flooding of New Orleans, the Great Depression) present a special opportunity to bring together a punitive coalition and turn it loose on one's status rivals: To play the attribution game, one manufactures representations that promote mental coordination on the interpretation that one's status rivals are at fault – are indeed fitness suppressors of the community at large. This serves as a triggering coordinative signal for those who want to take action against the blamed – that is, it triggers outrage (Tooby, Cosmides, and Price 2006). The blameworthy are picked by an emerging power-based consensus. If an attack on rivals is framed as punishment for a moral transgression that injured the encompassing community, then it disarms defenders of the target of the attack. By standing up for the transgressor, they can be framed as defending moral transgression and injuring the community.

Welfare trade-offs, disgust, and the sorting game: Ejecting cheaters from exchange relationships is a process of disaffiliation. This is one component of a more general adaptive problem: filling one's finite association niches with individuals that have high association value, and removing individuals with low or negative association value. There are differential payoffs to playing this discriminative association game well or poorly (Tooby and Cosmides 1996). Depending on who the actor's associates are, the actor may be helped or exploited, may incur positive or negative externalities, may accrue changes in status, and so on. In dyadic games, affiliation is under direct individual control, but in social networks, your associates' choices influence the actualization of your own preferences. You may be forced to associate with your friend's friends, if you are to maintain your relationship with your friend. This makes conflicts over network affiliation or group membership a second order moral game – and an n-party exchange. The stakes of competitive exclusion and differential affiliation are high, with displacement and ostracism at one extreme and valued centrality at the other.

Several families of pre-existing adaptations were co-opted into adaptations for the discriminative association game. Disgust is the emotion program that evolved to recognize, evaluate, and motivate avoidance of harmful things, and the output of adaptations for discriminative association is motivated avoidance. That is why actions (and characteristics) can lead persons to be seen as disgusting.

Adaptations for computing and responding to WTRs are a second family of programs involved in discriminative association games. Humans are subject to kin selection, reciprocity, retaliation, bargaining, and other selection pressures which make it important to place weight (under certain conditions) on the welfare of the other as well as the self. Experimental evidence supports the prediction that humans evolved architectures that compute specific WTRs for each social relationship – WTRs that determine which self-benefiting choices, and which other-benefiting choices the actor will make (Tooby et al. 2008; Delton et al. forthcoming). Humans have complementary adaptations which use observations of others behavior to infer the WTRs that others are using. Low WTRs from others to self trigger anger and disgust; WTRs from the self to another that are too low trigger guilt and (if public) shame; and so on (Tooby et al. 2008; Sell, Tooby and Cosmides 2009).

To fill one's finite association niches with others' whose WTRs toward you are low is a fitness mistake – you will rarely be helped, and often exploited. That is, WTR machinery delivers information that should guide behavior in the discriminative association game. The expression by others of a high WTR toward you (and those you value) elicits affection and affiliation; the expression of low WTRs toward you (and those you value) elicits disgust (if the person can be ejected or avoided) or anger (if they cannot). Since it is advantageous to be seen as harboring a high WTR toward others, individuals dissemble by behaving more favorably when they are being observed, or when the cost is low. Someone's WTR-based association value is therefore set by the minimum WTR they are caught expressing – it reveals the true but hidden magnitude of how little they value others – a representation that should be sticky or "staining." Someone who is capable of severely damaging affiliates in pursuit of trivial personal gains is a threat to be avoided. Actions toward ingroup members that express unusually low WTRs elicit the shared value project of avoidance and exclusion. But such acts are only useful for discriminative association if they are intentional, and WTR concepts help us define what intentionality in this domain means. According to the WTR theory of intentionality, intentionality is computed as a tool to help the judger infer a maximum upper bound on the WTR that the actor is using toward the other person. If I choose to benefit myself by 1 unit of welfare, at a cost to you of 50 units, and I know these costs and benefits, then others can infer that my maximum WTR is lower than .02, a very low WTR. This theory predicts that I will be seen as intentionally depriving you of 50 units, just to get myself 1 unit. In contrast, if I choose an option that benefits me by 1 unit, and benefits you by 1 unit (over an option that benefits neither one of us), we expect I will not be judged to be intentionally helping you, because no (positive) WTR toward you from me can be inferred – I might have done it just to get myself 1 unit, regardless of how this impacted you. Moral credit should show the reverse effect – if the act benefits the self as well as others, it should be seen as less praiseworthy, and my helping you less intentional. Experiments on the so-called *side effect* are consistent with this view – that is, foreseen but negative side effects on third parties of self-interested choices are seen as intentional, but foreseen but positive side effects are not (Knobe 2003). According to WTR theory, one function of intentional attributions is moral inferences about WTRs. In short, blame and credit are partly functions of imputed WTRs, and mental coordination that targeted persons are blameworthy can be mobilized in the discriminative association game to trigger their elimination from the social unit.

Playing moral games defensively: For humans, it is important not only to have adaptations to play moral games offensively, but also defensively. Offensive moral warfare involves attempting to influence others to modify their behavior so that it conforms to your preferences – a process that gains special force when allies are recruited. One set of preferences may involve social exclusion of targets. However, at least as important as offensive play is the complementary process: Individuals have to conduct themselves to minimize retaliation or exclusion from others for any moral missteps. Incautious actions expose individuals to severe or even fatal sanctions by empowered moral coalitions. Individuals can stigmatize themselves, be found at fault for a negative outcome, or be identified as a violator of a moral understanding, whether explicit (e.g., a law) or implicit. A course of action is in the defensive moral domain if it might draw an negative evaluative response, exclusion and/or a punishment from a sufficiently empowered and mentally coordinated number of social actors in the community. The goal of defensive adaptations is to guide behavior in the actor so that it minimizes others' pretexts for moral attack, and maintains others' valuations of the self. Moreover, they seem better designed to win in the assortment game, for example by advertising adherence to restraints that increase the attractiveness of the individual as a close social partner (e.g., would you choose to live with someone who would kill you to save 10 others?). The moral sense operating in the self systematically departs from maximizing general social utility, nor do moral judgments of others' behavior map on to utility maximization (Tooby and Cosmides, 1979).

From the point of view of defensive adaptations, something is a moral issue if others deem it to be one. Blame, condemnation, ostracism, and punishment are endemic to small-scale communities, and very much to be feared. How can they be avoided? First, as already discussed, our psychological architecture should be equipped with a moral sense designed to assimilate and weight others' values, in proportion to their social power and the likelihood of surveillance. (The moral sense will also integrate outputs from the individual's altruistic adaptations, since both put weight on others' welfare.) Second, the computational problems inherent in launching a moral attack are formidable. Defensive moral psychology is designed to make those computational problems more intractable, in order to offer less traction to potential antagonists. Hence, many evolved features of our defensive moral psychology are counterparts to the cognitive coordination problems faced by those on the moral offensive. One obvious application of this is the fact that our evolved moral psychology treats sins of omission as less culpable than sins of commission, making them safer to commit and easier to get away with. When in doubt, do nothing. Similarly, humans are inclined to hide self-interested actions under other publicly valued guises; to voice public support for reigning values; to see where general sentiment lies before publicly committing oneself, and so on. If accused of transgressions we are designed to plead lack of intentionality, shift blame, attack accusers as hypocrites, and intimidate or retaliate against those who are mobilizing the moral attack.

Conclusion

The set of evolved programs that enable and drive warfare and politics strongly overlap with the set of evolved programs that drive human morality. The mapping of these evolved programs and their embedded circuit logics is only in its infancy, and we have only sketched out some of the known or predicted features of our coalitional and moral psychologies. However, progress in this enterprise holds out the possibility of gradually throwing light on some of the darkest areas of human life.

References

Alexander, R. D. 1979. *Darwinism and human affairs*. Seattle: University of Washington Press.

Andrea, J., and A. J. Sedlak. 1979. Developmental differences in under-standing plans and evaluating actors. *Child Development* 50(2):536–60.

Aumann, Robert. 1976. Agreeing to disagree. *Annals of Statistics* 4(6):1236–9.

Aumann Robert and Adam Brandenburger. 1995. Epistemic conditions for Nash equilibrium. *Econometrica* 63(5):1161–80.

Baumeister, R. F., and K. L. Sommer. 1997. What do men want? Gender differences and the two spheres of belongingness. *Psychological Bulletin* 122:38–43.

Boehm, C. 1992. Segmentary 'warfare' and the management of conflict: Comparison of East African chimpanzees and patrilinieal–patrilocal humans. In *Coalitions and Alliances in Humans and Other Animals*, edited by A. H. Harcourt and F. M. B. de Waal, 137–73. Oxford: Oxford University Press.

Boehm, C. 1999. *Hierarchy in the forest: The evolution of egalitarian behavior.* Cambridge, MA: Harvard University Press.

Bowles, S. 2006. Group competition, reproductive leveling, and the evolu-tion of human altruism. *Science*, 314:1569–72.

Chagnon, N. 1983. *The Yanomamo.* New York: Holt, Rinehart & Winston.

Cosmides, L. and J. Tooby. 2000. Consider the source: The evolution of adaptations for decoupling and metarepresentation. In *Metarepresentations: A multidisciplinary perspective*, edited by D. Sperber, 53–115. New York: Oxford University Press.

Cosmides, L. and J. Tooby. 2005. Neurocognitive adaptations designed for social exchange. In *The Handbook of Evolutionary Psychology*, edited by D. M. Buss, 584–627. Hoboken, NJ: Wiley.

Chwe, M. S. 2003. *Rational ritual: Culture, coordination, and common know-ledge.* Princeton: Princeton University Press.

Darwin, C. 1871. *The descent of man, and selection in relation to sex.* London: John Murray.

Delton, A., L. Cosmides, and J. Tooby. (forthcoming). *The psychosemantics of free-riding.*

Delton, A., J. Tooby, L. Cosmides, D. Sznycer, and J. Lim. (forthcoming). *Welfare trade-off ratios.*

Ermer, E. 2007. Coalitional support and the regulation of welfare tradeoff ratios. Dissertation, University of California, Santa Barbara.

Ermer, E., L. Cosmides, and J. Tooby. 2008. Relative status regulates risky decision-making about resources in men: Evidence for the co-evolution of motivation and cognition. *Evolution and Human Behavior* 29:106–18.

Freud, Sigmund. 1927[1923]. *Das Ich und das Es, Internationaler Psycho-analytischer*, translated as *The Ego and the Id* by Joan Riviere. London: Hogarth Press and Institute of Psycho-analysis.

Haidt J., C. McCauley, and P. Rozin. 1994. Individual differences in sen-sitivity to disgust: A scale sampling seven domains of disgust elicitors. *Personality and Individual Differences* 16(5):701–13.

Harner, M. 1972. The *Jivaro: People of the sacred waterfalls*. Berkeley: University of California Press.

Hauser, M. 2006. *Moral minds*. New York: Harper Collins.

Heider, Karl 1970. *The Dugum Dani*. Chicago: Aldine Publishing Company.

Henrich, J. and F. Gil-White. 2001. The evolution of prestige. *Evolution and Human Behavior* 22(3):165–96.

Hobbes, T. 1651. *Leviathan, The Matter, forme and power of a common wealth ecclesiasticall and civil*. London: Andrew Crooke and William Cooke Publishers.

Hrdy, S. B. 1980. *The langurs of Abu*. Cambridge, MA: Harvard University Press.

Hume, D. 1751. *An enquiry concerning the principles of morals*. London: A. Millar.

Hutcheson, F. 1728. *An essay on the nature and conduct of the passions and affections, with illustrations upon the moral sense*. Dublin: J. Smith and W. Bruce.

Ip, G. W., C. Y. Chiu, and C. Wan. 2006. Birds of a feather and birds flocking together: physical versus behavioral cues may lead to trait- versus goal-based group perception. Journal of Personality and Social Psychology 90(3):368–81.

Keegan, J. 1994. *A history of warfare*. New York: Random House.

Keeley, L. H. 1996. *War before civilization: The myth of the peaceful savage*. New York: Oxford University Press.

Knobe, J. 2003. Intentional action and side effects in ordinary language. *Analysis* 63:190–3.

Kuran, T. 1998. *Private truths, public lies: the social consequences of preference falsification*. Cambridge, MA: Harvard University Press.

Kurzban, R., J. Tooby, and L. Cosmides. 2001. Can race be erased? Coalitional computation and social categorization. *PNAS* 98(26):15387–92.

LeBlanc, S. A. 1999. *Prehistoric warfare in the American Southwest*. Salt Lake City: University of Utah Press.

LeBlanc, S. A. and K. Register. 2003. *Constant battles: The myth of the peaceful, noble savage*. New York: St. Martins Press.

Lee, R. and I. DeVore. 1976. *Kalahari hunter-gatherers*. Cambridge, MA: Harvard University Press.

Lieberman, D., J. Tooby, and L. Cosmides. 2007. The architecture of human kin detection. *Nature* 445(7129):727–31.

Lieberman, D., J. Tooby, and L. Cosmides. 2003. Does morality have a biological basis? An empirical test of the factors governing moral senti- ments relating to incest. *Proceedings of the Royal Society London (Biological Sciences)* 270(1517):819–826.

Lewis, David. 1969. *Convention: A philosophical study*. Oxford: Blackburn.

Manson, J. H., and R. W. Wrangham. 1991. Intergroup aggression in chimpanzees and humans. *Current Anthropology* 32(4):369.

Maynard Smith, J. 1964. Group selection and kin selection. *Nature* 201:1145–7.

Maynard Smith, J. 1977. Parental investment: A prospective analysis. *Animal Behaviour* 25:1–9

Olson, M. 1965. *The logic of collective action: Public goods and the theory of groups.* Cambridge, MA: Harvard University Press.

Pemberton, M. B., C., A. Insko, and J. Schopler. 1996. Memory for and experience of differential competitive behavior of individuals and groups. *Journal of Personality and Social Psychology* 71:954–66.

Price, M. E., L. Cosmides, and J. Tooby. 2002. Punitive sentiment as an anti-free rider psychological device. *Evolution and Human Behavior* 23:203–31.

Rofe, Y. 1984. Stress and affiliation: A utility theory. *Psychological Review* 91:235–50.

Sahlins, M. 1961. The segmentary lineage: An organization of predatory expansion. *American Anthropologist* 63:322–45.

Sell, A., L. Cosmides, J. Tooby, D. Sznycer, C. von Rueden, and M. Gurven. 2009. Human adaptations for the visual assessment of strength and fighting ability from the body and face. (Plus electronic supplemental material). *Proceedings of the Royal Society B (Biological Sciences)* 276(1656):575–84.

Sell, A., J. Tooby, and L. Cosmides. 2009 Anger, strength, and the logic of formidability. *Proceedings of the National Academy of Sciences.* Published in online Early Edition, 3 August 2009.

Sherif, M. 1966. *In common predicament: Social psychology of intergroup conflict and cooperation.* Boston: Houghton-Mifflin.

Sidanius, J., and F. Pratto. 2001. *Social dominance.* Cambridge: Cambridge University Press.

Smirnov, O., H. Arrow, D. Kennett, and J. Orbell. 2007. Ancestral war and the evolutionary origins of "heroism." *The Journal of Politics* 69:927–40. Cambridge: Cambridge University Press.

Tajfel, H., and J. C. Turner. 1979. An integrative theory of intergroup conflict. In *The Social Psychology of Intergroup Relations*, edited by W. G. Austin and S. Worchel, 33–47. Monterey: Brooks Cole.

Tiger, L. 1969. *Men in groups.* Toronto: Thomas Nelson and Sons Ltd.

Tooby J. and I. DeVore. 1987. The reconstruction of hominid behavioral evolution through strategic modeling. In *Primate Models of Hominid Behavior*, edited by W. Kinzey, 183–237. New York: SUNY Press.

Tooby, J., and L. Cosmides. 1979. Adaptationist approaches to moral phenomena. *Institute for Evolutionary Studies Technical Report* 79–1.

Tooby, J., and L. Cosmides. 1988. The evolution of war and its cognitive foundations. *Institute for Evolutionary Studies Technical Report* 88–1.

Tooby, J., and L. Cosmides. 1996. Friendship and the banker's paradox: Other pathways to the evolution of adaptations for altruism. In *Proceedings of the British Academy*, 88:119–43.

Tooby, J., and L. Cosmides. 2000. Cognitive adaptations for kin-based coalitions: human kinship systems at the intersection between collective action and kin selection. *Current Anthropology* 41(5):803–4.

Tooby, J., and L. Cosmides. 2008. The evolutionary psychology of the emotions and their relationship to internal regulatory variables. In *Handbook of Emotions*, edited by M. Lewis and J. M. Haviland-Jones, 3rd edition, 91–115. New York: Guilford.

Tooby, J., L. Cosmides, and M. Price. 2006. Cognitive adaptations for n-person exchange: The evolutionary roots of organizational behavior. *Managerial and Decision Economics* 27:103–29.

Tooby, J., L. Cosmides, A. Sell, D. Lieberman, and Sznycer, D. 2008. Internal regulatory variables and the design of human motivation: A computational and evolutionary approach. In *Handbook of approach and avoidance motivation*, edited by A. J. Elliot, 251–71. Mahwah, NJ: Lawrence Erlbaum Associates.

Tooby, J., L. Cosmides, and H. C. Barrett. 2005. Resolving the debate on innate ideas: Learnability constraints and the evolved interpenetration of motivational and conceptual functions. In *The Innate Mind: Structure and Content*, edited by P. Carruthers, S. Laurence, and S. Stich, 305–37. New York: Oxford University Press.

Turney-High, H. 1949. *Primitive war*. Columbia: University of South Carolina Press.

Woodfine, P. 1998. *Britannia's glories: The Walpole ministry and the 1739 War with Spain*. Woodbridge, UK: Royal Historical Society/Boydell Press.

Wilson, M. L., M. D. Hauser, and R. W. Wrangham. 2001. Does participation in intergroup conflict depend on numerical assessment, range location, or rank for wild chimpanzees? *Animal Behaviour* 61:1203–16.

Wilson, M. L., and R. W. Wrangham. 2003. Intergroup relations in chimpanzees. *Annual Review of Anthropology* 32:363–92.

Wrangham, R. W. and D. Peterson. 1996. *Demonic males: Apes and the origins of human violence*. New York: Houghton Mifflin.

Zimmerman, L. 1981. *The Crow Creek Site massacre: A preliminary report*. US Army Corps of Engineers, Omaha District.

9

Homo Sapiens – Homo Socious: A Comparative Analysis of Human Mind and Kind

Henrik Høgh-Olesen

> Mapping the Rubicon between man and beast is an onerous, perennial task.

First of all, it is muddy and stormy waters we are mapping, and on top of this, the general continuity between us and the rest of the animal world, makes the contours even more blurred. Then one's vain efforts will most certainly encounter a mixed reception. People in general tend to have strong feelings on this issue, colleagues will disagree, and time will prove us wrong.

However, a book as this one, that takes a comparative perspective on its subject, is more or less obliged to confront this task, and at least outline the species–specific behaviors, social and moral practices and psychological processes that appear to be uniquely human. In the following, I shall try to honor this obligation.

This chapter will survey and comparatively analyze the similarities and differences of four central behavioral fields related to:

1. complex symbolic activities
2. tool making and tool use
3. culture and social transmission
4. morality and sociality

As in the rest of the book, the main focus will be on our moral and social capacities. However, since these characteristics are situated in a unique language-using, tool-producing and culture-accumulating organism, these other features will also be reviewed and compared.

Today we know with certainty that nonhuman animals communicate and use tools. Complex mental processes related to memory and foresight (Oswath 2009), and some form of "theory of mind" (Hare et al. 2000, 2001; Hare and Tomasello 2004) may also be found outside the human species, as may moral inclinations such as altruistic and empathic behaviors (cf. de Waal this volume); but still these capacities may be substantially more complex on the human level, as well as different in kind, which may have interesting consequences on human sociality.

If we look at social cognition, it is obvious that the human brain is not simply an enlarged chimpanzee brain (Smedt, Cruz, and Braeckman 2009). Instead, natural selection seems to have favored a more collaborative kind of sociality in our species, involving – among other things – large-scale, high-risk cooperation among strangers, as well as third-party altruistic punishments and rewards. The finer nature of these characteristics will be treated later; however, we can now say that humans do seem to be an *ultra-social* species, and that a more precise generic designation to *Homo sapiens sapiens* could be *Homo socious sapiens*: Man the socially thinking animal.

But let us not anticipate events. First we will take a comparative look at our symbolic behaviors, from language and art to cults and rites.

Symbolic Capacities

Language

Language is a system to translate meanings into signals and signals into meanings (Hurford 2007, 3). For a long period it was cherished as a species-specific marker common to humans only, but now this bastion has also been challenged.

We have long known that a wide range of earth, air, and sea-living animals use sounds and calls in order to attract mates or conspecifics, or to signal danger (Eibl-Eibesfeldt 1970). So far, however, referential communication and not least syntax (i.e., the ability to create new meanings through the rearrangement of discrete vocal elements) has been viewed as a strictly human hallmark.

Nevertheless, studies of several species – for example, domestic fowl (*Gallus gallus*) (Evans and Evans 1999), black–capped chickadees (*Poecile atricapillus*) (Templeton et al. 2005*)*, vervet monkeys (*Cercopithcus aethiops)* (Cheney and Seyfarth 1990), surricats (*Suricata suricata)* (Manser 2001) and California ground squirrels (*Spermophilus beecheyi*) (Leger et al. 1980) – have documented qualitatively and quantitatively different alarm calls in response to different predators, specifying, for instance, whether the danger is aerial or terrestrial.

Other studies have shown that putty–nosed guenon monkeys (*Cercopithecus nictitans*), as well as gibbons (*Hylobatidae*) use combinations of calls, and rearrange their cries in order to relay new and specific information to one another. Different sounds were combined to create more complex sequences specifying for example whether a threat was a leopard, a serpent, or an eagle, and the responses of conspecifics demonstrated that these syntactic differences were meaningful – when somebody shouts "leopard," climb up a tree; when somebody shouts "eagle," hide under a bush (Arnold and Zuberbühler 2006; Clarke, Reichard, and Zuberbühler 2006).

Some species may even incorporate a range of more descriptive information about a predator besides its spatial whereabouts. Prairie dogs (*Cynomys gunnisoni, Cynomys ludovicianus*) encoded information into their alarm calls specific to the color of clothes (grey, green, orange, blue) and general shape (male/female, tall/small, slim/round) of humans acting as potential predators in their territory. When some of these humans, in another set of experiments, started to either feed the prairie dogs or fire a gun, these individual references were also encoded in distinct calls whenever these persons later appeared (Slobodchikoff et al. 1991; Frederiksen and Slobodchikoff 2007).

Admittedly, this is not speech in the human sense, but it certainly is a close forerunner, and one could argue that these species may have some sort of "lexical items" or referential sounds related to central life–categories that one can point to or act out. Something equivalent to our nouns ("eagle," "air predator"), verb phrases ("watch out for...") and simple specifying adjectives related to physical properties.

Apparently no grammatical items (prepositions, conjunctions, articles, or auxiliary verbs like "can," "may," "will" and "should") are found, in sharp contrast to human language, where up to half of the words are purely grammatical items, with no physical reference that one can point to (Diamond 2006, p.153).

Language-trained chimpanzees *(Pan troglodytes)* and bonoboes *(Pan paniscus)* are able to understand semantic content, as well as, grammatical syntax, and they are quite good at utterances with present time imperative force ("Give me this or that"), but considerably more reticent than humans at giving information about events that happened yesterday or earlier. Information related to the future beyond the next few minutes seems to be more or less closed land as well, although the renowned Kanzi has been known to remind Sue Savage-Rumbaugh to give him the treat that he was promised the day before (Hurford 2007, 50; Savage-Rumbaugh 1986).

Captive, language-trained dolphins *(Tursiops truncates)* easily understand and react to complex instructions like: "Put the ball on your left in the basket on your right" the first time they are presented, just as they do not react to semantically meaningless instructions, but look expectantly at the instructor for further information. Referential gestures like pointing are spontaneously understood, and they are able to see and react to symbolic representations as TV exposures (even to carry out orders presented through TV), just as they are able to recognize themselves in mirrors and TV presentations (Herman 2006).

These are specially trained animals, so what we see here are well stimulated potentials for syntactical, grammatical and semantic understanding, rather than natural capacities. Yet, if we mix these insights with the natural capacities found in the free-living species presented before, a picture begins to emerge, which questions the Chomskyan "Big bang theory of language": First there was nothing, and then – after a major mutation in the human line sometime in the Pleistocene period – language emerged (Chomsky 1972; 1995). Instead, the new evidence suggests that some of the building blocks of human language and speech can be found in other species (even species outside the primate line), and consequently must have a much longer and more continuous evolutionary history than Chomsky's classical theory presumes.

Human language may be unique in its grammatical and syntactic complexity, as well as in its ability to signify abstract matters and relations involving unobservable mental and physical causes. Thus, language allows us to communicate with detail and precision on far more complex subject matters, and to cultivate and share far more complex and diverse social information and relations than other species.

Likewise, we may be the only species to process and reinterpret our first order perceptions into abstract, higher-order principles and categories, as Penn et al. (2008) argues. But, at least to this writer, these symbolic and abstract capacities rest on a staging of more basic linguistic and cognitive forerunners, which we share with some other species – see, for instance, Pepperberg's grey parrot studies (1987, 1988, 2006). This, however, may not be the case for all our symbolic, social behaviors.

If we take a closer look at some of our more complex, referential, symbolic actions, something uniquely human seems to appear. Unlike all other species, we produce art, we bury our dead, and we conduct complex religious ceremonies directed at unseen powers. Something exceptional is happening.

Art, Cult, and Rite

In a period some 40,000 years ago, when we were fully occupied with satisfying our most basic needs (Maslow 1970), we went out of our way and into deep inaccessible caves to adorn and decorate them from floor to ceiling! And it was not even the game that we survived on that was painted. These Paleolithic hunters had reindeer and grouses in their stomachs, and horses, bisons, and bears on their minds, as Leakey (1995) put it. Furthermore, these caves were not our domestic quarters, but ritualistic spaces that we often traveled long to reach, and used for special tribal activities and initiations (Pfeiffer 1985).

And why bury our dead? No other animal does that (elephant graveyards are only found in Tarzan books, should anyone be in doubt), and also within the human line this practice is a rather late achievement. Excavations from Atapuerca in Spain suggest that archaic *Homo sapiens*, some 300,000 years ago, may have tugged dead tribesmen into caves and collectively thrown them into deep shafts where scavengers could not reach them. But individualized interments, where a deceased is placed in a grave, are first known from about 100.000 years ago (Eliade 1995, v. 1).

With burials came awareness of death and of self, and where there are burial rites and offerings (in the form of weapons, food, goods, and gifts) this awareness is further intensified. Death is no longer just a physical fact – something that happens – it is conceived as a transmission from one mode of being into another. Now a reflective and narrative mind with a natural propensity to causality

> **Behavioral field 1:** Complex symbolic behavior

- Grammatical items with no physical reference
- Syntactic complexity – Ability to signify abstract matters, unobservable mental and physical causes
- Art
- Burial rites
- Cults and religions
- Quest for origin, meaning, ontological status

> **Mental preconditions:** *Self-reflective, narrative, social mind with the ability to abstract and symbolize higher order categories and relations*

Figure 9.1   Human characteristics – behavioral field 1

perception – and projection of meaning, purpose, and mind into the meaningless, coincidental, and mindless (Heider and Simmel 1944; Mischotte 1963; Boyer 2002) – has started to seriously ponder the human conditions and to answer the perennial questions of who we are, why we are here, and what will happen in the afterlife. In other words: the quest for meaning, origin, and ontological status, so typical to our species, has now become an all-pervading part of human existence.

These rites also suggest that a higher sense of individuality, self-identity, and self-consciousness, together with a deeper kind of personal and tribal bonding, may have arisen. The deceased must have had a very strong personal presence – he must have been "somebody" to someone – to survive as a lasting impression among the living, and he must have been *alive* to such a degree that he simply cannot die, but has to live on in another sphere (Figure 9.1 sums up the differences).

In short: With the rise of modern *Homo sapiens*, a new and more complex social/tribal mind seems to have seen the light of day, and there is even more evidence to support this presumption.

Technology

Many animals use and produce simple tools (Barnard 2004), but here a few examples will suffice. New Caledonian crows (*Corvus moneduloides*), living in their natural environments, are consummated tool makers and users, and may, under laboratory conditions, for instance, bend a piece of wire into a hook in order to pull food out of a pipe (Weir et al. 2002; Hunt 2000). Recently, they have even been shown to spontaneously solve a demanding meta-tool task, in which a short tool is used to extract a longer tool that can be used to obtain meat (Taylor et al. 2007).

Meta-tool use – for example, the use of simple stone tools to make more complex tools – was one of the major innovations in our own history, and to many an indication of the "cognitive leap" that initiated technological evolution in hominines. This capacity, so far only found in humans and apes, has now also been documented outside the primate line.

Dolphins and whales may practice "sponge-carrying" in their foraging tactics, which involves finding and tearing off conical marine sponges from the substrate, placing the sponge in the rostrum and using it to ferret fish from the sea floor (Smolker et al. 1997). Elephants may show the highest frequency and diversity of tools outside the primate line. They brake off branches, leaves, and sticks in order to make flyswatters, fans, and backscratchers, and they throw stones and sticks at antagonists. In a 100-hour field study of African savannah elephants (*Loxodonta africana*), Chervalier-Skolnikoff and Liska (1993) observed as many as 9 types of tool use, with an average of 1.45 acts per hour.

Chimpanzees have special *tool kits*, that is, repertoires of tools used in special areas (hygiene, agonism, extractive foraging, etc.). Sometimes they mash leaves to manufacture a sponge, throw rocks and sticks at antagonists (Goodall 1986), strip and bend branches to fish termites (Sanz, Morgan, and Gulick 2004), or even produce 'spears' with sharpened points to hunt bush babies (*Galago senegalensis*) hiding in tree holes (Pruetz and Bertolani 2007). Several of these tools are not only made but also reused and transported from one place to another. Moreover, they have *tool sets* – tools used in a necessary functional sequence to achieve goals and to solve problems (McGrew 2004), such as the "termite tool set" which includes puncturing sticks (that are often kept and carried and especially used for subterranean nests) followed by modified twigs with brush-tip fishing probes made in one end (Sanz, Morgan, and Gulick 2004).

The complete chimpanzee tool kit may be as complex as the simplest tool kit known to modern humans, such as the one used by the aboriginal Tasmanians (McGrew 1992), but in spite of its relative complexity something is conspicuously missing: So far, no animal has been seen to spontaneously combine two items to make one new tool. What is even more conspicuous is that apparently none of our hominid ancestors did that either!

If we look into the toolboxes of *Homo habilis, Homo erectus*, and archaic *Homo sapiens* (2 million – 150,000 BC), no multi-component tools, no special-purpose tools, and no socially marked tools are found, just as we do not find any manifestations of art or decoration in their remains. In fact, almost nothing happens between the invention of the drop-shaped hand axe 1.4 million years ago, and until modern Homo sapiens set off the Paleolithic revolution less than 60,000 years ago. Then the axe is connected with a wooden shaft, the spear with a spear thrower, and the bone hook with a line and a stick. Then our technical skills are fused with our knowledge of the natural world in the production of special-purpose tools and weapons that take into account, for instance, that the skin of elephants and rhinos is tougher than the skins of deer and birds. Then these things become beautifully decorated and hereby loaded with social information about the possessor, and the group to which he belongs. And, as suggested by Mithen (1998), all these material differences may very well indicate, that a new, functionally integrated and generally reflective mind or brain has developed, with the ability to mentally combine information (social, technical, and natural-historical) stored in different brain systems, previously not in communication with each other (Figure 9.2 sums up the differences).

Yet, the fact that all these complex cultural patterns have only been found in our species, does not imply that culture as such is a strictly human phenomenon. That depends entirely on how culture is defined.

Behavioral field 2: *Complex, combinatory tool making*

- Multi-component tools
- Special-purpose tools
- Socially marked tools

Mental preconditions: *Functionally integrated, generally reflective mind combining information stored in various brain systems*

Figure 9.2   Human characteristics – behavioral field 2

Culture

If we, as De Waal (2001, 30–1), simply define culture as *"the non-genetic spreading of habits,"* and insist that the rest is nothing else than *"embellishment,"* or as Laland and Hoppit (2003, 151) maintain that culture is *"those group-typical behaviour patterns shared by members of a community that rely on socially learned and transmitted information,"* then a number of species, from birds and whales to elephants and primates can be granted a membership to "the culture club."

In a review of social transmission of foraging behavior, Lefebvre and Palameta (1988) documented 97 examples of socially learned variation in animals as diverse as fish, lizards, sparrows, and baboons. One study gathering data from six long-term chimpanzee studies from across Africa reported 39 different cultural features (Whiten et al. 1999), and recently Zapolsky (2006) has convincingly documented how a distinctive social tradition of low aggression and high affiliation was established, passed on to the following generations, and socially transmitted to newcomers in a group of wild anubis baboons (*Papio anubis*).

However, other researchers (Zihlman and Bolter 2004) insist that we maintain a strict dividing line between tradition and culture, and that the transmission of knowledge through symbols with an abstract reference (which allows cultural learning to take place without the physical presence of living models) is the defining basis of culture proper. Yet others (Bergman 2006) suggest that we leave out socially functional and ecologically functional behaviors, and hereby the patterns that appear as responses to demographic and environmental contingencies.

Personally, I fail to see what is gained by this exclusivity. Why reserve the concept of culture to the highest order of human complexity? Such restrictive definitions not only exclude inquiries by biologists and comparative psychologists into questioning whether or not other species have culture; but also preclude an exploration of the evolutionary roots of human culture and of humans' place in nature! And besides, who would insist that, for example, the Indian or the Egyptian culture is independent of such ecological factors as the monsoon, the desert, or the Nile?

The environmental forces both evoke (Tooby and Cosmides 1992), afford, and select for (cultural, as well as, natural selection) specific adaptive behaviors and cultural strategies that are passed on through generations. However, I fail to see why these specific group patterns should be less cultural than other patterns. A much more fertile approach would be to start out with a few descriptive and common denominators that most of us would agree with, and which would allow us to compare human cultural patterns to discrete and group-specific patterns found in other species. Something like the following (inspired by Potts 2004):

Culture: Descriptive common denominators

1. Culture is a system of non-genetic information transfer between generations and among individuals of the same generation.
2. Culture is manifested as discrete forms (i.e., readily identifiable behaviors, artifacts, mental outputs, or social organizations) distinctive of particular populations.
3. These distinct forms show geographic and temporal differentiation inside a species.
4. There is a potential for change across generations.

Cumulative Culture

Other species may have different cultural features, but a distinctive feature of human culture is its *cumulative* nature. Behaviors and artifacts are transmitted, modified, and further developed over many generations, leading to more complex artifacts and behaviors. Even an instrument as simple as a spear consists of several components and requires several meta-tools such as scrapers, wrenches, knives and hammers for its manufacture, and such complex innovations are not invented by individuals, but evolve gradually over many generations.

Evidence of cumulative culture in nonhuman animals remains minimal and controversial (Richerson and Boyd 2005; Marshall-Pescini and Whiten 2008). Our complex symbolic capacities allow us to store and stockpile vast repositories of social information, and another important factor may be our ability to acquire novel behaviors through observational learning and imitation. The last two abilities are also found in a range of other species, but much more seldom and in less sophisticated forms (Richerson and Boyd 2005). A well described incidence of cultural accumulation occurred, when the famous potato-washing Japanese macaques (*Macaca fuscata*) also began to wash wheat and rice, and later in the following generation started to dig waterholes, when the tide was low, so that they did not have to walk too far, in order to wash and salt their groceries (Matsuzawa 2003). But until now, the scientific registration of such incidences has been limited, and experimental approaches with, for instance chimpanzees, indicate that they, like most other animals, are conservative and hesitant in adopting new habits.

Marshall-Pescini and Whiten (2008) showed, that young chimpanzees (age 2–8 years) were able to learn and copy a honey-dipping technique demonstrated by a familiar human: they had to use their index finger to slide open a trap door, whilst with their other hand they had to insert a rod to reach the honey. Yet when they were later shown a more efficient probing technique, built cumulatively on the first one (using the same rod to poke a bolt in the side of the honey pot, allowing the lid to go off so that not only more honey but also peanuts could be reached), nobody upgraded to this more efficient technique despite excessive series of demonstrations (exceeding 200). Instead, they seemed to be stuck on the fishing technique they initially learned, inhibiting cumulative social learning, and possibly constraining the species' capacity for cumulative cultural evolution.

The jury is still out on this question and awaiting more evidence, but so far, complex cumulative culture, where an artifact, through the endless modifications of generations, is transformed from a spear to a missile-carrying spacecraft, appears to be a uniquely human feature. And there are other differences.

Culture is sharing by learning, and human culture differs from the cultures of nonhuman species in what it is that can be shared, and a substantial part of human culture (from religion and marriage to the latest hip thing in fashion) consists of "social constructions,," which cannot be reduced beyond the common intentional states and agreements of the individuals making up these forms (Plotkin 2007). A sum of Euros is not just a unit of currency, it is also an agreement among a group of individuals to use it as the basis for trading relationships, and such imagined worlds and symbolic tokens, made real by collective agreements only, are not seen in other species.

Culture's single most adaptive feature is that it allows the gradual, cumulative assembly of adaptations over generations, adaptations that no single individual could evoke on their own (Richerson and Boyd 2005). But it is difficult to pin down exactly what it is that causes this difference between us and other species in cultural ability.

At least four interrelated factors may be involved: First, it is the same functionally integrated brain and mind that allows us to picture and produce multi-component tools, that also makes it possible for us to generate cultural accumulations. Second, other cognitive derivates of this mind, related to our ability to abstract and synthesize higher order categories, may be in play as well. Then, humans

---

Behavioral field 3: *Culture and social transmission*

- Cumulative culture
- Social constructions made real by collective agreements
- Vast repositories of information stored in sign-systems
- Social transmission without the physical presence of
  living models

Mental preconditions: *Complex symbolic capacities.*
Cognitive ability to abstract and synthesize high-order
categories. Ultra-social mind with ToM

Figure 9.3   Human characteristics – behavioral field 3

have languages, and hereby complex symbolic capacities for spoken
and written sign-systems, which allow us to store and stockpile vast
repositories of information and to socially transmit knowledge without the physical presence of living models. And last, but not least,
cumulative culture may be a derived side-effect of our ultra-social
human mind (see next section). Humans have "theory of mind"
(ToM), that is, the ability to attribute intentional mental states to
others, whereby they simply cannot help joining forces, sharing perspectives, and taking part in each others' projects. This is imperative
for the spreading and accumulation of knowledge, as well as for collaborative ventures (Figure 9.3 sums up the perspectives).

Sociality and Morality

Collaboration and Shared Intentionality

In a headline-making study, comparing chimpanzees, orangutans
(*Pongo pygmaeus*), and 2.5 years old human children on a comprehensive battery of cognitive tests, Herrmann et al. (2007) showed that
children and apes had very similar cognitive skills for dealing with
the physical world, but that children had more sophisticated skills
than any of the ape species for dealing with the social world.

Other researchers (Boesch 2007; De Waal, Boesch, Horner, and
Whiten 2008) have questioned these findings and objected that when a
human experimenter provides the social cues, the apes are at a disadvantage (and this may be especially crucial in the social tasks). Furthermore,
they point out that the differences between the setups for children and
apes in these tests are manifold, making comparisons difficult.

This is undoubtedly true, but that does not change the fact that a growing number of studies indicate how important features of human sociality are not to be found in the rest of the animal world, not even among our closest primate relatives.

Tomasello and colleagues have launched a theory, which states that the decisive difference between apes and us is that only humans have "shared intentionality" – that we are the only species that are: 1) biologically adapted to participate in collaborative activities involving shared goals and socially coordinated action plans, and 2) motivated to share emotions, experiences, and activities with conspecifics (Tomasello et al. 2005, 676).

Indeed, among apes and monkeys there are very few triadic interactions or communications about third entities or topics, and very few signals serve a declarative or informative motive. They usually do not point, show, or actively offer things to conspecifics, and generally they do not engage in simple tasks, such as carrying or building things, together. In the mother–infant dyad, as well, there does not seem to be any of the shared dyadic face-to-face engagements, or 'proto conversations' with turn-taking, which is so common to humans and their infants (Trevarthen 1974; Hobson 2002).

Warning and food calls left aside, apes and monkeys communicate almost exclusively with the purpose of getting others to do what they want. Human infants, in addition, also make gestures and talk in order to share information with others, just as they share their emotions freely, as when an infant points to a running dog to show her mother and squeals with delight. This unprompted sharing of information reveals a helpful, interested, other-directedness that seems natural to humans, but is almost absent in other species.

It may be fair to conclude that "shared intentionality," and socially coordinated actions are significantly more widespread and cognitively more elaborated in our species than among our nonhuman relatives. But is it also fair to conclude, as Tomasello and consorts do, that no convincing signs of shared intentionality are found outside the human line?

Many would disagree and throw incidences in strong defense of chimpanzees engaging in collaborative hunting with role division, coordinating territorial patrolling, and raids behind enemy lines (Boesch 2001; 2003; this volume), soliciting support during coalition formation (De Waal and van Hooff 1981), mediating reconciliation (De Waal and van Rosmalen 1979), or performing various helping behaviors such as holding a "ladder" for others to climb (Menzel 1972; De Waal 1982), etc.

Lately, even Tomasello and collaborators have presented evidence that young human-reared chimpanzees may volunteer to help familiar or unknown humans in obtaining an object beyond their reach, or assist a conspecific in gaining access to a room with food by removing a chain that only they can control (Warneken et al. 2007). Other species follow suit.

Rooks (*Corvus frugilegus*) cooperate to move a heavy platform loaded with food by pulling both ends of a string simultaneously, and share the food afterwards (Seed, Clayton, and Emery 2008). Species as diverse as hawks (*Parabuteo unicinctus*), social cetaceans (humpbacked whales, killer whales, dolphins), and lions (*Pantera leo*) hunt in groups of up to 10 individuals with coordinated movements and division of roles (some drive or flush, some block and surround, and some ambush), resembling the collaborative hunting seen in chimpanzees (Bednarz 1988; Gaydos et al. 2005; Rendell and Whitehead 2001; Connor, Heithaus, and Barre 1999; Byrne 1994; Boesch 2003).

Skeptics may object that what we see here are acts of opportunistic mutualism, in which everybody does their thing on the spur of the moment – a case of adequate reactive improvising – rather than cooperative endeavors governed by a shared plan, and this may be the case in some incidences. In other cases, it seems difficult not to see these complex, coordinated, collaborative, and group-initiated acts as expressions of shared intentions. But there are other differences.

Humans not only engage in complex large-scale cooperation, unparalleled in the rest of the animal world outside the eusocial insects – involving tens, hundreds, or even thousands of participants, united in super-groups, performing almost like "super-organisms," pursuing common goals through elaborate individual specialization and division of labor, and sometimes involving radical self-sacrifices for the benefit of the group. But most peculiarly, we do so with non-kin and total strangers, just as we trade systematically and exchange goods and services, accepting symbolic tokens such as money and stocks, based on a system of mutual trust.

Such large-scale and high-risk engagements with non-kin can only work if we can detect cheaters, social parasites, and non-reciprocators, and if defection is collectively sanctioned; that is, not only by the ones cheated, but also by third-parties watching or hearing about the deed.

Indeed, people do seem to (1) make spontaneous personality judg-ments (Haselton and Funder 2006) and to be endowed with cogni-tive and emotional cheater-detection mechanisms that react to even minor indications of cheating (Petersen, Sell, Tooby, and Cosmides, this volume; Cosmides 1989; Frank et al. 1993; Brown, Palameta, and Moore 2003; Pradel, Euler, and Fetchenhauer 2009); (2) keep score of (and gossip about) other people's behaviors; (3) use these reputation-scores to gauge the quality of potential partners and to cooperate electively with sharing and trustworthy individuals (Pradel et al. 2009; Norenzayan, this volume); and, most spectacularly, (4) practice third-party altruistic punishment and rewards ("strong reciprocity") toward group members as well as total strangers that they might never meet again, just to enforce the social norms that they abide by (Gintis 2000; Fehr, Fishbäcker, and Gächter 2002; Fehr and Fishbäcker 2004). We even have evidence that social and generous acts spontaneously inspire goodwill and reciprocal gener-osity, not only in the beneficiary, but also in unrelated third-parties (Weedekind and Milenski 2000).

Many species, from fish to nonhuman primates, are scorekeepers, and register others' behaviors toward them in order to predict future behaviors (Silk 2002; Dugatkin 2006). Chimpanzees may also learn the reputation of strangers by observing third-party interactions, and later use this information in their own interactions with the stranger (Subiaul et al., 2008). However, these scores are still limited to the individual's personal perceptions and experiences, whereas humans have language that allows them to share the scores of others, which makes it possible for large groups of non-kin, without day-to-day interactions, to reap the benefits of cooperation by monitoring each others' behaviors (via gossip), shunning or punishing cheaters, and rewarding team players. Besides, chimpanzees may be recruited to take part in conflicts and attacks involving kin or allies, but gen-erally they take a self-centered and opportunistic stance in relation to the on-goings of group life, and we still have no evidence of them rewarding a good deed done to others. Moreover, experimen-tal findings indicate that this should not be expected either, as the next paragraph will show.

Sharing, Reciprocity and "Other-Regarding Preferences"
As humans we simply are each other's means to the common goals, and the *human niche* – that is, the physical and social environment

that we have adapted to throughout history – is a niche characterized by considerable inter-dependence, collaboration, closely knit
relationships, intensive gift-giving, reciprocity, extended sharing
of resources and services, and radical self-sacrifices (Simmel 1950;
Becker 1956; Gouldner 1960; Rochat 2006; Høgh-Olesen 2006).

Comparatively speaking, our capacities to share are quite unique.
For instance, as humans we often take pleasure in simply giving
something to others and take delight in their joy. And when flooded
by beggars on holidays in less privileged parts of the world, we sometimes have to install cognitive counterstrategies – such as only carrying a certain amount of coins in our pockets – simply to restrain our
inclinations to share. In other species, sharing may be endured, but
it is hardly enjoyed, and they most certainly do not need cognitive
counter strategies in order to keep things for themselves. Reciprocal
exchanges are also found in a number of other species, from vampire
bats and whales to primates (Høgh-Olesen 2006), but in humans
reciprocity runs through our social exchanges as such, permeates all
aspects of our social life – outside the most intimate parental-care
relations – and takes on unique species-specific forms (Simmel 1950;
Becker 1956; Gouldner 1960).

In a cross-cultural study from the USA, Japan, and Sweden on
subjects' attitude to receiving donations. An experimental game
situation was set up in which they could receive financial help from
their coplayers, with different obligations attached to these donations. Gerken et al. (1975) found that there was a curve-linear relationship between the degree of obligations attached to a donation
and the beneficiary's sympathy for the benefactor, and that the highest sympathy was rewarded to the benefactor who wanted equal reciprocity for his help (see Figure 9.4).

Contrary to what we would expect, the subjects in these
countries do not gladly just receive donations without obligations. This strange fact is an interesting expression of some of the
social-hierarchic complexities that regulate human relations. The
unrequited gift or help breaks the social symmetry between people
and is thereby in danger of releasing a number of negative moods
in the beneficiary, from inferiority to suspicion ("Something for
nothing! What's he up to?"); most importantly, the gift maintains
the beneficiary in what Homans (1961) named "an unpleasant *tension of obligation.*" Moreover, this tension seems to be a human emotion only, as it is not found with our closest relatives among the
primates, who – as we shall later see – show no aversion whatsoever

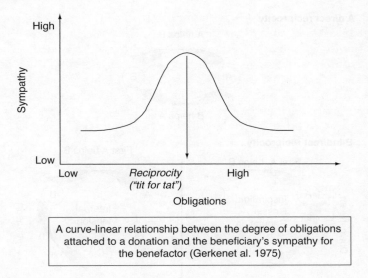

A curve-linear relationship between the degree of obligations
attached to a donation and the beneficiary's sympathy for
the benefactor (Gerkenet al. 1975)

Figure 9.4 Obligations and sympathy in three cross-culture human sample

to exchanges that only benefit themselves (Silk, Brosnan, Vonk
et al. 2005).

The fact that this particular tension, in our species acts as a real
social psychological motivator can be seen in yet another strange and
uniquely human phenomenon known as *'reparative altruism'*. A person who has received help which cannot be returned, will later on
be more inclined to help a total stranger, than a person who has not
previously received any help, or who could reciprocate a generous
act to the original benefactor (Krebs 1970). This phenomenon – also
known as "upstream indirect reciprocity" (Nowak and Sigmund
2005; Alexander 1987) – has perplexed biologists and game theorists
just as much.

Direct "tit for tat" reciprocity where A helps B, and B returns
the favor, makes immediate sense (see Figure 9.5). Classic "downstream indirect reciprocity," where A helps B and later receives help
from C, who has observed or heard of the deed, also works, because
generous acts inspire goodwill and generosity in the ones that wit-
ness such acts (Alexander 1987; Weedekind and Milenski 2000), and
because a good reputation among gossiping, social-hierarchic beings
may result in hardcore evolutionary benefits related to reproduction
and resources as the anthropological data suggests (Kaplan and Hill

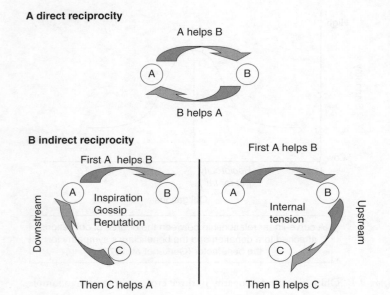

Figure 9.5   Direct and indirect reciprocity: The "upstream" version demands something more than inspiration, gossip, or reputation, and it is suggested that a more intrinsic motivator may be operating

1985; Patton 2000). But why reciprocate a total stranger something you have received from another?

Here, a more intrinsic motivator (in the form of an inner-organism tension) has to be operating, and to me this is yet another indication of how strong and "hardwired" the urge to reciprocate may be.

It is almost as if something like a "fixed action pattern" (FAP) is released by a key-stimulus (Tinbergen 1951; Lorentz 1981). When the reciprocity program is released by the key-stimuli of helping and sharing, an urge to reciprocate develops, and in the absence of a proper benefactor a stand-in may be found in order for this program to deploy its behaviors and release the built-up inner-organism tensions (see Figure 9.6).

Chimpanzees do share, but it is first and foremost passive sharing as a response to intense begging – it is rarely unsolicited and never egalitarian as in our hunter-gatherer societies (Nissen and Crawford 1936; De Waal 1989; 1997; Boesch 2001a; Høgh-Olesen 2010). Therefore, a prey killed alone and without the other's knowledge will not be shared but eaten on the spot (Knauft 1991), whereas

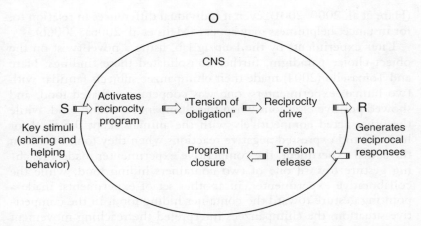

Figure 9.6   Intrinsic FAP-like reciprocity program explaining "reparative alturism"
             Notes: S = stimuli, O = organism, CNS = central nervous system,
             R = response

the human impulse clearly is to *actively* share what we have with others, and a prey killed by a hunter is brought to the common home base and divided among the tribesmen (Barret et al. 2002; Hawkes 1991).

Likewise, reciprocity comes not only in direct and indirect forms, but also in simple and complex forms. With the norm of active sharing, humans move from the simple, responsive, "tit-for-tat reciprocity," found among our *Pan* relatives (Packer 1977; Seyfarth 1980; De Wall and Luttrell 1988; De Waal 1989; 1997; Brosnan and De Waal 2002; Melis Hare and Tomasello 2008), toward a more complex, proactive "golden rule reciprocity," that may be unique to our species, in which the sharing initiative is clearly placed upon the individual: "*You* have to give in order to receive!" Moreover, hard-wired neuro-endocrine feed-back systems seem to reinforce this behavioral normativity, since the centers associated with reward in the brain (*nucleus accumbens, caudate nucleus, ventromedial frontal and orbitro frontal cortex, rostal anterior cingulated cortex*) simply light up when we choose to help or cooperate, as Rilling et al. (2002) neurological studies has shown. This means that a good deed "does good" both outside and inside the organism.

Experimental studies further develop these differences. Several studies indicate that generally chimpanzees are naturally motivated to act competitively rather than cooperatively in food related situations

(Hare et al. 2000; 2001), even if individual differences in relation to, for instance, helpfulness may appear (Melis et al. 2006a; 2006b).

Later experiments by the Leipzig lab, using a novel twist on the object-choice paradigm, further consolidated these findings. Hare and Tomasello (2004) made their chimpanzee subjects familiar with two human experimenters: one was cooperative, shared food, and showed positive emotions when the chimpanzees found food, while the other acted competitively with the animals, kept the food for himself, and expressed negative reactions when they found food. In the actual experiment, the competitive experimenter made a reaching gesture toward one of two containers hiding food, while the collaborative experimenter, in another set of experiments, made a pointing gesture toward the container hiding food. In the competitive situation, the chimpanzees interpreted the reaching movement quite well, and tried to grab the food container before the competitors reached it. However, in the collaborative situation, the chimpanzees did not understand it, and so only chose the correct container at a near chance level. The difference between their predominantly correct responses to a competitor and their random responses to a human co-operator were highly significant ($P = 0.009$). Later replications, comparing a human co-operator with a chimpanzee competitor, showed the same differences.

The lessons learned seem to be that even if chimpanzees do seem to be able to read the intentions, or at least the behavioral goals of others, they do not expect those intentions or goals to be cooperative. Instead, these kinds of intentions often seem to be a closed book to them. So even if this line of experiments presents experimental evidence of "theory of mind" in chimpanzees, it is a special, restricted kind of ToM that anticipates that others – at least in situations related to food – will have competitive rather than cooperative intentions. More generally, a number of studies indicate that their "other-directedness" may be quite different to ours.

When chimpanzees are given a choice between a food reward for themselves, or the same reward for themselves and a visible, well-known, but unrelated conspecific in an adjoining cage, they show no other-regarding preferences (Silk et al. 2005; Jensen et al. 2006). They are highly observant and motivated to receive the food reward themselves, but seem indifferent to the opportunity to deliver cost-free rewards to others, even when these rewards could be released, after they have consummated their own reward, and after intense begging gestures and sounds from the other chimpanzee (Vonk et al. 2008).

Similar experiments with young children show that their other-regarding preferences develop strongly between the ages of three and eight and take the form of inequality aversion. At ages 3–4, most children behave selfishly, and fail to choose the other-regarding possibility above chance level, whereas most children at age 7–8 prefer resource allocations that remove disadvantageous as well as advantageous inequality, and this is even more so if the other player is an ingroup member (Fehr, Bernhard, and Rosenbach 2008).

Capuchin monkeys (*Cebus apella*), chimpanzees, and cotton top tamarins (*Saguinus Oedipus*) may at times display an aversion to disadvantageous inequity (Brosnan and de Waal 2003; Brosnan, Schiff, and De Waal 2005; Wolkenten et al. 2007; Fletcher 2008; Neiworth et al. 2009; however see also Bräuer, Call, and Tomasello 2006; Jensen, Call, and Tomasello 2007; and Bräuer, Call, and Tomasello 2009 for critical replications), but so far only humans have been shown to actively avoid advantageous inequality!

The benchmark test for examining other-regarding preferences and sensitivity to fairness is the *ultimatum game*, in which two players interact to decide how to divide a sum of money. The first player proposes how to divide the sum, and the second player can either accept or reject this proposal; but if he rejects, neither player receives anything.

When this game is played among humans, the proposer typically offers 40–50 percent of the windfall, and offers below 20–30 percent are routinely rejected by the responder (Camerer 2003; Henrich et al. 2005), suggesting that humans have an aversion to inequitable outcomes and punish offers that are too low. When an adapted mini-version of this game was played among chimpanzees, in which the proposer can choose between two pre-set offers which the responder can then accept or reject (by collaborating or not, in drawing in two food trays with different numbers of raisins), chimpanzees, in contradiction to humans, did not:

a. take outcomes affecting the responder into account;
b. make fair offers when given the opportunity; nor,
c. refuse to accept unfair offers from conspecifics.

In short: they did not show any other-regarding preferences or sensitivity to fairness and behaved according to traditional economic models of self-interest and rational maximization (Jensen, Call, and Tomasello 2007).

Other-regarding preferences and inequality aversion are decisive to the ability to achieve and maintain cooperation in large groups of genetic strangers. If an individual cares for the welfare of other group members, this individual is more likely to refrain from free-riding in cooperative projects; and if he is endowed with an aversion to inequality, he is more likely to monitor and punish free-riding in others. These inter-species differences are probably important in explaining why humans are so exceptionally cooperative – so "ultra-social" – compared to other primates.

New evidence may still modify or change this picture, but so far data suggests that chimpanzees are considerably more competitive than humans, and that other-regarding preferences (and perhaps also reputational concerns), proactive sharing, complex "golden rule reciprocity," large-scale cooperation, and third-party sanctioning – in short our *Homo socious* characteristics – are derived properties of humans that have evolved after *Homo* and *Pan* diverged.

Morality – from "Gut-Feelings" to "Ought-Scenarios"

Sociality and morality are communicating vessels, and the latter stems from the fact that we, as social creatures, are each others' means to common goals, and hence rely on a support system for our survival. A solitary organism has no need for moral rules, nor does a creature that lives among others without mutual dependency.

As students of Plato and Kant, we may have learned that morality is a strictly human phenomenon, depending on the faculty of pure reason and founded on higher cognitive and cultural processes. Consequently, we become moral creatures only by opposing our basic nature. Today, comparative studies and modern neuroscience show that many of our highest moral, altruistic, and sympathetic inclinations may be evolutionarily anchored in mammalian sociality, and based on pre-programmed, emotional, and neuro-endocrine feedbacks – operating as spontaneous "gut-feelings" – rather than pure reason, and just as selected for as our more selfish impulses (Krebs, this volume; De Waal 1996; 2006; this volume; Rilling et al. 2002; Greene and Haidt 2002; Chapman et al. 2009).

Hamilton's *kin selection theory* (1964) states that genes for altruism can evolve if altruism is targeted at kin. This explains why we, and many other species, help, care, and make costly sacrifices for those genetically close to us. Trivers' *reciprocal altruism theory* (1971) posits that genes for altruism can evolve if altruism and vengeance are targeted at those who do and do not return favors. This explains why so many social exchanges in humans – and a variety of other species, from worms (*Ophrocha diadema*), sea bass (*Hypoplectrus nigrans*), and sperm whales (*Physeter macrophalus*) to vampire bats (*Desmodus roton-dus*), impalas (*Aepyceros melampus*), coatis (*Nasua nasua*), and primates in general – are governed by a reciprocity program (Høgh-Olesen 2006; Dugatkin 2000; Mesnic, Evans, and Taylor 2003; Wilkinson 1984; Romero and Aureli 2008; De Waal 1989; 1997).

However, as several researchers (Richerson and Boyd 2005; Haidt 2007) have noted, these basic mechanisms cannot explain the extra-ordinary degree to which people cooperate with strangers they will never meet again, as well as make sacrifices for large groups of non-kin. Reciprocity may explain the cooperation of smaller social units with day-to-day interactions over longer periods, but for large-scale cooperation among strangers to take place, some of the above-mentioned mechanisms related to indirect reciprocity (score-keeping, reputation gossiping) and third-party altruistic punishments and rewards, found in humans only, have to play an important role. This has led the same researchers to assume that group-selective proc-esses in humans may have evolved a kind of "tribal overlay" in our species – that is, a coevolved set of cultural practices and moral intui-tions that are not about how to treat other individuals (kin selection and reciprocal altruism take care of that), but about how to be a part of a group competing with other groups (Haidt 2007) These generally cooperative dispositions were superimposed onto human psychology, without eliminating those older social instincts that favor friends and kin, and this renders us susceptible to an inherent conflict between other-regarding and public-minded concerns, as well as giving us more selfish and nepotistic dispositions that other species are spared with (Richerson and Boyd 2005). There are also other moral dilemmas that appear to be distinctly human.

That many of our highest moral impulses, rather than "pure rea-son," are anchored in our mammalian and primate sociality, and based on spontaneous, emotional intuitions and "gut-feelings," does not exclude the possibility that some of our moral choices may be both exclusively human and strictly rational. Take for instance the famous trolley dilemma (see Figure 9.7). Here, most people choose without hesitation to press a shift that will lead a runaway trolley from one track, where it would have killed five innocent people, to another track, where only one innocent person will be killed. In other words: Sacrificing one to save five.

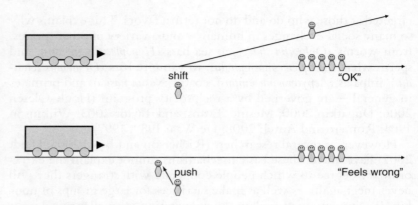

Figure 9.7   The Trolley dilemma

However, when they have to save the five by actually pushing this person onto the tracks themselves, a clear majority refuses flatly to do so. The reason given is that it simply does not feel right, and a fMRI scanning of their brain activity shows that a number of old mammalian brain areas (more specifically, the *Precuneus* area) are activated during this kind of problem solving (Greene and Haidt 2002), lending support to the above-mentioned idea that substantial parts of our morality may be anchored in mammalian sociality.

But what about the few rationalists who ignore their gut-feelings and still decide to sacrifice one to save five by pushing one onto the tracks?

A fMRI scanning shows that these subjects: (1) take a longer time to decide, and (2) show more activity in prefrontal brain areas, and hereby more cognitive processing before making the decision. And this morally rational choice, in which higher cognitive processes apparently overrule more basic programs, could be an example of a moral choice, which no other social animal than us would be able to make!

Let us widen the perspective slightly. It is possible for humans to have an organizing, "top-down" impact on some of their basic constituents – for example, when a child chooses to inhibit the spontaneous reflex of crying when hurt until others who can comfort are within sight; when a monk chooses celibacy; or when a mountaineer overrules basic needs for body temperature, oxygen, and food in order to climb Mount Everest. And this seems to be an essential difference.

Behavioral field 4: *Sociality and morality*

- Increased inclination to share and sacrifice, tension of obligation
- Complex, proactive "golden rule reciprocity"
- Other-regarding preferences
- Third-party altruistic punishments and rewards
- Large-scale, high-risk collaboration with non-kin and strangers
- Moral choices governed by "pure reason" and principles
- Moral projects governed by "ought-scenarios" for the future

Mental preconditions: *Ultra-social, other-directed mind: Hardwired neuro-endocrine programs of moral intuitions and sanctions, active sharing and reciprocity. Higher cognitive (prefrontal) top-down organization of basic programs*

Figure 9.8 Human characteristics – behavioral field 4

Thanks to this ability, humans can be motivated by "ought to" or "should,," and decide to "row a canoe against the stream,," metaphorically speaking – to lead lives governed by principles and values so important that they are worth dying for, and to strive to be impartial, courageous, responsible, honest, unselfish, and so on. Similarly, we can be tormented by complex, self-reflective emotions such as shame and guilt when we fail to live up to our standards. This makes up for a life other than a life ruled by instincts, desires, needs, and emotions, even if such a life can also be a social and intelligent one.

Apes may sometimes be helpful, caring, and brave, but that is not because they think they should be, and that is a crucial difference (Korsgaard 2006). Our neo-cortical superstructures have given us the ability to consider and reflect on any number of different scenarios for the future, and that gives us, as probably the only creatures, the ability to see before our mind's eye the world as it *could* be.

Figure 9.8 summarizes the human particulars.

Two Roads – Concluding Remarks

There is continuity between the rest of the world and us, but each species has its species-specific traits, and in this chapter I have tried to track down some of the human particulars.

However, things are progressing rapidly, and this applies especially to the areas of culture and sociality/morality. Research on tool use, collaboration, "theory of mind," and "mental time travels" is likewise gaining new momentum, thanks to the fascinating studies on rooks, crows, and scrub-jays conducted in Cambridge (Dally, Emery, and Clayton 2006; Seed, Clayton, and Emery 2008). So while you are reading these lines, studies currently under review, that are able to challenge or introduce light and shade onto the suggestions presented here, may already be pilling up. But that is just part of the game, and it shall not prevent us from summing up the conclusions reached so far. Figure 9.9 may recapitulate the main points.

The complex symbolic activities of art, cult, and rite, listed under Behaviour Field 1, still seem to be wholly unprecedented outside the line of modern *Homo*, but this may be due to an almost total absence of relevant comparative studies in this area. Apart from a few dubious examples of captive chimpanzees and elephants "painting" pictures (Stange 2009), and anecdotal incidences of chimpanzees performing so-called "rain dances" (when confronted with noisy natural phenomena like waterfalls and heavy showers) in the form of stylized power displays sometimes interpreted as an indication of awe (Goodall 1995), this area is more or less *terra incognita*. Aesthetic preferences may be functional to others than humans, but do other species show aesthetic sensibility and appreciation? We simply do not know.

Comparatively speaking, we are an ultra-social species, but this designation does not change the distinct Jekyll-and-Hyde nature – or, alternatively: the complementarity of human sociality, let alone the existential paradoxes that follow from this.

As biological organisms, it is in our nature to pursue and satisfy personal needs and interests, while at the same time – as group-living creatures – we are totally dependent on our conspecifics for survival. And as social-hierarchic creatures, coded for status rivalry, we have a strong inborn impulse to dominate, the counterpart of which is a strong inborn aversion against being dominated!

To maximize our personal gains and evolutionary chances, we unite in alliances In the course of evolution, outgroup hostility enhanced ingroup solidarity to the point that morality evolved, and all these characteristics leave man in a "brotherhood of tempered rivalry," as Wynne-Edwards (1963) formulated it.

It may not be part of our everyday awareness, but basically there are only two main roads to what we all want and need: We can fight and compete, or we can collaborate and share (Høgh-Olesen 2006). Thanks to our *Homo socius* characteristics – that is, our unique other-regarding preferences, our increased inclinations to proactive sharing, and our complex "golden rule" reciprocity, where the imperative

Human characteristics

Behavioral field 1
Complex symbolic behavior

- Grammatical items with no physical reference
- Syntactic complexity –Ability to signify abstract matters, unobservable mental and physical causes
- Art
- Burial rites
- Cults and religions
- Quest for origin, meaning, ontological status

Mental preconditions:
Self-reflective, narrative, social mind with the ability to abstract and symbolize higher order categories and relations

Behavioral field 3
Culture and social transmission

- Cumulative culture
- Social constructions made real by collective agreements
- Vast repositories of information stored in sign-systems
- Social transmission without the physical presence of living models

Mental preconditions:
Complex symbolic capacities. Cognitive ability to abstract and synthesize high-order categories. Ultra-social mind with ToM

"Mind" organizing

constituting "Nature"

Behavioral field 4
Sociality and morality

- Increased inclination to share and sacrifice, tension of obligation
- Complex, proactive, "golden rule reciprocity"
- Other-regarding preferences
- Third-party altruistic punishments and rewards
- Large-scale, high-risk collaboration with non-kin and strangers
- Moral choices governed by "pure reason" and principles
- Moral projects governed by "ought-scenarios" for the future

Mental preconditions:
Ultra-social other-directed mind: Hardwired programs of moral intuitions, active sharing and reciprocity. Higher congitive (prefrontal) top-down organization of basic programs

Behavioral field 2
Complex combinatoric tool making

- Multi-component tools
- Special-purpose tools
- Socially marked tools

Mental preconditions:
Functionally integrated, generally reflective mind combining information stored in various brain systems

Figure 9.9 Behaviors and capacities apparently unique to humans

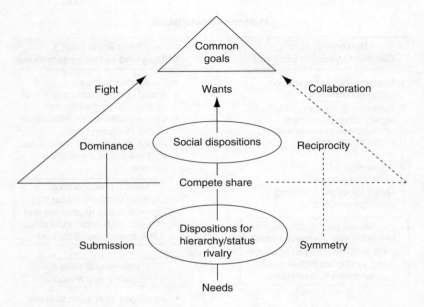

Figure 9.10   Two roads

to give, help, and share is clearly placed upon the individual – the collaborative road is chosen more often, and with more far-reaching consequences, in our species, than in any other species that we know of. This does make a difference (see Figure 9.10).

The broken lines indicate that the Homo socious characteristics mediate between the antagonistic forces in our social-hierarchical nature and provides us with a *collaborative* instrument to pursue *personal* goals (Høgh-Olesen 2006).

Humans travel and mingle in crowds, just as they engage in large-scale cooperation with strangers; whereas chimpanzees are xenophobic and lack any friendly ties between groups. And when we compare intra-group conflicts and killings, chimpanzees turn on their own, and fight aggressively, up to 200 times more frequently than humans in small-scale societies (Wrangham et al. 2006), who in turn have 2–3 times higher homicide rates (per 100,000 per year) than people living in modern societies (Kelly 2007).

All in all, we seem to have developed a set of socio-cognitive, inter-personal strategies that function as a bulwark against the more antagonistic impulses in our social-hierarchic nature: Our *sapiens* characteristics allow us to engage in complex problem solving and symbolic sanctioning, while the *socious* characteristics of human nature provides us with a functional alternative to the fight that still allows us to pursue *personal* needs and goals, but now in a *collaborative* way!

Again, this does not imply that modern humans are anything near the blissful pastoral envisioned by Rousseau in the introduction. We are exactly as selfish and self-sacrificing as it has paid off for us to be. But still we are, comparatively speaking, a much more peaceful, other-directed, and sharing species, operating according to slightly different socio-cognitive programs than, for instance, our closest relatives, the chimpanzees.

References

Alexander, R. D. 1987. *The biology of moral systems.* New York. Aldine.

Arnold, K. and, K. Zuberbühler. 2006. Semantic combinations in primate calls. *Nature* 441:303.

Barnard, C. 2004. *Animal behaviour.* England: Pearson Education.

Barret, L. R. Dunbar, and J. Lucett, 2002. *Human evolutionary psychology.* New York: Palgrave.

Becker, H. 1956. *Man in reciprocity.* New York: Praeger.

Bednarz, J. 1988. Cooperative hunting in Harris' hawks. *Science* 239:1525–7.

Bergman, T. J. 2006. Comments. *Current Anthropology* 47(4):648–9.

Boesch, C. 2001. Chimpanzee hunters! Chaos or cooperation in the forest? In *Model Systems in Behavioral Ecology*, edited by L. Dugatkin, 453–65. Princeton: Princeton University Press.

Boesch, C. 2001a. Cooperative hunting roles among Tai chimpanzees. *Human Nature* 13:27–46.

Boesch, C. 2003. Complex cooperation among Tai chimpanzees. In *Animal Social Complexity*, edited by F. B. M. De Waal and P. L. Tyack, chapter 4. Cambridge, MA: Harvard University Press.

Boesch, C. 2007. What makes us Human (Homo sapiens)? The challenge of cognitive cross-species comparison. *Journal of Comparative Psychology* 121(3):227–40.

Boyer, P. 2002. *Religion explained.* London: Vintage.

Bräuer, J., J. Call, and M. Tomasello. 2006. Are apes really inequity averse? *Proceedings of the Royal Society of London, B* 273:3123–8.

Bräuer, J., J. Call, and M. Tomasello. 2009. Are apes inequity averse? New data on the Token-Exchange paradigm. *American Journal of Primatology* 71:175–81.

Brosnan, S. F. and F. B. M. De Waal. 2002. Empathy: Its ultimate and proximate bases. *Behavioral and Brain Sciences* 25:1–72.

Brosnan, S. F. and F. B. M. De Waal. 2003. Monkeys reject unequal pay. *Nature* 425:297–9.

Brosnan, S. F., H. C. Schiff, and F. B. M. De Waal. 2005. Tolerance for inequity may increase with social closeness in chimpanzees. *Proceedings of the Royal Society of London, B,* 1560:253–8.

Brown, W. M., B. Palameta, and C. Moore. 2003. Are there nonverbal cues to commitment? *Evolutionary Psychology* 1:42–69.

Byrne, R. 1994. The evolution of intelligence. In *Behaviour and Evolution,* edited by P. Slater and T. Halliday, 223–65. Cambridge: Cambridge University Press.

Camerer, C.F. 2003. *Behavioral game theory: Experiments in strategic interaction.* Princeton, NJ. Princeton University Press.

Cheney, D. L. and R. M. Seyfarth. 1990. *How monkeys see the world.* Chicago: University of Chicago Press.

Chevalier-Skolnikoff, S. and J. Liska. 1993. Tool use by wild and captive elephants. *Animal Behaviour* 46:209–19.

Chapman, H. A., D. A. Kim, J. M. Susskind, and A. K. Anerson. 2009. In bad taste: Evidence for the oral origins of moral disgust. *Science* 323:1222–6.

Chomsky, N. 1972. *Language and mind.* New York. Harcourt Brace Jovanovich.

Chomsky, N. 1995. *The minimalist programme.* Cambridge, MA. MIT Press.

Clarke, E., U. H. Reichard, K. Zuberbühler. 2006. The syntax and meaning of wild gibbon songs. *Plos one* 1(1):e73

Connor, R. C., M. R. Heithaus, and L. M. Barre. 1999. Superalliance in bottlenose dolphins. *Nature* 371:571–2.

Cosmides, L. 1989. The logic of social exchange. Has natural selection shaped how humans reason? *Cognition* 31:187–276.

Dally, J. M., N. J. Emery, and N. S. Clayton. 2006. Food-caching western scrub-jays keep track of who was watching when. *Science* 312:1662–5.

Darwin, C. 1966 [1859]. *On the origin of species.* Cambridge, MA: Harvard University Press.

Darwin, C. 1998 [1874]. *The descent of man.* New York: Prometheus Books.

De Quervain, D. J. F., U. Fishbacher, V. Treyer, M. Schellhammer, U. Schnyder, A. Buck, and E. Fehr, 2004. The neural basis of altruistic punishment. *Science* 305:1254–8.

De Waal, F. B. M. 1982. *Chimpanzee politics.* London: Jonathan Cape.

De Waal, F. B. M. 1989. Food sharing and reciprocal obligations among chimpanzees. *Journal of Human Evolution* 18:433–59.

De Waal, F. B. M. 1996. *Good natured: The origins of right and wrong in humans and other animals.* Cambridge, MA: Harvard University Press.

De Waal, F. B. M. 1997. The chimpanzee's service economy: Food for grooming. *Evolution and Human Behaviour* 18:375–86.

De Waal, F. B. M. 2001. *The ape and the sushi master.* New York: Basic Books.

De Waal, F. B. M. 2005. *Our inner ape.* London: Grania Books.

De Waal, F. B. M. 2006. *Primates and philosophers.* Princeton, NJ: Princeton University Press.

De Waal, F. B. M., C. Boesch, V. Horner, and A. Whiten. 2008. Comparing social skills of children and apes. *Science* 319:569.

De Wall, F. B. M and L. M. Luttrell. 1988. Mechanisms of social reciprocity. *Ethology and Sociobiology* 9:101–18.

De Waal, F. B. M. and J. A. van Hooff. 1981. Side-directed communication and agonistic interactions in chimpanzees. *Behaviour* 77:164–98.

De Waal, F. B. M. and A. van Roosmalen. 1979. Reconciliation and consolation among chimpanzees. *Behavioral Ecology and Sociobiology* 5:55–66.

Diamond, J. 2006. *The third Chimpanzee.* New York. Harper Perennial.

Dobzhansky, T. 1962. *Mankind evolving: The evolution of the human species.* New Haven: Yale University Press.

Dugatkin, L. 2000. *Cheating monkeys and citizen bees.* Cambridge, MA: Harvard University Press.

Dugatkin, L.A. 2006. Trust in fish. *Nature* 441:937–8.

Eibl-Eibesfeldt, I. 1970. *Ethology: The biology of behavior.* New York: Holt, Rinehart & Winston.

Eliade, M. 1995. *De religiøse ideers historie,* vol. 1. København: Gyldendal.

Evans, C. S. and L. Evans. 1999. Chicken calls are functional referential. *Animal behaviour* 58:307–19.

Fehr, E., H. Bernhard, and B. Rockenbach. 2008. Egalitarianism in young children. *Nature* 454:1079–83.

Fehr, E., U. Fishbacher, and S. Gächter. 2002. Strong reciprocity, human cooperation and the enforcement of social norms. *Human Nature* 13:1–25.

Fehr, E. and U. Fishbacher. 2004. Third-party punishment and social norms. *Evolution and Human Behaviour* 25:63–87.

Fletcher, G. 2008. Attending to the outcome of others: Disadvantageous inequity aversion in male Capuchin monkeys. *American Journal of Primatology* 70:901–5.

Frank, R. H., Gilovicht, L. and Reagan, D. T. 1993. The evolution of one-shot cooperation: An experiment. *Ethology and Sociobiology* 14:247–56.

Frederiksen, J. K. and C. N. Slobodchikoff. 2007. Referential specificity in the alarm calls of the black-tailed prairie dog. *Ethology, Ecology and Evolution* 19:87–99.

Gaydos, J., S. Raverty, R. Baird, and R. Osborne. 2005. Suspected surplus killing of harbour seal pups (Phoca vitulina) by killing whales (Orcinus orca). *Northwestern Naturalist* 86:150–4.

Gerken, K. S., P. Ellsworth, C. Maslach, and M. Seipel. 1975. Obligation, donor resources and reactions to aid in three cultures. *Journal of Personal and Social Psychology* 31(3):390–400.

Gintis, H. 2000. Strong reciprocity and human sociality. *Journal of theoretical biology* 206:169–79.

Goodall, J. 1969. *My friends the wild chimpanzees.* Washington DC: National Geographic Society.

Goodall, J. 1986. *The chimpanzees of Gombe.* Boston: Bellknap Press.

Goodall, J. 1995. *The new chimpanzees.* National Geographic DVD.

Gouldner, A. Q. 1960. The norm of reciprocity. *American Social Revue* 25(2):161–78.

Greene, J. and J. Haidt. 2002. How (and when) does moral judgement work? *Trends in Cognitive Science* 16:517–23.

Haidt, J. 2007. The new synthesis in moral psychology. *Science* 316:998–1002.

Hamilton, W.D. 1964. The genetical evolution of social behaviour. *Journal of Theoretical Biology* 7:1–52.

Hare, B. E, J. Call, and M. Tomasello. 2001. Do chimpanzees know what conspecifics know? *Animal Behaviour* 61(1):139–51.

Hare, B. E., J. Call, B. Agnetta, and M. Tomasello. 2000. Chimpanzees know what conspecifics do and do not see. *Animal Behaviour* 59:771–85.

Hare, B. E. and M. Tomasello. 2004. Chimpanzees are more skilful in competitive than in cooperative tasks. *Animal Behaviour* 68:571–81.

Haselton, M. G. and D. C. Funder. 2006. The evolution of accuracy and bias in social judgment. In *Evolution and social psychology*, edited by M. Schaller, J. A. Simpson, and D. T. Kenrick, 16–37. New York: Psychology Press.

Hawkes, K. 1991. "Showing off": Test of another hypothesis about men's foraging goals. *Ethology and Sociobiology* 11:341–61.

Heider, F. and M. Simmel. 1944. An experimental study of apparent behaviour. *American Journal of Psychology* 57:243–54.

Henrich, J., R. Boyd, and S. Bowles, et al. 2005. "Economic Man" in cross-cultural perspective: Behavioural experiments in 15 small-scale societies. *Behavioral and Brain Sciences* 28:795–855.

Herman, L. M. 2006. Intelligence and rational behaviour in the bottle-nosed dolphin. In *Rational animals*, edited by S. Hurley and M. Nudds, chapter 20. Oxford: Oxford University Press.

Herrmann, E., J. Call, M.V. Hernandez-Lloreda, B. Hare, and M. Tomasello. 2007. Humans have evolved specialized skills of social cognition: The cultural intelligence hypothesis. *Science* 317:1360–6.

Hobson, R. P. 2002. *The cradle of thought.* New York: Macmillan.

Høgh-Olesen, H. 2006. The sacrifice and the reciprocity-programme in religious rituals and in man's everyday interactions. *Journal of Cognition and Culture* 6(3–4):499–519.

Høgh-Olesen, H. 2010. The will to sacrifice. Sharing and sociality in humans, apes, and monkeys. In A. W. Geertz (Ed.): *Origins of Religion, Cognition and Culture*. London: Equinox. In press.

Homans, G. C. 1961. *Social behavior: Its elementary forms.* New York: Hartcourt, Brace and World.

Hunt, G. R. 2000. Tool use by the New Caledonian crow. *EMU* 100:109–14.

Hurford, J. R. 2007. *The origins of meaning.* Oxford: Oxford University Press.

Jensen, K., J. Call, and M. Tomasello. 2007. Chimpanzees are vengeful but not spiteful. *PNAS* 104:1346–50.

Jensen, K., B. E. Hare, J. Call, and M. Tomasello. 2006. What´s in it for me? Self-regard precludes altruism and spite in chimpanzees. *Proceedings of the royal Society of London, B* 273:1013–21.

Kaplan, H. L. and K. Hill. 1985. Food sharing among Ache Foragers. *Current Anthropology* 26(2):223–40.

Keeley, L. H. 1997. *War before Civilization.* Oxford: Oxford University Press.

Kelly, R. C. 2007. *Warless societies and the origin of war.* Ann Arbor: The University of Michigan Press.

Knauft, B. M. 1991. Violence and sociality in human evolution. *Current Anthropology* 26(2):223–40.

Korsgaard, C. M. 2006. Morality and the distinctiveness of human action. In *Primates and Philosophers*, edited by F. B. M. De Waal, 103–23. Princeton, NJ: Princeton University Press.

Krebs, D. L. 1970. Altruism: An examination of the concept. *Psychological Bulletin* 73(4):258–302.

Laland, K. and W. Hoppit. 2003. Do animals have culture? *Evolutionary Anthropology* 12:150–9.

Leakey, R. 1995. *The origin of humankind.* New York: Basic Books.

Lefebvre, L. and B. Palameta. 1988. Mechanisms, ecology, and population diffusion of socially-learned food-finding behaviour in feral pigeons. In *Social Learning, Psychological and Biological Perspectives*, edited by T. Zentall and J. B. G. Galef, 141–65. Hillsdale, NJ. Lawrence Erlbaum Associates.

Leger, D. W., D.H. Owings, and D. L. Gilfand. 1980. Single note vocalizations of California ground squirrels. *Zeitschrift für Tierpsychologie* 52:227–46.

Lorenz, K. 1981. *The foundations of ethology.* New York: Springer Verlag.

Manser, M.B. 2001. The acoustic structure of suricate alarm calls varies with predator type and the level of urgency. *Proceedings of the Royal Society of London B* 268:2315–24.

Marshall-Pescini and A. Whiten. 2008. Chimpanzees (Pan troglodytes) and the question of cumulative culture: an experimental approach. *Animal Cognition* 11:449–56.

Maslow, A. H. 1970. *Motivation and personality*, 2nd edition. New York: Harper and Row.

Matsuzawa, W. 2003. Koshima monkeys and bossou chimps: Long-term research on culture in non-human primates. In *Animal Social Complexity*, edited by F. B. M. De Waal and P. L. Tyack, chapter 14. Cambridge, MA: Harvard University Press.

McGrew, W. C. 1992. *Chimpanzee material culture.* Cambridge: Cambridge University Press.

McGrew, W. C. 2004. *The cultured Chimpanzee.* Cambridge, UK. Cambridge University Press.

Melis, A. P., B. E. Hare, and M. Tomasello. 2006a. Chimpanzees recruit the best collaborators. *Science* 311: 1297–300.

Melis, A. P., B. E. Hare, and M. Tomasello. 2006b. Engineering cooperation in chimpanzees: Tolerance constraints on cooperation. *Animal Behaviour* 72(2):275–86.

Melis, A. P., B. E. Hare, and M. Tomasello. 2008. Do chimpanzees reciprocate received favours? *Animal behaviour* 76:951–62.

Menzel, E. 1972. Spontaneous invention of ladders in a group of young chimpanzees. *Folia Primatologica* 17:87–106.

Mesnic, S. L., K. Evans, and B. L. Taylor. 2003. Sperm whale social structure. In *Animal social complexity,* edited by F. B. M. De Waal and P. L. Tyack, chapter 6. Cambridge, MA: Harvard University Press.

Mischotte, A. E. 1963. *The perception of causality.* London: Methuen.

Mithen, S. 1998. *The prehistory of the mind.* London: Phoenix.

Neiworth, J. J., E. T. Johnson, K. Whillock, J. Greenberg, and V. Brown. 2009. Is a sense of inequity an ancestral primate trait? *Journal of Comparative Psychology* 123(1):10–7.

Nissen, H. W. and M. P. Crawford. 1936. A preliminary study of food-sharing behavior in young chimpanzees. *Journal of Comparative Psychology* 22:383–419.

Nowak, M. A. and K. Sigmund. 2005. Evolution of Indirect Reciprocity. *Nature* 437(27):1291–8.

Oswath, M. 2009. In Search of Inner Worlds. In *Human Characteristics: Evolutionary Perspectives on Human Mind and Kind,* edited by H. Høgh-Olesen, J. Tønnesvang, and P. Bertelsen, chapter 3, 44–64. Cambridge, UK: Cambridge Scholars Publishers.

Packer, C. 1977. Reciprocal altruism in Papio anubis. *Nature* 265:441–3.

Patton, S. Q. 2000. Reciprocal altruism and warfare. In *Adaptation and Human Behavior,* edited by L. Cronk, N. Chagnon and W. Irons., 417–37, New York: Aldine de Gruyter.

Penn, D. C., K. J. Holyoak, D. J. Povinelli. 2008. Darwin's Mistake: Explaining the discontinuity between human and nonhuman minds. *Behavioral and Brain Sciences* 31:109–78.

Pepperberg, I. M. 1987. Acquisition of the same/different concept by an African grey parrot (Psittacus erithacus). *Animal Learning and Behavior* 15:423–32.

Pepperberg, I. M. 1988. Acquisition of the concept of absence by an African grey parrot. *Journal of the Experimental Analysis of Behavior* 50:553–64.

Pepperberg, I. M. 2006. Ordinality and inferential abilities of a Grey parrot. *Journal of Comparative Psychology* 120:205–16.

Pfeiffer, J. E. 1985. *The creative explosion.* New York: Cornell University Press.

Plotkin, H. 2007. The power of culture. In *The Oxford Handbook of Evolutionary Psychology*, edited by R. Dunbar and L. Barrett, chapter 2. Oxford: Oxford University Press.

Potts, R. 2004. Sociality and the concept of culture in human origins. In *The Origins and Nature of Sociality*, edited by R. W. Sussman and A. R. Chapman, chapter 12. New York: Aldine de Gruyter.

Pradel, J., H. A. Euler, and D. Fetchenhauer. 2009. Spotting altruistic dictator game players and mingling with them: The elective assortation of classmates. *Evolution and Human Behavior* 30:103–13.

Pruetz, J. D. and Bertolani, P. 2007. Savanna chimpanzees, Pan troglodytes verus, hunt with tools. *Current Biology* 17(1–6):412–7.

Rendell, L. and H. Whitehead. 2001. Culture in whales and dolphins. *Behavioral and Brain sciences* 24:309–82.

Richerson, P. J. and R. Boyd. 2005. *Not by genes alone*. Chicago. Chicago University Press.

Rilling, J. K., D. A. Gutman, T. R. Zeh, G. Pagnon, G. S. Berns, and C. D. Kilts. 2002. A neural basis for social cooperation. *Neuron* 35:395–405.

Rochat, R. 2006. What does it mean to be human? *Journal of Anthropological Psychology* 17:100–7.

Romero, T. and F. Aureli. 2008. Reciprocity of support in Coatis (*Nasua nasua*). *Journal of Comparative Psychology* 122(1):19–25.

Sanz, C., D. Morgan, and S. Gulick. 2004. New insights into Chimpanzees, tools, and termites from the Congo Basin. *The American Naturalist* 164(5):567–81.

Savage-Rumbaugh, E. S. 1986. *Ape language: From conditioned response to symbol*. New York. Columbia University Press.

Seed, A. M., N. S. Clayton, and N. J. Emery. 2008. Cooperative problem solving in rooks (*Corvus frugilegus*). *Proceedings of The Royal Society B* 275(1641):1421–9.

Seyfarth, R. 1980. The distribution of grooming and related behaviours among adult female vervet monkeys. *Animal Behaviour* 28:798–813.

Silk, J. B. 2002. Kin selection in primate groups. *International Journal of Primatology* 23:849–75.

Silk, J. B., S. F. Brosnan, and J. Vonk, J. Henrich, D. J. Povinelli, A. S. Richardson, S. P. Lambeth, J. Mascaro and S. J. Shapiro. 2005. Chimpanzees are indifferent to the welfare of unrelated group members. *Nature* 437:1357–9.

Simmel, G. 1950. *The sociology of George Simmel*. Glencoe, IL: Free Press.

Slobodchikoff C. N., J. Kiriazis, and E. Creef. 1991. Semantic information distinguishing individual predators in the alarm calls of Gunnisons prairie dogs. *Animal Behaviour* 42:713–19.

Smedt, J. de, Cruz, H. de and Braeckman, J. 2009. Why the human brain is not an enlarged chimpanzee brain. In *Human Characteristics: Evolutionary*

Perspectives on Human Mind and Kind, edited by H. Høgh-Olesen, J. Tønnesvang, and P. Bertelsen, chapter 8, 168–81. Cambridge, UK: Cambridge Scholars Publishers.

Smolker, R. A., A. F. Richards, R. Connor, J. Mann, and P. Berggren. 1997. Sponge-carrying by dolphins (delphinidae tursiops): A foraging specialization involving tool use?. *Ethology* 103(6):454–65.

Stange, K. 2009. Art creation and appreciation: Uniquely human? In *Human Characteristics: Evolutionary Perspectives on Human Mind and Kind*, edited by H. Høgh-Olesen, J. Tønnesvang, and P. Bertelsen, chapter 1, 2–16. Cambridge, UK: Cambridge Scholars Publishers.

Subiaul, F., J. Vonk, S. Okamoto-Barth, and J. Barth. 2008. Do chimpanzees learn reputation by observation. *Animal Cognition* 11:611–23.

Taylor, A. H., G. R. Hunt, J. C. Holzhaider, and R. D. Gray. 2007. Spontaneous Metatool used by New Caledonian Crows. *Current Biology* 17:1504–7.

Templeton, C. N., E. Greene, and K. Davis. 2005. Allometry of alarm calls: Black-capped chickadees encode information about predator size. *Science* 308:1934–7.

Tinbergen, N. 1951. *The study of instinct*. Oxford: The Clarendon Press.

Tomasello, M., M. Carpenter, J. Call, T. Behne, and H. Moll. 2005. Understanding and sharing intentions! The origins of cultural cognition. *Behavioral and Brain Science* 28:675–735.

Tooby, J. and L. Cosmides. 1992. The psychological foundations of culture. In *The Adapted Mind*, edited by J. Barkow, L. Cosmides, and J. Tooby, 19–136. New York. Oxford University Press.

Trevarthen, C. 1974. Conversations with a two-month-old. *New Scientist* 62:230–5.

Trivers. R. L. 1971. The evolution of reciprocal altruism. *The Quarterly Review of Biology* 46:35–57.

Vonk, J., S. F. Brosnan, J. B. Silk, J. Henrich, A. S. Richardson, S. P. Lambeth, S. J. Schapiro and D. J. Povinelli. 2008. Chimpanzees do not take advantage of very low cost opportunities to deliver food to unrelated group members. *Animal Behaviour* 75:1757–70.

Warneken, F., B. Hare, A. P. Melis, and M. Tomasello. 2007. Spontaneous altruism by chimpanzees and young children. *PloS Biology* 5(7):e184.

Weedekind, C. and M. Milenski. 2000. Cooperation through image scoring in humans. *Science* 288:850–2.

Weir, A. A. S., J. Chappell, and A. Kacelnik. 2002. Shaping of hooks in New Caledonian crows. *Science* 297:981.

Whiten, A. J., W. Godall, T. McGrew, V. Nishida, V. Reynolds, Y. Sugiyama, C.E.G. Tutin, R. W. Wrangham, C. Boesch. 1999. Cultures in chimpanzees. *Nature* 399:682–5.

Wilkinson, G. S. 1984. Reciprocal food sharing in the vampire bat. *Nature* 308:181–4.

Wolkenten, M.V., S.F. Brosnan, and F. B. M. de Waal. 2007. Inequity responses of monkeys modified by effort. *Proceedings from the National Academi of Science. USA* 104:18854–9.

Wrangham, R. W., M. L. Wilson, and M. N. Muller. 2006. Comparative rates of violence in chimpanzees and humans. *Primates* 47:14–26.

Wynne-Edwards, V. C. 1963. *Animal dispersion in relation to social behaviour.* New York: Hafner.

Zapolsky, R. M. 2006. Social cultures among nonhuman primates. *Current Anthropology* 47(4):641–56.

Zihlman, A. L. and D. R. Bolter. 2004. Mammalian and primate roots of human sociality. In *The Origins and nature of sociality,* edited by R. W. Sussman and A. R. Chapman, 23–52. New York: Aldine de Gruyter.

Index